Y0-ARU-795

WAR CRIMES AND JUSTICE

A Reference Handbook

Other Titles in ABC-CLIO's

CONTEMPORARY WORLD ISSUES

Series

Agricultural Crisis in America, Dana L. Hoag
Biodiversity, Anne Becher
Endangered Species, Clifford J. Sherry
Environmental Justice, David E. Newton
Genetic Engineering, Harry LeVine III
Indoor Pollution, E. Willard Miller & Ruby M. Miller
Natural Disasters: Floods, E. Willard Miller & Ruby M. Miller
Natural Disasters: Hurricanes, Patrick J. Fitzpatrick
New Information Revolution, Martin K. Gay
Nuclear Power, Harry Henderson
The Ozone Dilemma, David E. Newton
Recycling in America, 2d Edition, Debra L. Strong
Tax Reform, James John Jurinski
Urban Sprawl, Donald D. Williams

Books in the Contemporary World Issues series address vital issues in today's society such as terrorism, sexual harassment, homelessness, AIDS, gambling, animal rights, and air pollution. Written by professional writers, scholars, and nonacademic experts, these books are authoritative, clearly written, up-to-date, and objective. They provide a good starting point for research by high school and college students, scholars, and general readers, as well as by legislators, businesspeople, activists, and others.

Each book, carefully organized and easy to use, contains an overview of the subject; a detailed chronology; biographical sketches; facts and data and/or documents and other primary-source material; a directory of organizations and agencies; annotated lists of print and nonprint resources; a glossary; and an index.

Readers of books in the Contemporary World Issues series will find the information they need in order to better understand the social, political, environmental, and economic issues facing the world today.

WAR CRIMES AND JUSTICE

A Reference Handbook

Howard Ball

CONTEMPORARY
WORLD ISSUES

ABC-CLIO

Santa Barbara, California • Denver, Colorado • Oxford, England

Library of Congress Cataloging-in-Publication Data

Ball, Howard, 1937-
War crimes and justice : a reference handbook / Howard Ball.
p. cm. — (Contemporary world issues)
Includes index.
ISBN 1-57607-899-X (hbk. : alk. paper)
1. War crimes. 2. War crime trials. 3. International criminal courts. 4. War (International law) I. Title. II. Series.

K5301 .B35 2002
341.6'9—dc21

2002014681

06 05 04 03 02 10 9 8 7 6 5 4 3 2 1

This book is also available on the World Wide Web as an e-book. Visit abc-clio.com for details.

ABC-CLIO, Inc.
130 Cremona Drive, P.O. Box 1911
Santa Barbara, California 93116-1911

This book is printed on acid-free paper ∞
Manufactured in the United States of America

Dedicated to the innocent victims of armed conflict

Victims are entitled to justice. Offenders deserve punishment. The world needs to establish a historic record of major international crimes, if for no other reason than to establish the truth and to educate future generations. Maybe then we can deter potential criminals and avoid the repetition of those crimes. Otherwise, we are condemned to repeat the mistakes of the past.
—Cherif Bassiouni

Contents

Acknowledgments, xiii
Preface, xv

Chapter 1 Introduction, 1
Defining War Crimes, 5
Establishment of International Laws of War, 10
Historical Perspective, 11
Legal Sources for the Laws of War, 12
International Ad Hoc War Crimes Tribunals Since 1945, 23
Conclusion, 26
References, 27

Chapter 2 The Pursuit of Justice: Current Issues, Controversies, and Possible Solutions 29
The Toll on Civilians Since 1945, 29
No Peace Without Justice: Current Issues, 31
Trying Heads of State, 32
Hybrid International Criminal Courts, 38
Truth and Reconciliation Commissions, 47
The Permanent International Criminal Court, 48
Conclusion, 57
References, 58

Chapter 3 International Laws of War: A Chronology of Major Treaties and Events in Armed Conflicts that Triggered their Adoption, 1856–2002, 61
Chronology, 62
Conclusion, 83
References, 83

Chapter 4 People and Events, 85

Chapter 5 Major Treaties and Reports, 107
Major Treaties (Excerpts), 107
Geneva Convention for the Amelioration of the Wounded and Sick of Armies in the Field, 1864, 107
Hague Declaration, II, IV, Final Act, 1899, 110
Hague Convention III, 1907, 119
Geneva Protocol for the Prohibition of the Use in War of Asphyxiating, Poisonous or other Gases, and of Bacteriological Methods of Warfare, 1925, 126
Treaty of Paris (Kellogg-Briand Pact for the Renunciation of War as an Instrument of National Policy), 1928, 127
Red Cross Convention Regarding the Amelioration of the Condition of Wounded and Sick of Armies in the Field, 1929, 129
Geneva Convention Relative to the Treatment of Prisoners of War, 1929, 132
Nuremberg Principles, 1946, 1950, 138
UN Convention on the Prevention and Punishment of the Crime of Genocide, 1948, 140
The Four Geneva Conventions, 1949, 143
Geneva Protocol I Additional to the Geneva Conventions of 12 August 1949 and Relating to the Protection of Victims of International Armed Conflicts, 1977; Geneva Protocol II Additional to the Geneva Conventions of 12 August 1949 Relating to the Protection of Victims of Non-International Armed Conflicts, 1977, 153
UN Statute of the International Criminal Tribunal for the Former Yugoslavia, 1993, 159
UN Statute of the International Criminal Tribunal for Rwanda, 1994, 174
Dayton Peace Accord, 1995, 178
Rome Statute of the International Criminal Court (ICC), 1998, 181
Major Reports/Rules/Speeches, 186
Prosecutor's Opening Statement, November 21, 1945 (part 4, pp. 98–102), 186
Red Cross Fundamental Rules of International
Humanitarian Law Applicable in Armed Conflicts, 1983, 187
"One Sad Night." A Poem by Hajrie Lajqi, 189
Text of Kosovo Peace Plan, June 1999, 190
Newsweek Article by Joshua Hammer, July 17, 2000, 193

U.S. President Bill Clinton's Speech Ratifying the ICC, December 31, 2000, 197
Press Release of the ICTR, 199
Official U.S. Letter Renunciating the ICC, May 6, 2002, 201

Chapter 6 Directory of Nongovernmental and Governmental Organizations, 203
Essay: "Non-Governmental Human Rights Organizations and International Humanitarian Law," Rachel Brett, 203
Directory, 207
Amnesty International, 207
Campaign to End Genocide, 208
Center for Economic and Social Rights, 208
Coalition for an International Criminal Court, 208
Coalition for International Justice (CIJ), 209
Derechos Human Rights, 209
Dr. Homa Darabi Foundation, 210
Doctors Without Borders (Medecins Sans Frontieres), 210
Human Rights Watch, 211
Institute of War and Peace Reporting (IWPR), 211
International Campaign to Ban Landmines (ICBL), 212
International Commission of Jurists (ICJ), 212
International Committee of the Red Cross (ICRC), 212
International Rescue Committee (IRC), 213
Lawyers Committee for Human Rights, 213
Organization of American States, 214
Peace Brigades International, 214
Physicians for Human Rights (PHR), 214
United Nations High Commissioner/Commission on Human Rights, 215
Witness Program, 215
World Organisation Against Torture, 215

Chapter 7 Selected Print and Nonprint Resources, 217
War Crimes and Justice: "Resources and Research Steps," Sandra J. Lamar, 217
Selected Print Resources, 224
Nonprint Resources, 230

Glossary, 239

Index, 247

About the Author, 261

Acknowledgments

I wish to acknowledge the excellent, untiring men and women who work with nongovernmental organizations (NGOs) such as Human Rights Watch, Amnesty International, Doctors Without Borders, and the International Committee of the Red Cross. These NGOs and others have worked hard to provide humanitarian assistance to the innocent victims of war and worked aggressively to achieve the plan and then the ratification of the world's very first permanent International Criminal Court (ICC), which began operating on July 1, 2002. In addition, these NGOs have provided the world with data necessary to move toward the creation of the ICC as well as to provide the two functioning ad hoc international criminal tribunals (the former Yugoslavia and Rwanda) with vital data regarding the commission of war crimes, crimes against humanity, and genocide..

Such research efforts provide all who are interested in war crimes and justice—students, teachers, researchers, practitioners, and jurists—with detailed examinations of the many wars that have occurred since the end of World War II. Some of these NGOs are listed in this reference work. All are easily contacted via the Internet and e-mail. All of them have made extensive use of the Internet, and their findings are available to billions of persons across the globe. They provide the world community with the most vital of services in assisting the victims of war and in the gathering of information and data that ensures that these tragedies of war—whether civil or regional—are revealed to the world.

Finally, I want to acknowledge the wonderful support I have had, for forty years, from my best friend, my wife, Carol. She has always understood and supported in so many ways my need to attack injustices, whether in Mississippi or Bosnia, and to inform the public about them.

Howard Ball
Richmond, Vermont

Preface

> The balance between vengeance and forgiveness is in many ways the balance between too much forgetting and too much remembering.
>
> —U.S. Supreme Court Justice Sandra Day O'Connor

This war crimes reference book underscores a number of realities. Until 1945, the matter of punishing perpetrators of war crimes and other crimes against humanity was a dead issue. As Richard Goldstone noted, "Prior to World War II, the victims of [war crimes] and human rights abuses were not the subject of international concern." This leads to another somber reality: the culture of impunity for those perpetrators who planned, ordered, and implemented these crimes. Furthermore, a majority of those who have been victims of war crimes and crimes against humanity have been innocent noncombatants, that is, civilians—women, children, the elderly. In 1900, 90 percent of the dead and wounded in war were military personnel; in 2000, less than 25 percent of the dead and wounded in any war—civil or regional—were military personnel.

Until the 1945 Nuremberg and 1946 Tokyo international military tribunals, there existed no international criminal justice process by which justice was meted out to the perpetrators of war crimes and other crimes against humanity. Since the convictions and punishment of some of the leading Nazi and Japanese political and military leaders, the world has seen more than 250 wars, both large and small. Tens of millions of innocent persons have been victimized during these conflicts. In almost all of these battles war crimes, crimes against humanity, and genocide occurred. Yet it was not until the 1990s that the third ad hoc international criminal tribunal—the 1993 International Criminal

Tribunal for the Former Yugoslavia—and fourth—the 1994 International Criminal Tribunal for Rwanda—were created to mete out justice to those who perpetrated war crimes and on behalf of all those innocent persons whose deaths cried out for some kind of justice.

However, the world community has come to realize the need to provide for a permanent international criminal justice system. In July 2002, the International Criminal Court (ICC) came into being, headquartered in The Hague, Netherlands. And as Justice Goldstone has written, "The twenty-first century will witness the growth of an international criminal justice system and victims of war crimes will no longer be ignored" (Goldstone 2000, 138).

There can be no lasting peace in any region or nation that has suffered the cruelty and the horror of war crimes and crimes against humanity unless there is justice for the victims. As Justice O'Connor has noted, there is the need to balance vengeance with forgiveness. The ICC is the world's effort to end the culture of impunity that has existed far too long. This book is the effort to portray the events and the personalities that have moved the world community to perceive and to act on the necessity of creating a *permanent* international criminal justice system.

1

Introduction

In Nelson DeMille's *Up Country*, a contemporary novel about Vietnam, the major character is Paul Brenner, a detective in the U.S. Army Criminal Investigation Division who was traveling in North Vietnam to discover who killed a U.S. Army lieutenant and three Vietnamese civilians in 1972. He has just been given the dead officer's wallet:

> I opened it and went through it. There were some military payment certificates and a few more family photos—Mom and Pop, two teenage girls who looked like his sisters, and an infant who could be the child of the deceased. There were a few other plasticized odds and ends in the wallet: the Geneva Convention card, the card that listed the Rules of Land Warfare, and another card with the [American] Rules of Engagement. Lots of rules in war. Most of them don't mean shit except Rule One, which was, "Kill him before he kills you." (DeMille 2002, 497)

In the novel, during a battle between belligerents, unspeakable horrors take place in accordance with DeMille's Rule One. It is essentially before and after such bloodshed that the rules of war come into play. For the most part these laws of war focus on the protection and treatment of injured belligerents, prisoners of war (POWs), civilians, and civilian property. (In 1900, 90 percent of the wounded and dead in war were soldiers and sailors; in 2000, 75 percent of the wounded and dead in war were civilians.)

War crimes directed at these sets of human beings are not merely modern realities. Whether it was the poisoning of springs and wells to kill the enemy, showing no quarter to a defeated enemy in the field, mistreating POWs, laying siege to undefended towns populated by civilians, or intentionally killing groups of people, young and old alike, because of race, color, religion, or ethnicity, the world has for centuries experienced war, war crimes, and acts of brutality that violated accepted customs and conventions of war and the "conscience" of humanity.

The excessiveness, the brutal reality of "total" warfare, leads to the creation of laws of war to mitigate war's horrors. *Jus in bello*—the laws of war and armed conflict—is the effort of civilized societies to regulate the conduct of war. These laws of war, whether customary norms of behavior that attempt to proscribe certain indefensible actions taken in war or treaties and conventions that do the same, are violated in every war by combatants on both sides. Such persons are war criminals, subject to punishment for the crimes they commit during war. What follows are two stories that illuminate the nature of war crimes. In some respects, they are quite similar; in another way they are very different.

Former U.S. Senator Bob Kerrey (D–NE), currently the president of the New School University in New York City, is an unindicted, unpunished war criminal. On the night of February 25, 1969, Kerrey, a 25-year-old U.S. Navy lieutenant who had been in Vietnam for less than a month, led a squad of six other Navy SEALS of the Delta Platoon, Seals Team One, Fire Team Bravo (nicknamed Kerrey's Raiders), on a raid of a hamlet, Thanh Phong, in Vietnam's eastern Mekong Delta. The area was in Vietcong-controlled territory. Their objective: to capture a local Vietcong official. Around midnight, Kerrey and his men rounded up and brutally killed almost two dozen unarmed women and children.

American military law (in this case, as incorporated in the Navy's Rules of Engagement manual) is explicit in regard to the treatment of persons detained in enemy territory:

> A commander may not put his prisoners to death because their presence retards his movements or diminishes his power of resistance by necessitating a large guard, or by reason of their consuming supplies, or because it appears certain that they will regain their liberty through the impending success of their forces. It is likewise unlawful for a commander to kill his prisoners on grounds of self-preservation, even in the case of airborne or commando operations, although the circumstances of the operation may make necessary rigorous supervision of and restraint upon the movement of prisoners of war.

Kerrey's seven-man team disregarded the laws of war. The SEALs quickly rounded up the civilians, placed them in one of the village huts, and then fired more than 1,200 rounds of ammunition into the hooch, which was 25–30 feet in front of them. The gunfire lasted only a minute or so, during which a war crime occurred. Afterward, they left the area and returned to base. The after-combat report noted that Kerrey's Raiders killed 21 Vietcong. Kerrey was awarded the Bronze Star for the mission; his citation also noted the deaths of 21 Vietcong.

Although there were 122 court-martial convictions for war crimes arising from the conflict in Vietnam, Kerrey and his SEAL team never faced U.S. military justice. Indeed, less than a month later, in what turned out to be Kerrey's final commando raid on suspected Vietcong, he lost part of a leg and was transported back to the United States. In 1970, he was awarded America's highest military award, the Medal of Honor, for his bravery on his last combat mission.

Nine months after Thanh Phong, at another Vietnamese village, My Lai, U.S. troops under the command of U.S. Lieutenant William L. Calley Jr. slaughtered at least 350 innocent villagers. Calley was convicted of the premeditated murder of 22 unarmed civilians and was sentenced to life at hard labor. He served only three years under house arrest at Fort Benning, Georgia, before being pardoned by President Richard M. Nixon.

For decades, Kerrey was routinely introduced as a valiant war hero until the Thanh Phong atrocity was publicly revealed in 2001. In a way, Kerrey was relieved: "This [memory] haunted me, [it] is killing me. I'm tired of people describing me as a hero and holding this [memory] inside." He continued:

> [Thanh Phong] was not a military victory. It was a tragedy, and I had ordered it. How, I have anguished ever since, could I have made such a mistake? Though it could be justified militarily, I could never make peace with what happened that night.

Although Senator Kerrey was never prosecuted for violating one of the laws of war, others who have engaged in military actions since 1945 have been indicted, tried in a war crimes tribunal, and convicted for war crimes.

Dusko Tadic was the first person brought to trial before three judges sitting in The Hague in the ad-hoc International Criminal Tribunal for the Former Yugoslavia (ICTY), created in 1993 by the

United Nations (UN), for alleged war crimes he committed during the Serb-Muslim war in Bosnia-Herzegovina (1992–1995).

Tadic was born in the Serb-populated town of Kozarac, in northwestern Bosnia. He was a married man with two daughters. Before the three Yugoslavia wars began in 1991, he owned and ran a cocktail lounge and was a part-time karate instructor. He was friendly with Muslims and Croats who lived in his town. He was forty years old when he committed his war crimes against his former neighbors and friends. Stirred by Yugoslavian President Slobodan Milosevic's tirades about the need for a "Greater Serbia," Tadic banned Muslims from his bar. He compiled a list of prominent Muslim intellectuals—religious, business, and political leaders who were targeted for execution as part of the Serb ethnic cleansing of Bosnia once the war began in 1992.

He fled Bosnia toward the end of the war. However, he was arrested by German authorities in 1994 and sent to The Hague, the site of the UN-created ICTY, for indictment and trial for war crimes. Tadic was charged with violations of the laws and customs of war for the murder and torture of more than one hundred Bosnian Muslim and Croat civilians and POWs. (Importantly, Tadic was also charged with one count of rape. It was the first time in history that rape had been prosecuted as a war crime.)

His trial began in May 1996. The prosecutors charged him with 132 separate counts, most of them involving actions he took as the commander of Bosnian Serb paramilitary forces who ran Omarska, the notorious Serb prison camp. It was the most brutal of the four Bosnian Serb concentration camps established to detain, torture, sodomize, rape, and then execute Muslim and Croat enemies. Between May and August 1993, it was the holding place for more than 10,000 enemy combatant POWs and civilians. Most of the detainees were executed by the Bosnian Serb paramilitary forces and their bodies thrown into mass graves.

There were more than 115 witnesses who testified against Tadic. The trial transcript ran to more than 6,000 pages. POWs as well as local civil leaders were tortured, raped, sexually mutilated (the biting off of prisoners' testicles, for example), executed, and buried in unmarked killing fields. One year later, in May 1997, Tadic was found guilty of eleven counts of violating the laws and customs of war. He was sentenced to twenty years' imprisonment.

The major difference between these two examples of war crimes is that the Kerrey incident was a war crime that did not reflect U.S. military and political policy, whereas Tadic's war crimes did. His actions were in line with the Serbian governmental policy—boldly announced time and again by President Slobodan Milosevic—of ethnically cleansing the areas in Yugoslavia where a majority of Serbs resided. This does not mean that Kerrey's war crime should not have been punished. However, the primary judicial authority for initiating such action against him is the U.S. military, not an international war crimes tribunal.

"What is the law which governs an army invading an enemy's country?" asked the U.S. Supreme Court after the U.S. Civil War, in *Dew v. Johnson.* "It is not the civil law of the invaded country; it is not the civil law of the conquering country; it is *the law of war*" (emphasis added). Customs and laws of war were created to subject war's excesses to some kind of ethical and legal constraint and to punish those who committed war crimes. War crimes are very serious offenses against the enemy, in violation of internationally recognized laws of war, whether they are enemy combatants or civilians.

According to U.S. military manuals, "All war crimes are subject to the death penalty, although a lesser penalty may be imposed." However, in the aftermath of all wars, some war criminals are convicted for their crimes while many others escape justice.

Defining War Crimes

The formal definition of the term "war crimes" is narrower than many would expect. For example, crimes against humanity and genocide are not war crimes. Nevertheless, as a review of section 8 of the 1998 Rome Statute shows (see excerpt below), the laws and customs of war cover most imaginable cruelties that have been committed during wars since the beginning of civilized society. And as new military technologies of killing are created, the *jus in bello* will evolve to take these new techniques of murder into account.

War crimes lead to individual criminal responsibility once war has begun. Kerrey's Raiders committed a war crime against enemy civilians. Tadic and his paramilitary unit, following governmental policy, committed a number of war crimes against enemy POWs and civilians.

Thus war crimes are grievous wrongs committed by individuals during and after armed conflict against other individuals—whether combatants, POWs, or innocent civilians—that violate the laws and customs of war. They also include intentional acts against the property of the enemy's civilian population, including the destruction of cultural and religious buildings, works of art, and other valuable artifacts.

The 1998 Rome Statute of the International Criminal Court (ICC; see part II [Jurisdiction, Admissibility, and Applicable Law] and article 8 [War Crimes]) is the most comprehensive contemporary enumeration of war crimes. It is a list that incorporates violations of the laws and customs of war that date back centuries before the Christian era. The Rome Statute defines "war crimes" in the following manner:

> 2. . . . "War crimes" means: c. Grave breaches of the Geneva Convention of August 12, 1949, namely:
>
> (i) Wilful killing;
>
> (ii) Torture or inhuman treatment, including biological experiments;
>
> (iii) Wilfully causing great suffering, or serious injury to body or health;
>
> (iv) Extensive destruction and appropriation of property, not justified by military necessity and carried out unlawfully and wantonly;
>
> (v) Compelling a prisoner of war or other protected person to serve in the forces of a hostile Power;
>
> (vi) Wilfully depriving a prisoner of war or other protected person of the rights of fair and regular trial;
>
> (vii) Unlawful deportation or transfer or unlawful confinement;
>
> (viii) Taking of hostages. . . .
>
> b. Other serious violations of the laws and customs applicable in international armed conflict, within the established framework of international law, namely, any of the following acts:
>
> (i) Intentionally directing attacks against the civilian population or against individual civilians not taking direct part in hostilities;
>
> (ii) Intentionally directing attacks against civilian objects, i.e., objects which are not military objectives;
>
> (iii) Intentionally directing attacks against personnel, installations, material, units or vehicles involved in hu-

manitarian assistance, . . . as long as they are entitled to the protection given to civilians or civilian objects under the international law of armed conflict;

(iv) Intentionally launching an attack in the knowledge that such attack will cause incidental loss of life or injury to civilians or damage to civilian objects or widespread, long-term and severe damage to the natural environment which would clearly be excessive in relation to the concrete and direct overall military advantage anticipated; attacking or bombarding, by whatever means, towns, villages, dwellings or buildings which are undefended and which are not military objectives;

(v) Killing or wounding a combatant who, having laid down his arms or having no longer means of defense, has surrendered at discretion;

(vii) Making improper use of a flag of truce, or the flag or military insignia and uniform of the enemy or of the UN, . . . resulting in death or serious personal injury;

(viii) The transfer by the Occupying Power of parts of its own civilian population into the territory it occupies, or the deportation or transfer of all or parts of the population of the occupied territory within or outside this territory;

(ix) Intentionally directing attacks against buildings dedicated to religion, education, art, science, or charitable purposes, historic monuments, hospitals, and places where the sick and wounded are collected, provided they are not military objectives;

(x) Subjecting persons . . . to physical mutilation or to medical and scientific experiments of any kind which are neither justified by the medical, dental, or hospital treatment of the person concerned nor carried out in his or her interest, and which cause death to or seriously endanger the health of such person or persons;

(xi) Killing or wounding treacherously individuals belonging to the hostile nation or army;

(xii) Declaring that no quarter will be given;

(xiii) Destroying or seizing the enemy's property unless such destruction or seizure be imperatively demanded by the necessities of war;

(xiv) Declaring abolished, suspended or inadmissible

in a court of law the rights and actions of the nationals of the hostile party;

(xv) Compelling nationals of the hostile party to take part in the operations;

(xvi) Pillaging a town or place, even when taken by assault;

(xvii) Employing poison or poisoned weapons;

(xviii) Employing asphyxiating, poisonous, or other gases, and all analogous liquids, materials, or devices;

V. Employing bullets which expand or flatten easily in the human body, such as bullets with a hard envelope which does not cover entirely the core or is pierced with incisions;

(xx) Employing weapons, projectiles, and material and methods of warfare which are of a nature to cause superfluous injury or unnecessary suffering, . . . provided [they] are the subject of a comprehensive prohibition and are included in an annex to this Statute;

(xxi) Committing outrages upon personal dignity, in particular humiliating and degrading treatment;

(xxii) Committing rape, sexual slavery, enforced prostitution, forced pregnancy, enforced sterilization, or any other form of sexual violence also constituting a grave breach of the Geneva Conventions;

(xxiii) Utilizing the presence of a civilian or other protected persons to render certain points, areas, or military forces immune from military operations;

(xxiv) Intentionally directing attacks against buildings, material, medical units and transport, and personnel using the distinctive emblems of the Geneva Conventions in conformity with international law;

(xxv) Intentionally using starvation of civilians as a method of warfare by depriving them of objects indispensable to their survival, including wilfully impeding relief supplies as provided for under the Geneva Conventions;

(xxvi) Conscripting or enlisting children under the age of 15 years into the national armed Forces or using them to participate actively in hostilities.

c. . . .Any of the following acts, in an armed conflict not of an international character [does not apply to internal disturbances and tensions such as riots], committed against persons taking no active part in the hostilities, including members of armed forces who have laid down their arms and those placed *hors de combat* by sickness, wounds, detention, or any other cause:

(i) Violence to life and person, in particular murder of all kinds, mutilation, cruel treatment and torture;

(ii) Committing outrages upon personal dignity;

(iii) Taking of hostages;

(iv) The passing of sentences and the carrying out of executions without previous judgment pronounced by a regularly constituted court, affording all judicial guarantees which are generally recognized as indispensable. . . .

e. Other serious violations of the laws and customs applicable in armed conflict not of an international character, within the established framework of international law, namely, any of the following acts:

(i) Intentionally directing attacks against civilian population . . .;

(ii) Intentionally directing attacks against buildings, etc. using the distinctive emblems of the Geneva Conventions in conformity with international law;

(iii) Intentionally directing attacks against . . . humanitarian assistance;

(iv) Intentionally directing attacks against buildings dedicated to religion, art, etc.;

(v) Pillaging a town or a place, even when taken by assault;

(vi) Committing rape, sexual slavery, etc.;

(vii) Conscripting or enlisting children under the age of 15 years, etc.;

(viii) Ordering the displacement of the civilian population;

(ix) Killing or wounding treacherously a combatant adversary;

(x) Declaring that no quarter will be given;

(xi) Subjecting persons in the power of another party to the conflict to physical mutilation or to medical or scientific experiments, etc.;

(xii) Destroying or seizing the property of an adversary unless such destruction or seizure be imperatively demanded by the necessities of the conflict;

3. Nothing in paragraphs 2 (c) and (e) shall affect the responsibility of a Government to maintain or re-estab-

> lish law and order in the State or to defend the unity and territorial integrity of the State, by all legitimate means.

This definition of war crimes, our most recent, covers deliberate acts taken against the enemy whether in an international conflict between nation-states or in military actions taken by belligerents in a civil war. This lengthy enumeration, however, does not exhaust the definition. When new battles are fought, new kinds of war crimes will be perceived, and the laws and customs of war will be modified to take these new brutalities into account in order to prohibit them from being used in the future.

The 1899 and 1907 Hague Conventions (see below) contained, in their preambles the so-called Martens clause. Professor Feodor de Martens was a Russian delegate at the 1899 peace conference at The Hague and introduced the clause to resolve a specific disagreement between large nation-states and smaller ones.

This clause recognized that even the most comprehensive listing of war crimes was necessarily incomplete.

> Until a more complete code of the laws of war has been issued, the high contracting parties deem it expedient to declare that, in cases not included in the Regulations adopted by them, the inhabitants and the belligerents remain under the protection and empire of the principles of international law, as they result from the usages established between civilized nations, from the laws of humanity and the dictates of the public conscience.

The Martens clause has been restated in the 1949 and 1977 Geneva Conventions. International tribunals, such as the International Military Tribunal at Nuremberg in 1945 and the International Court of Justice in 1996, concluded that the Martens clause was customary law with a normative status in its own right.

Establishment of International Laws of War

After the first armed conflicts in history, the creation of the laws and customs of war immediately followed. Human nature being what it is, shedding blood—whether for money, clan, king, village, ideology, or love of country—involves deliberate acts of excessive cruelty and destructiveness directed primarily at the enemy's combatants and civilian populations. Because of the reality of reciprocity and reprisals in war, rules were established to limit the type and extent of violence that occurred during the preceding war. War crimes are the violations of these rules of war. Individuals who plan or commit them are subject to punishment according to their own nation's military rules manual or, if captured, by the enemy's military regulations, which can in part lay out the limits of aggressive behavior in wartime.

Historical Perspective

Ordinarily in the beginning, warfare concluded with the sacking of the cities and towns of the defeated army and the slaying of noncombatants, including women, children, and the elderly. Desecration of fallen bodies was common. Customs of war were pronounced to restrain such wanton action. Thus, instead of slaying the defeated enemy, the defeated were brought into slavery or were swapped for those soldiers who had been captured. Although no quarter was the early norm in war, society's humanistic principles decreed that quarter be given when ransom was paid. After the practice of selling prisoners commenced, quarter was extended if the enemy was asleep, running away from battle, naked, defenseless, or holding his hands prayerfully while asking for mercy.

Religious beliefs were incorporated into the customary norms of wartime behavior during the Middle Ages. If one side was seen as "pagan," then cruel and excessive practices were tolerated. Conflicts between religious coequals (i.e., two Christian nations or two Muslim nations) did not reflect excessive violence. However, wars between two unequal nations (e.g., a Christian versus a Muslim nation) were bloodier and much less forgiving for the vanquished. In 1179, for example, Pope Alexander III requested that enslavement of conquered nations be limited to non-Christians.

During the eleventh century, church leaders created the so-called Truce of God, a customary principle that prohibited warfare on certain days and barred the killing of priests, women, pilgrims, and merchants. (The Peace of God, by contrast, protected Christian noncombatants caught in a war between two Christian nations.)

During the Middle Ages, customary principles recognized four kinds of warfare, including the actions permissible in each one. There was *bellum Romanum*—war by a Christian nation against a pagan nation. No quarter was given, and the slaughter of soldiers and noncombatants was not considered to be a war crime. *Bellum hostile* was war between Christian nations, and the customary restraining principles included avoidance of treacherous, extreme battlefield tactics, the paroling of prisoners, and the protection of noncombatants. There also developed rules and customs for siege warfare (e.g., cities were not sacked when the occupants surrendered) and for *guerre couvette*—war between two feudal lords.

Limitations on the conduct of armed conflict date back to the ancient Greeks, the first to place limits in law on how armed conflict should be conducted. For example, enemy dead had to be returned after the battle ended, prisoners were ransomed rather than killed, civilians were protected, and sacred truces were made to allow Olympic games to take place. As well, brutal treatment of wounded prisoners were prescribed in the Hindu Code of Manu (c. 200 B.C.E.), and similar prohibitions eventually found their way into Roman and European custom.

The first recorded account of a war crimes trial was that of Sir William Wallace in 1305 in an English court. He was charged with and convicted of waging a war of extermination against the English people, "sparing neither age nor sex, monk or nun." Through the nineteenth century, there were hundreds of cases in which national military commissions tried and convicted enemy nationals for breaches of the customary principles and laws of war. During the Franco-Prussian War of 1870–1871, for example, the Germans executed hundreds of French irregulars for violations of the laws of war.

Legal Sources for the Laws of War

The rules of war are a fundamental part of international law today and have existed since the ancient civilizations of China, India, Greece, and Rome. They are primarily found in written treaties between nations (laws) and in the unwritten societal norms and customs that addressed the actual conduct of war. These prescriptive norms and treaties have, for centuries, been accepted by all civilized nations. There are also international and domestic judicial decisions by courts and judges that have led to the development of the laws of war. Legal scholars have also contributed to the development of the customs and principles of the law of wars.

Laws of war are also found, at least since the nineteenth century, in the manuals of military law all nations write, publish, and distribute to their military leaders for further dissemination to their military forces. Finally, and primarily in the last half of the twentieth century, laws of war were crafted and ratified under the auspices of international organizations such as the United Nations.

Customary Norms and Principles of War

The customary law of war was the earliest obligation placed on belligerents. It is the result of general and consistent practices followed by states, arising from a sense of moral and legal obligation that is part of a nation's history and tradition. Customary laws have deep roots and reflect the nation's fundamental values.

Contemporary multilateral written laws of war, codified in treaties and conventions and ratified by nation-states, are a relatively recent innovation in the international law of war. Most treaties incorporate the earlier customary norms that prescribed certain war time behavior.

For centuries, state practices were followed to limit the more extreme methods and tactics of warfare. The customary norms limiting wartime behavior consisted of general pronouncements based on the moral, religious, or legal beliefs of the nation. Over the millennia these restraining practices turned into general principles or norms of behavior recognized by all civilized nations. War is nasty business, but leaders of the warring nations adhered to prescriptions that attempted to ameliorate the worst practices.

Customary norms—laws of war—are consistent actions or inactions by nations over time during hostilities. By the eighteenth century, soldiering was a profession, and mercenary forces, paid by the nation for services, were to heed customary norms of warfare. Nations came to accept these restrictions and constraints on military behavior toward enemy belligerents, enemy civilians, and POWs, occupation of territory, taking of property, and the like. Bilateral treaties began to contain sections that codified customary norms of behavior in wartime. Since the middle of the nineteenth century, groups of nation-states have come together to see if agreements could be written and ratified that would, based on customary limiting principles, restrain the conduct of war. At such meetings, the nations' representatives utilized and incorporated some of these lasting customs and principles of behavior into international law.

A primary effect of customary law is that when a norm, principle, rule, or custom that criminalizes a particularly atrocious action taken during war is accepted as customary, it binds all civilized states. When a restraining principle becomes customary—when it is repeatedly employed to restrict certain practices during an armed conflict—a civilized state is bound to follow that limitation when waging war.

These customary norms of wartime behavior had their origin in the time of the Chinese warrior Sun-tzu (sixth century B.C.E.). The Hindu Code of Manu (c. 200 B.C.E.) and the ancient Greeks viewed these customary behaviors in war as law. These three streams of customary norms were incorporated into Roman Law. Because warring parties generally followed certain principles or norms of wartime behavior, over time they became law that limited wartime extremism even if they had never been written down.

Warring parties regard the ruling as binding on them. It was, for centuries, customary for a state to declare war against their opponent; not to do so is a violation of the customs of law. Since the ancient Greeks, it has been a violation of the customs of war to poison the enemy's wells. The most fundamental limiting custom or principle is that belligerents do not have unlimited freedom to use any means to injure the enemy. This basic norm lies at the heart of many treaties ratified in the nineteenth and twentieth centuries. It was incorporated into the 1874 Brussels Declaration, the 1880 Oxford Manual, and formally codified in the 1899 and 1907 Hague Conventions and the 1949 Geneva Conventions and 1977 Protocols.

Derived from this fundamental customary principle are two important corollaries: proportionality and discrimination. The former, proportionality, is the custom that establishes criteria for limiting the use of force, whether it is the proper response—reprisal—to a specific military action by the enemy or the general response by one nation to another nation's commencing war against its people or territory. The discrimination principle deals with the methods, tactics, weaponry, and targeting of the response. It is impermissible to target, for example, noncombatants and military personnel who are *hors de combat* (wounded, sick, or unable to participate in battle).

Three other customary principles incorporate and balance the ideas of proportionality and discrimination. These are military necessity (the minimum use of force necessary to defeat the enemy), humanity (minimum expenditure of time, life, and physical resources to defeat an enemy), and the principle of chivalry (under which dishonorable or treacherous conduct is forbidden in war).

Codification of the laws of war began in the middle of the

nineteenth century. These new covenants did not displace the preexisting principles and norms of armed hostilities, for many of these customary norms were incorporated into the written treaties, including the 1998 Rome Statute. (An important note: A treaty or statute that embodies existing general practices of customary law is binding on states not party to the treaty.) The 1998 Rome Statute, ratified by the requisite number of parties in April 2002, established the permanent International Criminal Court. It will be binding on the nation-states that signed the statute. Equally important, because the Rome Statute incorporates customary law, it will also be binding on all those states who have not yet ratified or who refuse to ratify the statute. This is so because customary law has been acknowledged as binding on all civilized nation-states.

Written International Agreements

Practical actions by warring nations, beginning with the ancient Chinese, Hindi, Greek, and Roman leaders, led to the establishment of customary rules and principles of wartime behavior. The Westphalia Treaty, promulgated in the seventeenth century, established in law the concept of state sovereignty. It underscored the nation-state's power to declare and make war. From the seventeenth century to the middle of the nineteenth century, states entered into bilateral treaties. For example, the 1785 Treaty of Amity and Commerce between the United States and Prussia contained two sections that made explicit the two nations' commitment to certain fundamental rules if war broke out between them: the immunity of merchants, women, children, and other noncombatants. The second article focused on the proper treatment of POWs.

By the middle of the nineteenth century, war no longer meant armed clashes with small mercenary armies doing the fighting for kings, feudal lords, or popes. The transition from earlier forms of war and what was to become known as "total" war can be seen in two wars involving hundreds of thousands of belligerents: The Crimean War (1854–1856), in which Russia clashed with the Turkish Ottoman Empire, Great Britain, and France; and the U.S. Civil War (1861–1865).

The Crimean War exhibited dreadful communications, logistical nightmares, and nonexistent medical conditions that the belligerents addressed a decade later in the United States. The Crimean War began because of a disagreement between French and Russian religious leaders regarding access and control of two holy places in Palestine: Nazareth and Jerusalem. The Russians sent troops to "protect" these two cities, and the Russian navy destroyed a small fleet of Turkish ships, killing all survivors. Both England and France sent military forces into the Balkans and into the Crimea to confront the Russians.

The war began in March 1854 with British and French troops scoring victories against the retreating Russian forces. The decisive battle was fought at Sevastopol, a major Russian navy base in the Crimea. The allied forces laid siege to the base, using the harbor of Balaklava as their supply point. The siege and accompanying battles lasted more than a year, and during that time disease and starvation took an enormous toll on the allied forces. Thousands starved to death even though food supplies were only six miles away. Many more thousands died due to the absence of medical personnel and the needed medicine; wounds were left untreated, and diseases such as cholera and dysentery ravaged the troops. During the winter of 1854–1855, four times as many soldiers died from disease as from enemy action. One British regiment of more than 1,000 soldiers was reduced to a total of seven men by January 1855.

It was not until Florence Nightingale and 38 nurses were posted to the battleground that conditions and facilities were improved. By the end of the war she was a legendary figure. However, more allied soldiers died of starvation and disease and untreated wounds than were killed by the Russians. The capture of Sevastopol by the British and French in September 1855 led to the Treaty of Paris (February 1856), which ended the war.

Within the decade, the world experienced a different type of war: total war, with masses of men conscripted to serve in the state's military forces, using new technology, new communications links between commanders and their troops, new supply logistics to quickly get equipment, food, and materiel to the troops, and new weapons of mass destruction. Total war has become the reality in the twentieth century. It is the product of three significant changes: technological developments in the weaponry of war, administrative improvements in the fighting of war, and the heightened presence of ideology as a factor accounting for total war.

By the middle of the nineteenth century, as seen especially in U.S. Civil War battles, the world saw the technology of the age of industrialism impacting modern warfare. Unlike in the Crimean War, by the 1860s there emerged new forms of military organization that sought to incorporate the technological changes into new methods of warfare. New military tactics developed that changed the ways enemies engaged in war. For the first time, military combatants were conscripted into military service by their governments. Total mobilization for total war was speeded up due to the draft and the use of new means of transporting men and materiel. The logistics of fighting war improved because of the new management and the new means of waging war.

New weapons were used in the Civil War: rapid-firing machine guns; artillery and mortars; submarines as battle weapons; and cannons that lobbed projectiles many miles behind enemy lines, inflicting casualties on combatants and noncombatants indiscriminately. The telegraph allowed military commanders to communicate, and railroads transported soldiers from the rear to the front lines and supplied troops in the field with needed medical, food, military supplies. By the turn of the twentieth century, there was the full-blown emergence of what President Dwight D. Eisenhower, speaking in the late 1950s, had identified as the "military-industrial complex." In Western nation-states, weapons research and development was in the hands of industrial giants such as Krupp in Germany, DuPont in the United States, Vickers in Great Britain, and Schneider-Creusot in France.

Propaganda reflecting the ideological differences between enemy forces also became a new feature of total war at the turn of the twentieth century. Whether it was the American battle cry "Remember the *Maine!*"—used to stir up the American public during the Spanish-American War (1898)—or the allies' use of emotional descriptions of the Germans in World War II two decades later—the "Huns' Rape of Belgium"—propaganda became a significant instrument in total war. It brought the combatant and the noncombatant together in a shared hatred of a wanton and brutal enemy.

As a direct consequence of the emergence of total war, with its devastating impact on the men who fought the battles and on the civilian population miles behind the lines, the nineteenth century saw a new practice emerge: codification of the laws of war in the form of multilateral treaties or conventions. The codification placed into binding treaties customary laws of war as well as other restraints that emerged in light of the changing character of war.

The first major multilateral treaty limiting the activities of belligerents in wartime was the 1856 Paris Declaration that dealt with limits on maritime war. Others followed. The 1864 Geneva Convention on the treatment of the wounded and the sick in the field was followed by the 1868 St. Petersburg Declaration prohibiting explosive projectiles. The use of such bullets was prohibited because of the need to "alleviate as much as possible the calamities of war, that is, uselessly aggravating the sufferings of disabled men and were contrary to the laws of 'humanity.'"

At the turn of the twentieth century, there were the 1899, 1904, and 1907 Hague peace conferences. They led to a number of limits on the conduct of war on land and at sea. The protection of the individual—whether a combatant or a civilian—and protection of the property of the enemy were highlights of both treaties. Protections were especially extended to wounded, sick, or shipwrecked combatants and included medical care and "humane and decent treatment" for POWs.

The conclusion of World War I led to the 1919 Treaty of Versailles. In article 1, the League of Nations was created to prevent another world war. In part, it stated that "the maintenance of peace requires the reduction of national armaments to the lowest point consistent with national safety." Between 1919 and the beginning of World War II, many efforts were made by the international community to peacefully settle all percolating conflicts between nations. The end of World War II saw additional international agreements that were signed and ratified by many nation-states, often under the auspices of the United Nations.

The conclusion of World War II saw the punishment of the leaders of Nazi Germany and Japan through the creation of ad hoc international military tribunals, the first such courts created to try military and political leaders for waging aggressive war, war crimes, and crimes against humanity. Four judges (one each from the four major Allies—France, Great Britain, Russia, and the United States) sat in Nuremberg, Germany; eleven judges (representing the Allied nations who defeated the Japanese) presided in Tokyo. After the majority of those indicted were found guilty and their sentences carried out, the world acknowledged these activities by universal acceptance of a new set of international laws of war: the Nuremberg Principles (1946) and the Convention Against Genocide (1948).

In succeeding generations, new international treaties have addressed the behavior of belligerents during civil wars and have attempted to ban new kinds of military weapons, such as chemical weapons and landmines. There as yet has been no international treaty that expressly prohibits the use of nuclear weapons as tactical instruments of war. There has, however, been discussion as to whether the use of such weapons is an example of the customary principle prohibiting unnecessary suffering.

Judicial Decisions

The decisions of national and international judicial tribunals have also had an impact on the development and implementation of the international laws of war. After World War II, for example, national courts and military courts-martial heard infinitely more cases involving alleged war crimes by Nazi and Japanese military and political leaders and others—convicting thousands and executing many of them for war crimes—compared to the tribunals at Nuremberg and Tokyo.

The major national civilian courts have recognized and validated the impact of international law on domestic law. For example, the U.S. government, in its very first year of existence (1789), passed the Alien Tort Act. It stated that all "U.S. district courts shall have original jurisdiction of any civil action by an alien for a tort only, committed in violation of the law of nations or a treaty" of the United States. Federal courts have validated such legislation. Furthermore, the U.S. Supreme Court has consistently validated the applicability of international law. In *United States v. Armistad* (1841), the Court applied international law. Slaves aboard a Spanish ship mutinied and killed all the Spanish crew and officers. Captured and brought to the United States, the slaves were charged with piracy. The Spanish government demanded that the slaves be returned to Spain for punishment. However, an international treaty prohibited the international slave trade. The Court applied international law and concluded that the African slaves were free men and should be returned to their homeland.

Domestic (national) courts have proven to be ineffective in rendering justice against their own military when it has been accused of committing war crimes. For example, in 1919, after the conclusion of World War I and after an investigating committee spent over a year examining allegations about German war crimes, the allies identified 901 German officers and men as probable war criminals. Their offenses included:

- Deportation of noncombatants to Germany;
- the sack of Louvain, Belgium;
- first-ever use of poison gas on the Ypres battlefield (1915);
- sinking of the *Lusitania* (1915), other neutral passenger ships, and hospital ships (e.g., the *Dover Castle* and the *Llandover Castle*) by U-boats;
- execution of civilians;
- torture of Belgian children;

- execution of English nurses;
- taking hostage noncombatants and executing some;
- rape of noncombatants in occupied territory;
- destruction and pillaging of the Rheims Cathedral; and
- giving no quarter to French soldiers who surrendered.

Because of the U.S. rejection of an international war crimes tribunal to try the alleged perpetrators, the allies allowed Germany to try these indicted war criminals in Germany's highest national court, the Reichsgericht. Not surprisingly, the German court dismissed 870 cases. Only about 30 trials were conducted, and most of the accused military personnel involved in the alleged war crimes were acquitted by the judges. The victorious allies were outraged by what the British Foreign Office called a "scandalous failure of justice."

This kind of national behavior of judges was not lost to the Allied leaders who had to determine how and where Nazi war criminals should be punished at the conclusion of World War II. The pressure was on to create an international tribunal to deal with the defeated Nazi leadership. The task of this new innovation, the International Military Tribunal in Nuremberg (IMTN) in international law was to identify those laws of wars allegedly violated by the Nazis, determine guilt or innocence, and then mete out judgments—including the death penalty.

At the opening of the post–World War II IMTN in 1945, the Allies' chief prosecutor, U.S. Supreme Court Justice Robert Jackson, recalled the World War I Reichsgericht actions. Jackson said: "Either the victors must judge the vanquished, or we must leave the defeated to judge themselves. After the First World War we saw the futility of the latter course."

The Impact of Political Philosophers on the Laws of War

Another foundation for the establishment of the laws of war or armed conflict is reflected in the writings of a host of scholars and philosophers. They have interpreted and written about the importance of many of the customary principles that try to limit inhumanity and superfluous suffering during war. Of course, one major problem is that men, including political theorists, will give different interpretations to the same customary principle.

Nevertheless, the teachings of such writers as Hugo Grotius (1583–1645), whose humanism was reflected in *On the Law of War and Peace* (1625), which called for the regulation of the conduct of war; Charles de Secondat, Baron de Montesquieu (1689–1755), who held, in *The Spirit of the Laws* (1748), that to murder—to show no quarter—to POWs was contrary to all humane laws; and Jean-Jacques Rousseau (1712–1778), who wrote that POWs must not be held in dungeons or prisons or put in irons but placed in a healthy environment and repatriated at the conclusion of hostilities—all were valuable to the statesmen who drafted the first multilateral treaties.

Military Law Manuals

After the U.S. Civil War began, President Abraham Lincoln asked professor Francis Lieber, a German lawyer who fled Europe during the aborted revolutions of 1848, to draft a manual that would enumerate valid behavior of the Union troops when confronting Confederate armed forces.

Lieber, a naturalized U.S. citizen and a professor at Columbia University's law school, crafted one of the world's earliest military manuals, *Instructions for the Government of Armies of the United States in the Field*. It was one of the very first efforts to codify the laws of land warfare for use by military commanders and the men under them. Promulgated as General Orders No. 100, Adjutant General's Office, Washington, D.C., by Lincoln on April 24, 1863, it provided the U.S. military, for the very first time, with information about the constraints on warfare that had evolved over the centuries. (It was replaced in 1914 by the U.S. Army's field manual *Law of Land Warfare,* which incorporated the basic structure and premises of Lieber's *Instructions* and is still in force in the U.S. military.)

Lieber's *Instructions* was a guidebook for "honorable belligerents." It reflected the advances of civilization "during the last centuries, so has likewise steadily advanced, especially in war on land," the customary principles and laws of war of civilized nations. It had ten sections, including how POWs and deserters were to be treated (section 3), a definition of partisans, that is, armed enemies not belonging to the enemy army and how they were to be treated when captured (section 4), the meaning of safe conduct, treatment of spies and traitors, abuses of flags of truce (section 5), the treatment and exchanges, including paroles, of POWs, "who shall be fed upon plain and wholesome food, whenever practicable, and treated with humanity" (sections 6 and 7), and the protection of the public and private property of the enemy, protection of noncombatants, "especially women," of religion, of the arts, and of sciences (section 2).

President Lincoln issued the *Instructions* to all his military commanders and sent copies to the commanders of the Confederacy. It became the essential code of military conduct for both sides during the Civil War and even today represents the core of the nation's code of military conduct. The *Instructions* became a model for other nation-states and led to the proliferation of "rule books" throughout Europe in the last decades of the nineteenth century.

Such manuals have joined the customary principles and laws of war and hostile belligerents engaged in battle. The Netherlands issued its version of Lieber's *Instructions* in 1871, France in 1871, Serbia in 1879, Spain in 1882, Portugal in 1890, and Italy in 1896. The basic purpose of such manuals was to emphasize what was considered to be appropriate conduct during hostilities. A U.S. Navy manual entitled *Commander's Handbook on the Law of Naval Operations* states: "The law of armed conflict is not intended to impede the waging of hostilities." Its purpose was (and is) to ensure that the violence of hostilities is directed toward the enemy's forces and is not used to cause purposeless, unnecessary human misery and physical destruction.

Another, briefer, and more specific type of manual—Rules of Engagement instructions—is issued to all military personnel before engaging in specific military actions. These manuals summarize the conduct of the military operation and reflect what the issuing state considers to be the basic rules of lawful conduct during war. For example, the U.S. military issued the *U.S. Rules of Engagement for Operation Desert Storm* (for the 1991 Gulf War) and the *U.S. Rules of Engagement for Operation Enduring Freedom* (Afghanistan, beginning in 2001).

International Bodies and Governmental and Nongovernmental Organizations

Since the end of World War I, international governmental organizations, the League of Nations (1920–1946), and especially the United Nations (1945 to the present) have played an important role in the continued clarification, development, creation, and implementation of the laws of war. The United Nations has played and continues to play a very significant role in the clarification, development, and implementation of the laws of war. It was involved in drafting the 1948 Genocide Convention and, more recently, in the drafting of the 1998 Rome Statute.

The first major nongovernmental organization (NGO)—still a major player in the twenty-first century—to contribute to the development of a more humane law of war was the International

Committee of the Red Cross (ICRC). Its founder, Count Henri Dunant, was a Swiss citizen who was shocked at the lack of treatment for the wounded in the Battle of Solferino, Italy, of 1859. It was a military engagement fought in Lombardy between Austria and an allied French and Piedmontese army. In the battle, 14,000 Austrians and 15,000 allied soldiers were killed and wounded. Because of nonexistent medical facilities on both sides, injured combatants that could have been saved died of their wounds. Dunant organized emergency aid services for the wounded on both sides. In 1862, he proposed the formation of voluntary medical relief services in all nations and proposed an international agreement dealing with the treatment of war wounded.

In 1864, another Swiss humanist, Gustave Moynier, president of the Geneva Welfare Society, issued a call to the leaders of the European nations to address the problems Dunant had witnessed and wrote about in his 1862 book, *A Memory of Solferino*. Twelve nations met in Geneva in 1864 and signed the Geneva Convention for the Amelioration of the Wounded and Sick of Armies in the Field. This convention created the ICRC, provided "inviolable" protection for medical staff and volunteers to care for the wounded in the field, called for humane treatment of the wounded and POWs, and created a distinctive emblem for all those who treated the wounded—a red cross on a white background. (In 1901, Dunant received the first Nobel Prize for his humanitarian work.)

Currently, there are hundreds of internationally organized NGOs keenly and intimately involved in the clarification and development of new international laws and customs of war. Contemporary NGOs focusing on this issue include Amnesty International, Doctors Without Borders, and Human Rights Watch.

International Ad Hoc War Crimes Tribunals Since 1945

In November 1945, the world's very first international war crimes tribunal, the International Military Tribunal at Nuremberg, began its difficult task. This was unprecedented in world history, as almost two dozen military, industrial, and governmental leaders of Nazi Germany were indicted and tried (most were convicted) for their involvement in the planning, ordering, and execution of a plan of conquest—waging an aggressive war—that led to the fall of nine nations of Western Europe between 1939 and 1945. In executing Adolf Hitler's plan for world domination, his surrogates—and the military and industrial forces under their command and control—committed war crimes and crimes against humanity on such a grotesque scale that the victorious Allied nations had to conduct such a trial so that history could record the horrors of the Third Reich.

After the defeat of Japanese forces in the Pacific, the eleven victorious Allies created the International Military Tribunal–Far East, which convened in Tokyo. Almost two dozen leading Japanese military and governmental leaders (excluding Emperor Hirohito of Japan) were indicted, tried, and convicted of planning, ordering, and waging aggressive war, committing war crimes, and committing crimes against humanity. By the end of 1948, the tribunals had concluded their work. The allies executed a majority of the Nazi and Japanese leaders within a month of their convictions.

These two tribunals established the legal and moral precedent that individuals are responsible for actions taken during war—against combatants, POWs, and civilians. The traditional defenses used to explain violations of the laws and customary principles of the laws of war—following "superior orders" or "sovereign immunity"—were categorically rejected in these international war crimes trials. The decisions of these tribunals created legal standards in international law. These addressed (1) the applicability of both customary law and the written laws of war; (2) individual responsibility for acting in accord with these laws of war; and (3) punishment for those individuals found guilty of committing war crimes and crimes against humanity in violation of the laws of war. In December 1946 the world community codified the Nuremberg Principles in international law.

Soon thereafter, UN members attempted to create a permanent international criminal court with jurisdiction to indict and bring to justice those who waged aggressive war and committed war crimes, crimes against humanity, and, after the 1948 Genocide Convention was ratified, the crime of genocide. However, because the Cold War between the Soviet Union and the United States began at the same time, the movement to create a permanent war crimes tribunal was a dead letter until 1989.

In 1989, the world experienced the crumbling of the communist bloc led by the Soviet Union. The Berlin Wall that divided East and West Germany came down; the Solidarity movement in Poland ended communism in that country; and Czechoslovakia, Hungary, Bulgaria, Romania, the Baltic states all achieved sudden freedom from communism. Finally, the Soviet Union itself collapsed. Given these events, there were renewed calls for the creation of a permanent international criminal court. By the Summer of 1998, after no less than five planning conferences sponsored by the United Nations had led to the crafting of a statute creating a permanent international criminal court, more than 125 nations met in Rome and ratified the Rome Statute. It was ratified in April 2002 and entered into force in July 2002.

However, while these planning sessions were taking place in Geneva and in New York in the 1990s, many wars—regional and internal—continued to take their toll of innocent lives and continued to evidence clear signs of war crimes, crimes against humanity, and genocide during the same time. Across the world—in East Timor, Cambodia, Bangladesh, Afghanistan, Sierra Leone, Burundi, Rwanda, and the Balkans—millions of innocent civilians were caught up in the fighting and were tortured, maimed, and executed by military forces.

Great pressure was brought to bear on the United Nations to create additional ad hoc international criminal tribunals to punish those who committed brutal war crimes and genocide. In 1993, the United Nations addressed the wars in the former Yugoslavia when it established the International Criminal Tribunal for the Former Yugoslavia. An independent prosecutor was charged with indicting, arresting, and bringing to trial those leaders responsible for committing crimes against humanity, war crimes, and genocide in the Balkan Wars between 1991 and 1999 in the Serb-Croat war, the Serb-Bosnia-Herzegovina war, and Kosovo battles. The ICTY began its work in The Hague, Netherlands, in 1995. By 2002, more than 90 persons were indicted for war crimes and dozens had been tried, including the former president of Yugoslavia, Slobodan Milosevic.

The fourth ad hoc international war crimes court was created by the United Nations one year later. The International Criminal Tribunal for Rwanda (ICTR) was created to address the murders of almost 1 million Tutsis by Hutu paramilitary forces over three months during the civil war in Rwanda. Since the ICTR began its work in Arusha, Tanzania, in 1997, 70 people have been indicted—among them nuns, priests, radio broadcasters, paramilitary leaders, and leaders of the Hutu government; nine have been tried and convicted, and 17 were on trial in early 2002.

Both the ICTY and the ICTR will continue to hear cases brought by the chief prosecutor (Carla Del Ponte of Switzerland in 2002) throughout the first decade of the twenty-first century.

The international laws and customary principles of the laws of war have been dramatically enhanced and expanded during the twentieth century.

The victorious allies of World War I could not agree on the implementation of the articles of the Versailles Treaty, which called for Kaiser Wilhelm II of Germany to stand trial for war crimes. However, the victorious Allies in 1945 did not hesitate to change and broaden international law to ensure that those who were responsible for the most heinous war crimes imaginable would not go unpunished.

The concept of impunity for dastardly actions against enemy belligerents and civilians was rejected by the world in 1945. And by 1998, most nations agreed that war crimes, genocide, and crimes against humanity had to be addressed by the rule of law of the international community. The result was the ratification, in April 2002, of the permanent International Criminal Court—the world's first—with an independent prosecutor and jurisdiction to indict and try individuals accused of committing the most serious war crimes: grave breaches of the laws of war, crimes against humanity, and genocide.

The decisions of these four ad hoc international military/criminal tribunals—Nuremberg, Tokyo, Yugoslavia, and Rwanda—have played and will continue to play a major role in applying the laws of war to particular circumstances. The creation of the permanent ICC will, optimally, further clarify the content and scope of application of the laws of war. Its opinions—judicial precedent—will become new international understandings of war crimes and the vehicle through which perpetrators will be punished for violating the laws of war.

Conclusion

Generally, the laws of war constrain the kind of violence permitted during war—regardless of its scope—against military combatants, POWs, neutrals, spies, guerillas, and civilians. There are no less than four subcategories of the laws of war. These are:

1. Rules concerning the status of combatants. The laws of war outline the status of those who can lawfully engage in combat and how combatants who are hors de combat must be treated by their opponents.
2. Rules that attempt to circumscribe the conduct of hostili-

ties and the methods of killing. How military combatants conduct themselves during military engagements is the second category of the laws of war. The limits of pain inflicted on enemy combatants, "treacherous and superfluous" wounds, and how military forces deal with enemy spies are some of the issues addressed by treaties and customary law.

3. Rules dealing with the behavior of the occupying power when in enemy territory. This category deals with constraints on the manner in which the occupying power governs the people in the territory it conquered.
4. Rules pertaining to the treatment of neutrals, civilians, works of art, religious artifacts, truces, armistices, and the like. This category discusses the laws of war pertaining to the status of neutral nations and their citizens, as well as the behavior of the belligerents under a truce and during an armistice.

Violations of these laws of war—whether a treaty violation or violation of customary principles of armed conflict or a violation of a nation's military code of action on a battlefield—is considered to be a war crime. The alleged perpetrators of the war crime are subject to trial by a national military tribunal or an international tribunal convened to hear the evidence and to determine guilt or innocence of the accused. Inherent in the emergence of these customs and treaties are the overriding goals of making wars more humane and denying impunity for those who order others to commit war crimes and for those who commit them.

References

Akehurst, Michael. *A Modern Introduction to International Law.* London: Allen and Unwin, 1977.

Armstrong, David Armstrong, Lorna Lloyd, and John Redmond. *From Versailles to Maastricht: International Organization in the Twentieth Century.* New York: St. Martin's Press, 1996.

Ball, Howard. *Prosecuting War Crimes and Genocide: The Twentieth Century Experience.* Lawrence: University Press of Kansas, 1999.

Bardakjian, K. *Hitler and the Armenian Genocide.* Cambridge, MA: Harvard University Press, 1985.

Bassiouni, Cherif, and Ved P. Nanda, eds. *Crimes and Punishment.* Vol. 1

of *A Treatise on International Criminal Law.* Springfield, IL: Charles C. Thomas, 1973.

Berry, Nicholas O. *War and the Red Cross: The Unspoken Mission.* New York: St Martin's Press, 1997.

Buchanan, Rosmarie. "Battling the Crimes of War." *Student Law* (May 1993).

DeMille, Nelson. *Up Country.* New York: Warner Books, 2002.

Friedman, Leon, ed. *The Law of War: A Documentary History.* 2 vols. New York: Random House, 1972.

Glass, James M. *"Life Unworthy of Life:" Racial Phobia and Mass Murder in Hitler's Germany.* New York: Basic Books, 1997.

Goldstone, Richard J. *For Humanity: Reflections of a War Crimes Investigator.* New Haven, CT: Yale University Press, 2000.

Goodman, Walter. "Sorting Out War Crimes and Tangles of History." *New York Times,* May 13, 1996, p. 21.

Gutman, Roy. *Crimes of War.* New York: Norton, 1999.

Harris, Marshall, R. Bruce Hitchner, Michael P. Scharf, and Paul R. Williams, "Bringing War Criminals to Justice." In *Century Foundation Report: Making Justice Work.* New York: Century Foundation Press, 1998.

Holbrooke, Richard. *To End a War.* New York: Random House, 1998.

Howard, Michael, George J. Andreopoulos, and Mark R. Shulman, eds. *The Laws of War: Constraints on Warfare in the Western World.* New Haven, CT: Yale University Press, 1994.

Lewis, Anthony, "No Peace Without Justice." *New York Times,* November 20, 1995.

Morrison, Fred L. "The Significance of Nuremberg for Modern International Law." In "Symposium: Nuremberg and the Rule of Law: A Fifty Year Verdict." 149 *Military Law Review* (Summer 1995).

Neier, Aryeh. *War Crimes: Brutality, Genocide, Terror, and the Struggle for Justice.* New York: Times Books, 1998.

Prinz, Barrett. "The Treaty of Versailles to Rwanda: How the International Community Deals with War Crimes." 6 *Tulane Journal of International and Comparative Law* (Spring 1998).

Weisburd, Mark A. *Use of Force: The Practice of States Since World War Two.* University Park: Pennsylvania State University Press, 1997.

Willis, James F. *Prologue to Nuremberg: The Politics and Diplomacy of Punishing War Criminals of the First World War.* Westport, CT: Greenwood Press, 1982.

2

The Pursuit of Justice: Current Issues, Controversies, and Possible Solutions

Since 1945, the world has experienced more than 250 armed conflicts of all kinds. Almost 90 million persons, primarily innocent civilians, have died during the course of these military actions. The primary problem for the international community has been to seek a way to punish those who violate the international laws and customs of war. More than 75 percent of those killed by violators of the laws of war have been innocent civilians caught in harm's way or targeted victims of ethnic cleansing. Equally important for the maintenance of international justice is the need to develop an operating international criminal justice institution that would punish perpetrators as well as inhibit those who plan, organize, and implement armed actions from developing policies that lead to war crimes, crimes against humanity, and genocide.

The Toll on Civilians Since 1945

Rexhap Bislimi was a 33-year-old accountant who lived in Urosevac, Kosovo Province, Serbia. He was an ethnic Albanian, married with children, and not involved with the Kosovo rebellion. He had been an active member of the Human Rights Council of Kosovo, founded in 1990 to seek a peaceful resolution of the status of Kosovars within the Serb Republic. During the spring and summer of 1998, after the Yugoslav army swept into sections of Kosovo to beat down the uprising, Serbian "security police officers" followed; the fates of Rexhap Bislimi and other like him were sealed.

The military and security forces, under the command of President Slobodan Milosevic, shelled cities and small towns in

Kosovo, driving hundreds of thousands of Kosovo civilians from their homes. In early July 1998, Serb security forces entered Rexhap's town, rounded up all the local civic and political leaders and professional persons, and systematically tortured and killed them in an effort to discover the whereabouts of rebels leaders and arms caches.

On July 6, 1998, Rexhap was dragged to the local police station and unmercifully beaten by Serb special-unit men. The last time his mother, Hava Bislimi, saw her son was when he was brought back the following day to the family garden, "his face battered with bruises," given a shovel, and ordered to dig up the weapons on the property. "Reeling from beatings at the police station," Rexhap was "too weak to follow the orders." Neighbors were then brought in to dig for the arms, allegedly buried on the Bislimi property.

Failing to find any arms, the Serb security police told Rexhap to look at the house where he had been born. "'This is the last time you will see it,' the Serbian officers were overheard saying as they marched him out of the gate." Six weeks later, on August 21, 1998, after repeated tortures and beatings by the special units, Rexhap Bislimi was dead.

Rexhap was never charged with committing any crime. He was not given an attorney to defend his interests. He was held in local prisons while his family was denied the opportunity to visit. It was obvious that the Serbs did not want to allow the family to see Rexhap because he was undergoing daily tortures and beatings. Weekly the family would try to see Rexhap, and weekly they would be prohibited from visiting.

During an official visitation day toward the end of August 1998, his mother noticed an ambulance pull up to the prison while she waited to see if she could see her son. She again was not able to see her son because, she was told, he was being interrogated. Later, a sympathetic doctor at the hospital in Pristina, the provincial capital, got word to Rexhap's family that he was in very bad condition. The family rushed to the hospital, but another friendly medic told them that Rexhap was in "such bad shape, you don't want to see him." They were also told that there was a chance to save Rexhap's life if they bought some medicine to stop Rexhap's internal bleeding. The family spent 1,000 marks for the drugs and lined up blood donors from the family.

The next day, when they arrived with the medicine and the blood donors, the family was told that Rexhap Bislimi died the preceding day. The official death certificate stated that death was caused "by [repeated] blows to the head and body." His belongings were returned to the family: "a watch, his identity card, his wallet with a dollar bill tucked inside."

Thousands of ethnic Albanians attended Rexhap Bislimi's funeral. The deceased accountant's children, wife, and mother led the march to the cemetery. Afterward, the grandmother recounted a conversation she had with her granddaughter. To console her son's oldest daughter, Ardita, then six years old, the grandmother told her that Rexhap had gone to Germany. But the child had seen enough not to believe it. "No," Ardita replied, according to her grandmother, "my father has gone to the graveyard."

Since 1945, there have been almost 300 wars, the majority of them civil wars in the Third World. As a consequence of the proliferation of these kinds of war, the laws of war have been modified in the effort to criminalize certain actions taken by the belligerents. Since 1945, the phrase "no peace without justice" has entered the language of the international community. The essential meaning of this phrase goes to the ethical core of the laws of war: Unless persons are punished for committing war crimes, crimes against humanity, and/or genocide, the cycle of hatred and revenge will continue. Only when those who have suffered the outrages of war crimes have seen the oppressors brought to justice will there be the opportunity for peace in their nation.

No Peace Without Justice: Current Issues

In the 1990s and the early twenty-first century, new developments in the international laws of war suggest that the international community now recognizes the relationship between justice and the maintenance of peace. In the last decades of the twentieth century, four major innovations underscored the importance of providing justice for those who have suffered from crimes of war and other actions.

First, at both the national and international legal levels, two efforts were undertaken to try former heads of state for war crimes committed by their military and paramilitary forces against civilians as well as prisoners of war. Legal actions were instituted against Augusto Pinochet of Chile, the former head of state, and Slobodan Milosevic of Serbia, who was indicted by the International Criminal Tribunal for the Former Yugoslavia (ICTY) while still sitting as head of state of Yugoslavia. Although General Pinochet in the end avoided war crimes charges in a national court due to his advanced age and poor health, such was not the case for Milosevic. He was indicted for sixty-six violations of the laws of war for actions taken in the three Bosnian wars; his trial began before three ICTY judges sitting in The Hague in February 2002.

Second, there have been at least five efforts, some successful, to address war crimes through an internationalized national court created to hear war crimes cases and to mete our justice to those found guilty of war crimes and crimes against humanity in Sierra Leone, East Timor, Kosovo, Afghanistan, and Cambodia. Third, since 1983 twenty-five nations who survived civil war tried to move ahead, emotionally and psychically, through the creation and implementation of Truth and Reconciliation Commissions (TRCs). Finally, there was the creation, in 1998, of the world's first permanent international criminal court, the International Criminal Court. It was given jurisdiction to hear cases involving war crimes, crimes against humanity, and genocide. It was ratified in April 2002 and entered into force in July 2002.

Trying Heads of State

Near the turn of the twenty-first century, two powerful dictators—one a general and the former head of state in Chile, the other the sitting president of Yugoslavia—were indicted or detained and held for trial for alleged violations of the laws of war, including war crimes, crimes against humanity, and genocide. This was the first time in history that a former head of state and a sitting head of state were confronted by legal accusations and possible trials for violating the laws of war.

Although one of them, General Pinochet of Chile, was able to avoid a trial because of illness and age, the precedent was established in national courts in Spain and in Great Britain: In the future, prosecutors could ask national tribunals to detain and, upon indictment, try former heads of state who allegedly violated the laws of war.

Augusto Pinochet

General Augusto Pinochet was the dictatorial head of state of Chile for more than seventeen years. Born in 1915, Pinochet was encouraged by his mother to choose a career in the military. His wife, Lucia, encouraged him to participate in politics as a leading military figure in Chile. He was violently anticommunist; as a young officer in the 1950s, he was involved in efforts to clamp down on the Communist Party of Chile. However, by 1970, with the ascent of power of the left-wing Popular Unity government led by Salvador Allende, he was promoted to the rank of general, and in June 1973 he was promoted to commander in chief by Allende, who trusted Pinochet.

That trust was misplaced, however, for in September 1973 Allende lost his life in a coup led by Pinochet. The new leadership of Chile was a military junta led by Pinochet. In the first months of the new regime, Pinochet ordered the purges, torture, and deaths of more than 3,000 supporters (with thousands more forced to flee Chile for their lives) of Allende's Popular Unity government. Pinochet closed parliament, banned all political and trade union activity, and in 1974 appointed himself president. He ruled Chile for seventeen years, from 1973 to 1990.

Initially there was support for his one-man rule. However, by the 1980s left-wing groups and parties had reorganized. His 1980 constitution set a timetable for elections in the country; it allowed for a referendum on whether or not Pinochet should be the sole candidate. In 1990, after the voters rejected that proposal and Pinochet had to allow civilians to enter the government, he stepped down as president. He did, however, remain as commander in chief of the armed forces and used that position to effectively block any radical left-wing policies from becoming law.

In 1998, Pinochet relinquished his military position and the following day took a seat in parliament as a senator-for-life, another position he created for himself in the 1980 constitution. In October 1988, he was arrested, while traveling in London, on a warrant from a Spanish prosecutor requesting Great Britain to extradite Pinochet to Spain to face murder charges. (He was charged with the extrajudicial killings of a number of Spanish citizens living in Chile—allies of Allende—after he took power.)

He immediately challenged the arrest and the High Court, sitting in London, ruled that the arrest was unlawful. The argument was that of sovereign immunity: As a former head of state, he was immune from prosecution.

However, in November 1998 the United Kingdom's highest court, the Law Lords, heard the case on appeal, dismissed the lower court order, and ruled that Pinochet must face the attempt to extradite him to Spain. In December 1998, Home Secretary Jack Straw rejected appeals by Pinochet's lawyers and ordered the extradition case to continue. Pinochet immediately challenged Straw's ruling before the Law Lords, which ruled that Pinochet must receive a new hearing on the question of sovereign immunity.

Between January and March 1999, Pinochet's lawyers argued before the Law Lords in their second effort to block his extradition to Spain. In March 1999, the Law Lords rejected the immunity argument but reduced the number of charges against him and asked Straw to reconsider his earlier decision to allow the extradite request to go forward. In April 1999, Straw ruled that Pinochet could not go free and allowed Spain to go ahead with the request. The Chilean supreme court, in August 1999, lifted Pinochet's immunity from prosecution for crimes he may have ordered while the country's head of state.

In October 1999, after Pinochet suffered two strokes, another U.K. court ruled that he could be extradited to Spain to stand trial for torture and other human rights violations. However, Home Secretary Straw, in late November, asked Pinochet to go to a hospital for another medical examination. Based on a poor medical prognosis, Straw, in March 2000, ruled that Pinochet was too ill to stand trial and would not be extradited to Spain. Pinochet was immediately whisked off to Chile, where he arrived at the airport to cheers from his supporters. Chilean Judge Juan Guzman, however, announced plans to pursue a prosecution against Pinochet in a national courtroom. Given the Supreme Court ruling in August 1999, removing Pinochet's immunity from such a prosecution enabled Guzman to prosecute. Only a judgment of poor health by the Chilean supreme court could block a future prosecution.

Although Pinochet was not brought to trial in Spain for war crimes and torture, "the fact that [he] was arrested while traveling abroad," said Amnesty International, "has [sent] a powerful message: no one is above international law, even when national laws protect you from prosecution. The UK courts have confirmed that people accused of crimes such as torture can be prosecuted anywhere in the world. They have also firmly established that former heads of state are not immune from prosecution for such acts."

Slobodan Milosevic

Slobodan Milosevic, the president of Yugoslavia from 1997 until his overturn and arrest in June 2001, was born on August 29, 1941, in Pozarevac, a small town in Serbia southeast of Belgrade. Both parents, a teacher of religion (father) and a fervent member of the Communist Party (mother), committed suicide when Milosevic was a young man. His uncle, an army general, also committed suicide. He married a childhood friend and fellow

Communist Party member, Mirjana Markovic. He received a law degree in 1964, although he never practiced. His wife took her Ph.D. in sociology and was, for many years, a faculty member at the University of Belgrade as well as a Communist Party leader.

While still a teenager, Milosevic became a member of the League of Communists of Yugoslavia. By 1984, he headed Belgrade's Communist Party organization. In 1987, he staged a coup in Serbia, becoming the president of the Serbian Communist Party. In 1989, he was elected president of Serbia. In 1992, he was reelected. In 1997, he was elected president of the truncated Federal Republic of Yugoslavia. It was a truncated nation because, after the 1980 death of Yugoslavia's leader since World War II, Josip Broz Tito, there developed a pathologic rupture in the nation due to serious ethnic conflicts between the republics that constituted the Yugoslavian nation. Under Tito, these ethnic differences were submerged and suppressed in the name of the communist ideal.

These clashes—among Croats, Muslims, and Serbs—led by 1990 to a number of the Yugoslavian republics declaring their independence. These dynamic actions led, beginning with the collapse of European communism in 1989, to a series of wars between Serbia and two of the breakaway republics, Croatia and Bosnia-Herzegovina, and between Yugoslavia and (through 1999) Kosovo, Serbia's once-autonomous southern province populated by a majority of Serbian Albanians.

Milosevic succeeded in his election bid in Serbia because he addressed the ethnic pride of Serbs, calling for the establishment of a "Greater Serbia" within the Yugoslav state. Yugoslavia's split began in May 1991 when Croatia and Slovenia declared their independence from the Milosevic-dominated Yugoslavian central government. On March 3, 1992, a third area, Bosnia-Herzegovina, declared its independence from Yugoslavia. At the time, the new republic contained 40 percent Muslims, 30 percent Serbs, and 18 percent Croats.

Bosnian Serbs, fearing that the new republic would become a fundamentalist Islamic nation, rebelled against the successful popular vote for independence (in which the Bosnian Serbs refused to participate), and in 1992 an armed struggle began between Bosnian Muslims and the Milosevic loyalists, the Bosnian Serbs. The Bosnian Serbs were much better equipped militarily and received military support from Milosevic's central government's army; they quickly took control of more than two-thirds of Bosnia-Herzegovina.

The Bosnian Serbs, with support from Milosevic, then launched a campaign of terror against the country's Muslim population. There was implemented a policy with the prosaic name of "ethnic cleansing." Bosnian Serb military and paramilitary units (such as Dusko Tadic's raiders) attempted, with some success, to purify Bosnia by expelling Muslims from the country. Ultimately this meant the expulsion, rape, torture, and murder of tens of thousands of Bosnian Muslims between 1992 and 1995 (when the Dayton Peace Accord ended the war). Sarajevo, the capital of the new republic and the site of the 1984 Winter Olympics, was placed under siege by the Bosnian Serbs for more than two years (March 1992 until the spring of 1994). Thousands of Muslim civilians lost their lives as a consequence of daily Bosnian Serb artillery and sniper fire during this two-year siege. The Dayton Peace Accord created a new government structure for Bosnia and crafted a separate Bosnian Serb state, Srpska. Postwar elections were held in Bosnia-Herzegovina in 1996 under supervision of troops from the North Atlantic Treaty Organization (NATO).

In 1999, in an effort to protect the Serb minority in Kosovo Province, the Yugoslavian army, under the direction of Milosevic, took military actions against the Kosovar Albanian majority population. Between March 24 and June 12, 1999, thousands of Albanian civilians were brutally murdered by the Yugoslavian military and, as in earlier wars, paramilitary Serb forces. In 1993, the United Nations created the ICTY to investigate the battles that took place in that country since 1991 and determine whether war crimes had been committed by the belligerents. By 1996, the ICTY was at work in The Hague, funded by the United Nations and fully staffed with a prosecutor's office and the appointment of trial and appellate judges. Its basic function was to prosecute those who ordered or engaged in war crimes during the wars in the former Yugoslavia.

Milosevic's fall from power began when the ICTY indicted him, in May 1999, for war crimes in Serbia and Yugoslavia since 1991. In September 2000, elections were held in Yugoslavia, and Milosevic's opposition candidate for president, Vojislav Kostunica, received more than 48 percent of the vote to 40 percent for Milosevic. On October 6, 2000, Milosevic conceded defeat and Kostunica was sworn in as the new president of Yugoslavia the following day. In April 2001, Milosevic was arrested for alleged criminal activity while still president. In late May 2001, he was charged by Yugoslavian authorities with covering up evidence of war crimes committed in Kosovo. Finally, under great pressure from the West, in late June 2001 the Yugoslavian government handed Milosevic over to the ICTY at The Hague. On November 23, 2001, the three sets of indictments against Milosevic were announced by the chief prosecutor in the case, Carla Del Ponte. Milosevic refused to accept the validity of the indictments, calling them a "supreme absurdity." On February 12, 2002, his trial began in the ICTY chambers at The Hague. At a minimum, given that the prosecution alone intended to bring almost 400 prosecution witnesses to testify against Milosevic, speculation was that the trial would last for at least two years.

All told, Milosevic faced 66 charges of grave breaches of the Geneva Conventions of 1949 (18 counts), violations of the laws and customs of war (22 counts), crimes against humanity (24 counts), and genocide (2 counts). These alleged crimes took place during three of the four wars Serbia engaged in between 1991 and 1999. Central to all these wars was the Serbian effort to ethnically cleanse these republics of all non-Serb ethnic groups—Muslims, Croats, and Kosovar Albanians—in order to create what Milosevic called his Greater Serbia. (The 1991 Serbian war with Slovenia quickly ended in defeat for Serbia and did not lead to war crimes charges against Milosevic.)

Thirty-two counts grew out of the 1991–1992 Serbian war with the breakaway republic of Croatia. Milosevic, as president of Serbia, ordered his military and paramilitary forces to forcibly remove the majority of Croats and other non-Serbs from one-third of the territory of Croatia, the Krajina region. The fighting ended in 1992 when United Nations (UN) forces entered Krajina and the Serb forces withdrew.

During the 1992–1995 war with Bosnia-Herzegovina, which began when Bosnian Muslims and Croats voted for independence in March 1992, many thousands of Bosnian Muslims were rounded up and forcibly removed from their homes; women were raped, and many people were slaughtered in Srebrenica.

Milosevic was also accused of ordering the multiyear siege of Sarajevo and other Muslim enclaves in the republic of Bosnia-Herzegovina. He was charged with twenty-nine counts of war crimes, including two counts of genocide, for policies and orders he issued during the three-year war. Only after NATO air attacks began against Bosnian Serbs did the leaders of Serbia, Croatia, and Bosnia-Herzegovina come to U.S.-sponsored peace talks at Dayton, Ohio, to grind out a complex peace treaty.

Milosevic was charged with five counts of war crimes violations when, as president of Yugoslavia in 1998, he ordered military and paramilitary forces into Kosovo province to brutally crack down on ethnic Albanians, the population majority in Kosovo. The Kosovo indictment accused him of forcing almost 1 million Albanians from their homes, which were then looted and burned. Almost 1,000 Kosovar civilians were murdered by Milosevic's forces. In late March 1999, NATO commenced almost three months of air strikes against Serb forces in Kosovo and against military targets in Belgrade, Yugoslavia, and other Serbian cities. On June 10, 1999, NATO suspended its bombing after Milosevic ordered his troops out of Kosovo.

In her opening remarks, ICTY prosecutor Del Ponte told the three judges that the Milosevic tribunal "gives the most powerful demonstration that no one is above the law or beyond the reach of international justice. . . . The [criminal] events themselves were notorious and a new term, 'ethnic cleansing,' came into common use in our language. Some of the incidents revealed an almost medieval savagery and a calculated cruelty that went far beyond the bounds of legitimate warfare."

Hybrid International Criminal Courts

By 2000, a number of hybrid internationalized criminal courts were created or proposed in the war-torn regions of Kosovo, Sierra Leone, and East Timor. Another effort, begun in 1997, to create such a court in Cambodia stalled in 2002 when negotiations broke down between UN representatives and the Cambodian government. Afghanistan's new leadership, in early 2002, also discussed the possibility of creating a war crimes tribunal to bring to trial Taliban leaders who committed war crimes. These hybrid tribunals were established to provide fair legal redress for serious criminal offenses and violations of the laws and customs of war committed there during their civil wars.

These innovative courts were composed of national as well as international judges and were created in an effort to provide justice for innocent victims of war crimes by applying, procedurally and substantively, either national or international laws of war.

The location, composition, and applicable law in this context may mean that there is no reliance on national courts for justice in these emotional trials while also establishing close ties with the state and new government of the state where the war crimes occurred. Hopefully, it may lead to both the perception and the reality of fair justice for victims and perpetrators alike.

If these innovative legal tribunals serve the cause of justice by meting out justice while showing the victims that there is no impunity for the war criminals, then there may be the alleviation of the need to create ad hoc international tribunals to try and judge alleged war criminals.

Sierra Leone

Sierra Leone is a small nation in West Africa bordered by Liberia, Nigeria, and Guinea that has been in the throes of civil war since March 1991. That month, the Revolutionary United Front (RUF) entered the country from Liberia, launching a rebellion to overthrow the corrupt one-party rule of the All-People's Congress (APC). The RUF was led by a former corporal in Sierra Leone's army, Foday Sankoh, who had been fighting the APC since 1971. It consisted of middle-class, populist-style students, unemployed youths, and Liberian mercenaries. The campaign turned into one of violence, and the RUF's principal aim seemed to be to control the country's diamond and mineral wealth.

Since 1991, the nation has been wracked with violence and governmental instability. In 1992, the APC leader was overthrown in a military coup by Captain Strasser, whose National Provincial Ruling Council ruled until it was overthrown in 1996 by his deputy, Brigadier Bio.

Elections—parliamentary and presidential—were held in February 1996, and Ahmad Kabbah, the head of the Sierra Leone People's Party (SLPP), won on a pledge to bring an end to the civil war. The RUF and the SLPP signed a peace accord in November 1996, called the Abidjan Accord. It was broken in January 1997 when fighting broke out again between the groups, with innocent civilians trapped between the battling forces.

In May 1997, Kabbah was overthrown and fled to Guinea after another coup led by Johnny Paul Koroma, an army major who headed the Armed Forces Revolutionary Council (AFRC). He suspended the constitution, banned political parties, and led by military decree. Widespread human rights abuses followed. In August 1997, a total economic embargo was placed on Sierra Leone by the Economic Community of West African States (ECOWAS). In October 1997, the UN Security Council imposed mandatory sanctions against Sierra Leone, including an embargo on arms and oil imports.

ECOWAS peacekeeping military forces, largely Nigerian troops, in February 1998 drove the AFRC from the capital, Freetown. The next month, President Kabbah was reinstated and, with the help of the ECOWAS military, was able to regain control of two-thirds of the nation. In January 1999, the RUF, now in alliance with the AFRC and others, attacked Freetown and committed massive human rights abuses, which included severing the hands of hundreds of civilians, wide spread rapes, and the assassinations of many civilians. In July 1999, the government signed another peace accord with the RUF (which was to become a political party and participate in governing the country) in the city of Lomé, Togo. In addition, the treaty gave the RUF an "absolute and free pardon and reprieve to all combatants and collaborators in respect of anything done by them in pursuit of their objectives." The United Nations, ECOWAS, and the British Commonwealth were described as "moral guarantors" of the peace accord.

In October 1999, the United Nations established the United Nations Mission in Sierra Leone (UNAMSIL) with a final authorization of more than 17,000 troops to keep the fragile peace. Serious human rights abuses and war crimes continued. The RUF continued to rape, murder, mutilate, and torture thousands of civilians. It continued to abduct and train child soldiers, and because it controlled the diamond areas, it had the financial resources to arm its forces. After eight years of war, there were more than 50,000 extrajudicial killings, tens of thousands of mutilations, and savage, systematic rapes; an estimated 570,000 refugees fled the RUF into neighboring countries. In May 2000, the RUF, still led by Corporal Sankoh, took 600 UNAMSIL soldiers hostage, and full-scale fighting again broke out. In March 2001, the United Nations increased its peacekeeping force to 17,500 military personnel, including more than 1,500 crack British troops and troops from Bangladesh, Bolivia, Canada, China, the Czech Republic, Denmark, Egypt, France, and more than one dozen other countries.

Meanwhile, in October 2000 the United Nations, chagrined at the impunity given the RUF, proposed the establishment of a special court for Sierra Leone, consisting of Sierra Leone and foreign (i.e., UN-selected) judges, staff, and prosecutors. In addition, in the winter of 2000 the Sierra Leone government passed an act that created the Truth and Reconciliation Commission. The Lomé Treaty, in article 26, stated: "A Truth and Reconciliation Commission shall be created to address impunity, break the cycle of violence, provide a forum for both the victims and perpetrators of human rights violations to tell their story, get a clear picture of the past in order to facilitate genuine healing and reconciliation."

However, the amnesty granted the RUF was for actions taken between 1991 and November 30, 1996, the date of the first peace accord. The government and the United Nations agreed on the creation of the special court. The two parties agreed that the jurisdiction of the special court would cover crimes against humanity and grave breaches of the 1949 and 1977 Geneva Conventions, including murder, collective punishments, taking of hostages, attacks on human rights personnel, peacekeeping personnel, and the forced recruitment of children under the age of fifteen. In January 2002, the United Nations and Sierra Leone formally agreed to the establishment of the special court. The first person to face justice at the bench was Corporal Sankoh, the leader of the RUF. He had been held captive in Freetown since 1998, when British troops seized him and turned him over to government justice officials. He was brought before the court in March 2002 and charged with war crimes and crimes against humanity.

The main goal of the Truth and Reconciliation Commission in Sierra Leone was to heal the wounds of the nation. The special court was to operate as an international entity in accord with international criminal laws and customary principles. It would provide due process to persons indicted for grievous actions taken against civilians and combatants, and it would punish, with terms up to life imprisonment, those found guilty of these crimes against humanity and war crimes. The special court in Sierra Leone is another precedent in the effort to punish those who have committed grave violations of the laws and customary principles of the laws of war. It is the very first such hybrid court to actually sit and hear a case against an alleged war criminal.

East Timor

East Timor is a tiny territory once administered by Portugal lying between Australia and Indonesia in the Timor Sea. In 1974, Portugal sought to establish a provisional government and a popular assembly, which would determine the status of the non–self-governing territory. Civil war immediately broke out between those who wanted independence and those who wanted to become a part of Indonesia. Unable to control the fighting, Portugal withdrew.

In 1975, immediately after Portugal left, Indonesia invaded the area from its own territory of West Timor and integrated East Timor as its twenty-seventh province. For more than twenty-five years, until 1999, Indonesian troops occupied East Timor, subjecting its civilian population, as well as small bands of separatist guerillas, to some of the worst atrocities in modern times, according to BBC World News. Between 1975 and 1999, more than 25 percent of the population of East Timor—close to 400,000 persons—were murdered. Another 300,000 civilians became displaced refugees, fleeing into West Timor. Increased pressure from the United Nations led to a substantial development in 1999.

That year the Indonesian government agreed to allow the East Timorese to choose between independence and local autonomy within the Indonesian nation. Paramilitary units loyal to Indonesia, assisted by the army, used terror and execution to try to coerce the people to vote for local autonomy. The August 30 referendum, however, resulted in an overwhelming call for independence. (More than 98 percent of eligible voters decided, by a margin of 79 percent to 21 percent, to reject local autonomy.) The loyalist militias then went on a murderous rampage, killing hundreds of East Timorese and destroying many small villages. More than 80 percent of the territory's infrastructure was also destroyed by the rebels. As many as 500,000 were displaced from their homes, with 250,000 forced to leave East Timor. In late September 1999, a UN peace force was assembled and sent to East Timor. The executions and deportations quickly ended.

On October 25, 1999, the United Nations established the United Nations Transitional Administration in East Timor (UNTAET). The UNTAET mission has three major components until East Timor became a fully independent nation on May 20, 2002: (1) governance (including the reestablishment of basic services and law and order, with a functioning police force and a justice system) and public administration (including 1,600 UN civilian police); (2) humanitarian assistance and emergency rehabilitation; and (3) a military component with an authorized strength of about 9,000 troops and almost 300 military observers. Another UN agency established the Detainee Management Unit to review the detention of those loyalists and others suspected of serious offenses committed after the arrival of the multinational military in East Timor.

On November 15, 1999, the United Nations endorsed an international inquiry into alleged human rights violations in East Timor during the transition period that began in January 1999. The five-person International Commission of Inquiry panel, including Asian experts, arrived in East Timor on November 21, 1999, to begin work in East Timor and in the refugee camps in West Timor. And on December 3, 1999, the United Nations established the five-member Transitional Judicial Service, including three East Timorese and two international jurists.

By December 1999, inquiry commission members and the UNTAET military forces began to find unmarked graves throughout East Timor, the consequence of executions by loyalists and Indonesian paramilitary units operating in East Timor. A forensic specialist was brought in to begin work on the mass graves. Based on these and other findings of "serious violations" of human rights, the International Commission of Inquiry recommended that the United Nations establish an investigative-prosecutorial body and an international human rights tribunal, consisting of Indonesian and East Timorese jurists, to receive complaints, conduct trials, and sentence those found guilty.

Indonesia opted to conduct its own war crimes tribunal, however, and the human rights tribunal that began to hear cases in 2000 consisted of East Timorese and international jurists.

In September 2001, the internationalized tribunal, the UN–East Timorese Crimes Tribunal, filed the first indictments for "extermination" in East Timor (after the territory voted to secede from Indonesia in August 1999) against nine militiamen and two Indonesian soldiers. The suspects were accused of murdering sixty-five people in two massacres in September 1999. They segregated young men between sixteen and thirty, tied them up, and then shot and hacked them to death. In December 2001, ten of the defendants were sentenced, after trial and conviction, to jail terms up to thirty-three years for human rights violations. However, a continuing problem for the East Timor tribunal had emerged: All the suspects were living in Indonesia, and Indonesia was unwilling to return them to East Timor for trial and, after trial, for punishment.

A month after these initial indictments were handed down in East Timor, the nation's attorney general, in Jakarta, the capital of Indonesia, announced the appointment of twenty-three Indonesian jurists for Indonesia's first war crimes–human rights tribunal. That tribunal was installed in January 2002. There were twelve cases involving eighteen defendants, including army leaders, paramilitary leaders, and the former governor of East Timor—all charged with violence against East Timorese civilians between April and September 1999. No trial dates were announced.

By February 2002, the tribunal indicted ninety-nine war crimes suspects—basically pro-Indonesian militiamen and Indonesian soldiers—for crimes against humanity committed during East Timor's break with Indonesia in August 1999. The basic problem was that East Timor's request for extradition of the ten already sentenced to prison was denied: Indonesian officials have flatly refused to extradite anyone to East Timor to stand trial. An April 2000 memorandum of understanding between Indonesia and East Timor—in which Indonesia agreed to cooperate with the investigators and to extradite suspects—has gone unheeded.

Kosovo

In June 1999, after hostilities ceased in Kosovo because of an eleven-week series of NATO air strikes, a peace plan was developed by NATO and approved by the Serb parliament. It gave Kosovo "substantial autonomy within the Federal Republic of Yugoslavia." To achieve this independence, the Serbs agreed to the deployment in Kosovo "under UN auspices, of efficient international civilian and security presences, with NATO participation, to secure [a] safe environment for all the residents in Kosovo and enable the safe return of the displaced persons and refugees to their homes."

Kosovo came under international control in 1999. Its agencies and personnel—civilian, bureaucratic, humanitarian, and police—remain along with the military forces of NATO. The United Nations established an interim governmental administration until general elections were held in Kosovo, and a prime minister was chosen by the representatives. That authority, according to the peace deal, "will secure transitional authority during the time for the interim democratic and self-governing institutions, and establish conditions for peaceful and normal life of all citizens of Kosovo."

The international forces and bureaucracy remain in Kosovo because of the continued ethnic violence between Serbs and ethnic Kosovo Albanians (Muslims) since 1999. For example, UN police in February 2002 arrested two Serb males for the February 2000 grenade attack against Kosovo Albanians that killed eight Muslims. This attack occurred one day after Kosovo Albanians fired a rocket at a bus carrying Serbs, killing two and injuring three others.

There is also the internationalization of Kosovo's courts. International prosecutors and judges work in Kosovo under a system designed to prevent ethnic bias in these war crimes trials. In February 2002, the first trial began in the special court. The case involved a German volunteer fighter for the Kosovo Liberation Army (married to an ethnic Albanian) who was accused of killing a Serb in a bomb attack in April 2001 in the provincial capital, Pristina. The prosecutor, an American lawyer named Michael Hartmann, called the crime "ruthless revenge." The defendant, Roland Bartetzko, was charged with murder, attempted murder, and terrorism. (The trial was held in tight security, with UN police wearing flak jackets and armed with automatic weapons.) If convicted, he could face 20–40 years in prison.

This special court is a reflection of the difficulty nations have in providing justice for the victims of war crimes and the terrorism that ensues after peace has been achieved. Although general elections were held in November 2001, the United Nations still functions as the government, security, and justice systems for Kosovo citizens. A German politician, Michael Steiner, was the Yugoslav Province's UN governor in 2002. "We want the rule of law over the law of the jungle. We deny the right to violence," he said on his arrival in Pristina to take up his duties.

The main political parties in Kosovo failed to agree on a president, necessitating the continuing presence of the United Nations and NATO in the embattled province. In February 2002, three months after the elections, Governor Steiner urged the rival parties to come together on forming the new government. With hard brokering by Steiner, one month later, in March 2002, the four rival parties agreed on a new president and a government.

Moderate ethnic Albanian Ibrahim Rugova was selected as president. The newly elected prime minister was Bajram Rexhepi, a senior official of a rival political party. The final status of the province—independence or remaining as an autonomous province of Serbia, the dominant republic in Yugoslavia—loomed before the new government of reconciliation.

Cambodia

Between 1975 and 1979, Cambodia was governed by radical Communist Party leaders within the Khmer Rouge, led by a fanatical Cambodian communist named Pol Pot.

During "Pol Pot Time," almost 2 million Cambodian civilians, including a number of religious and ethnic minority groups living in Cambodia, were killed. The Cambodian killing fields were the last resting place for 40 percent of the country's population. In January 1979, Pol Pot's reign of terror ended when Vietnamese troops invaded Cambodia and forced the Khmer Rouge to flee. For almost two decades, the remnants of the Khmer Rouge remained hidden in the jungles to the north and west of Cambodia's capital, Phnom Penh.

During the latter half of the 1990s, the new Cambodian government, in an effort to put the past genocidal actions of the Khmer Rouge behind, granted amnesty to a number of the radical leaders of the old regime. At the same time, beginning in 1997, UN officials and leaders of other regional governmental organizations such as the Organization of American States Inter-American Commission on Human Rights, tried to create another novel internationalized court to put these radical leaders on trial for war crimes and genocide.

These two separate actions—amnesty and the creation of a special court to try the Khmer Rouge leaders—collided with each other. The United Nations proposed a hybrid tribunal, one that would include international as well as Cambodian judges. It was a court that would sit in Cambodia so that the millions of people who suffered at the hands of the Khmer Rouge would be able to see fair justice done. There would be one more Cambodian judge than international judges combined, giving Cambodia ultimate control over the outcome.

In August 2001, King Norodom Sihanouk signed a law establishing a special Khmer Rouge war crimes tribunal. However, the United Nations concluded that the complicated formula for a tribunal consisting of Cambodian and international representatives (judges and prosecutors) would not guarantee impartial justice. In February 2002, after negotiating for almost five years with Cambodian officials in the effort to create an impartial, fair war crimes tribunal to try the surviving leaders of the Khmer Rouge, the United Nations ended its efforts. The Cambodian negotiator in February 2002 refused to budge on his nation's view of the tribunal. He said, "It is not the time to talk about more concessions." As a consequence, decades after the Khmer Rouge reign of terror and genocide, not a single leader has been brought to trial. As the leaders, including Pol Pot, die of natural causes, many observers believe that the most wicked members of the Khmer Rouge will not live long enough to face justice for their crimes.

Afghanistan

During OPERATION ENDURING FREEDOM, the U.S.-allied military action against the radical fundamentalist Islamic Taliban government, the new Interim leader of Afghanistan, Hamid Karzai, promised the creation of a war crimes tribunal to pursue the perpetrators of war crimes, mass murders, and ethnic cleansing committed during the Taliban's five-year rule (1997–2001). (One particularly gruesome method of murdering ethnic enemies of the Taliban was to place 200–300 of them into airless storage containers, where they would very slowly die of suffocation. Hundreds of enemies were killed in this low-tech gas-chamber process.) However, in Afghanistan, as in Cambodia, provincial governors had already granted amnesty to hundreds of Taliban leaders and their followers.

Can a tribunal provide justice to the perpetrators of war crimes if successor political leaders provide amnesty to the killers? This was the seemingly insoluble contradiction in Cambodia, and it may be the same dilemma for the new government of Afghanistan.

Not necessarily in response to the conundrum, in March 2002 the George W. Bush administration announced its *Rules for Military War Tribunals,* which will be used to conduct trials for many of the hundreds of Al-Qaeda and Taliban prisoners held in detention from the U.S.-led war on terrorism. The rules require a unanimous verdict from a three-judge tribunal for the death penalty, allow the media to cover the proceedings, and provide the prisoners with military lawyers at government expense and/or civilian lawyers at their own expense. There will be the presumption of innocence, and defendants must be allowed to see the evidence presented against them by the prosecution. The standard of proof is the highest in U.S. jurisprudence: guilt beyond a reasonable doubt.

Truth and Reconciliation Commissions

An alternative to national and international war crimes tribunals is the concept of the Truth and Reconciliation Commission. TRCs are panels established to gather research, largely through testimony from victims and perpetrators, and to issue a report on human rights violation over a certain period of recent national history. They are not courts of law; testifying before a TRC will not lead to imprisonment for war crimes. They exist for a designated period of time, from one to three years, and develop processes and protocols for the protection of witnesses. The goal is to produce and circulate a final report that includes an account of past abuses of authority, including recommendations that promote national reconciliation and further legitimatize the existing governmental structure and its leadership.

Since 1982, when Bolivia established the National Commission of Inquiry into Disappearances, and 1983, when Argentina created the sixteen-member National Commission on the Disappeared, twenty-five nations have chosen to use the TRC format to purge the memories of the just-ended civil wars and move forward. These include Argentina, Bolivia, Burundi, Chad, Chile,

East Timor, Ecuador, El Salvador, Germany, Guatemala, Haiti, Malawi, Nepal, Nigeria, Panama, Peru, the Philippines, Sierra Leone, South Africa, South Korea, Sri Lanka, Uganda, Uruguay, the Federal Republic of Yugoslavia, and Zimbabwe. Another dozen nations have groups that have demanded the introduction of the TRC process into their country. Some of these nations are Bosnia-Herzegovina, Colombia, and Mexico.

For national leaders, the TRC is a way to promote healing and reconciliation between erstwhile enemies in a state. Victims as well as their oppressors testify. The victims will be heard by the community, whereas the perpetrators have the opportunity to confess their wrongs, be forgiven, and then be reintegrated into society. It was also hoped that having a TRC would prevent the repetition of earlier mistakes that led to armed conflict in the first place. The belief was that truth, justice, and reparation would lead to peace and that no nation could move forward without peace—even if it meant amnesty for alleged perpetrators of war crimes and crimes against humanity.

Some nations such as Sierra Leone have the TRC process as well as international tribunals for those who have committed the most heinous of war crimes. Some of the nations who have conducted TRC hearings, including Sierra Leone, had representatives from the international community as well as citizens from the nation conducting the TRC hearings.

The Permanent International Criminal Court

Since the Nuremberg and Tokyo war crimes tribunals ended their work in 1948, it has been a dream of international human rights advocates to see created a permanent world court that would try individuals for genocide, crimes against humanity, and crimes of war. The unfinished legacy of those World War II ad hoc tribunals has been the creation of such a permanent international criminal court that could hear cases involving grave violations of the laws and customs of war, and situations not remedied for any number of reasons, by national prosecutors.

The concept of a permanent international criminal court emerged in 1919, when the allies crafted the Versailles Treaty, signed reluctantly by Germany that same year. One of the hundreds of articles in the treaty called for the creation of an international criminal tribunal to try Germans accused of committing war crimes in violation of the Hague Treaties of 1899 and 1907. Given the unwillingness of the United States to actually implement that and other war crimes articles in the treaty (articles 227–230), as well as the desire of the victorious allies to forego implementation of article 227, no international criminal tribunal was created. In 1926, a permanent criminal court was again proposed in the League of Nations, but nothing came of it. During the interwar period (1920–1937), nothing further was proposed.

The horrors the world glimpsed at the end of World War II led the United Nations to reexamine the possibility of an international criminal court. After the ad hoc Nuremberg and Tokyo war crimes trials ended, and with the adoption of the Convention on the Prevention and Punishment of the Crime of Genocide in 1948, there was renewed interest in the creation of a permanent international criminal court with jurisdiction over actions of individuals that violated the Nuremberg Principles, the 1948 Genocide Convention, and the revised 1949 Geneva Protocols on the conduct of war on land and at sea.

Article VI of the 1948 Genocide Convention was, in certain respects, a watershed. It provided that persons charged with genocide "shall be tried by a competent tribunal of the State in the territory of which the act was committed or by such international penal tribunal as may have jurisdiction." This language introduced the world community to the concept of complementarity in international law.

A national prosecutor and court system has first crack at bringing to justice persons who commit war crimes, genocide, or crimes against humanity. Yet another consequence of the 1948 convention was the notion that such crimes were so universally abominable that an offender could be tried in the domestic criminal court of any nation: The brutal actions were considered crimes of universal jurisdiction, meaning that all who commit them can be tried in any court, even if the court has no connection with the crime. Complementarity and universal jurisdiction, finally, underscored the precedent that if nations are unwilling or unable to carry out a genuine investigation and prosecution, then a regional or international criminal tribunal has jurisdiction to investigate and, if appropriate, to prosecute. Because of the onset of the Cold War in the late 1940s, nothing more was said about a permanent international criminal court.

With the collapse of the Soviet Union in 1991, along with the freedom revolutions that took place across Eastern Europe, the idea of a permanent international criminal court was again the focus of conversation. In that year, the Trinidad and Tobago delegate, speaking for a group of sixteen Caribbean and Latin American countries in the UN General Assembly, called for the establishment of a permanent international court to prosecute international drug trafficking. On November 25, 1992, the General Assembly passed Resolution 47/33 requesting a UN agency to prepare a draft statute for such a permanent court.

In 1995, the United Nations established the UN Preparatory Committee (PrepCom). It was given the task of recommending whether further action by the United Nations on the question of establishment of a permanent court should take place. There were six PrepCom sessions between 1996 and early 1998; a drafting committee also met in the Netherlands in January 1998.

In July 1998, a draft statute was adopted and presented to UN Secretary-General Kofi Annan. The draft statute was 167 pages long, with 13 parts, 116 articles, and 478 bracketed passages, indicating words that were disputed by one or more states. It became the basis for the debates and bargaining at the United Nations Diplomatic Conference of Plenipotentiaries on the Establishment of an International Criminal Court, which convened in Rome during the summer of 1998. PrepCom had done a great deal of work since 1996; its efforts became the basis for discussions in Rome in 1998.

Of the 185 member states of the United Nations, 160 sent representatives to Rome for the International Criminal Court (ICC) conference. There were 235 accredited nongovernmental organizations (NGOs) in attendance at the deliberations that began on June 15, 1998, and ended on July 17, 1998. These NGOs were all under one organizational roof: the Coalition for an Independent Criminal Court (CICC). The workers for CICC were vital cogs in the final actions of the conferees. The CICC continually lobbied for the strongest, most independent ICC that could be created.

Additionally, the CICC served as the circulator of information to the delegates in Rome. A list of some of the groups illustrates the representational breadth of this important cohort, with its many hundreds of professional and volunteer workers who monitored every committee and subcommittee session during the six weeks of deliberation:

American Bar Association
Amnesty International
Association Internationale de Droit Penal
B'nai B'rith International
Baha'i International Community

Coordinating Board of Jewish Organizations

[President Jimmy] Carter Center

Center for the Development of International Law

DePaul Institute for Human Rights

European Law Students Association

Equality NOW

FN-Forbundet

Global Policy Forum

Human Rights Watch

Instituto Superiore Internazionale de Scienze Criminali

International Commission of Jurists

International Human Rights Law Group

Lawyers Committee for Human Rights

No Peace Without Justice

Parliamentarians for Global Action

Quaker UN Office

Transnational Radical Party

United Nations Association—USA

War and Peace Foundation

World Federalist Movement

World Order Models Project

These NGOs and their staffs were joined by the diplomatic plenipotentiaries from one hundred and sixty nations. Fifty years after the Nuremberg and Tokyo trials ended, fifty years after the Genocide Convention and the Universal Declaration of Human Rights were adopted by the United Nations, the fiftieth UN General Assembly placed on its agenda the establishment of the permanent International Criminal Court. However, the draft treaty that was the basis of the Rome sessions contained almost five hundred disputed options that the delegates had to resolve within the six-week period.

At the end of the conference in July 1998, the Rome Statute contained 128 Articles, up from 116 in the PrepCom draft. The section headings for the 13 parts of the PrepCom draft suggest the agenda for those in working in Rome:

Part 1. Establishment of the Court (articles 1–4), including general observations about its relationship with the United Nations.

Part 2. Jurisdiction, Admissibility, and Applicable Law (articles 5–20). This part contained many options for the delegates to discuss and choose among, regarding controversial issues such as the ICC's jurisdiction, core crimes, the trigger mechanism, the role of the prosecutor, complementarity, and the law to be applied by the ICC in deciding cases that come to it.

Part 3. General Principles of International Law (articles 21–34; General Principles of Criminal Law in the final draft). Individual responsibility for genocide and other war crimes, recognized at Nuremberg, was a conceptual anchor in this part of the draft statute. Draft article 23 (final treaty article 25) held that such individuals were individually responsible and liable for punishment for their crimes. In article 31 (draft and final versions), there were laid out exceptions to the individual responsibility: mental illness, intoxication, and threats to one's life.

Part 4. Composition and Administration of the Court (articles 35–53). This part essentially replicated the composition and administration of the two ad hoc tribunals of the 1990s in Yugoslavia and Rwanda. Articles in this section, borrowing from the two tribunals, discussed the role and functions of the Presidency, the Appeals Chamber, the Office of the Prosecutor, the Registry, and the qualifications of ICC judges.

Part 5. Investigation and Prosecution (articles 54–61). This dealt with the investigation and prosecution aspects of the international criminal justice process, including what process was due to those suspected of committing genocide and other crimes.

Part 6. Trial (articles 62–74). These articles addressed the various aspects of trial proceedings, including rights of the accused, protection of witnesses and victims, and the issue of reparation for victims.

Part 7. Penalties (articles 75–79). This limited punishment to imprisonment; the absence of the death penalty led to heated discussions in Rome.

Part 8. Appeal and Review (articles 80–84; Appeal and Revision in the final draft). This part addressed issues relating to the appeal and review of judicial decisions.

Part 9. International Cooperation and Judicial Assistance (articles 85–92).

Part 10. Enforcement (articles 93–101). State parties to the treaty had to enforce the judgments of the ICC by providing, at their discretion, prison facilities for incarcerating the convicted defendants.

Part 11. Assembly of State Parties (article 102). This part dealt with the oversight of the ICC divisions by states that ratified the Rome Treaty.

Part 12. Financing of the Court (articles 103–107).

Part 13. Final Clauses (articles 108–116). This part created parameters for states to file reservations and amendments of the ICC statute, review of the statute, and its ratification and entry into force.

In the end, the Rome Statute, adopted on July 17, 1998, by a vote of 120-7 (with 20 abstentions), resolved by majority vote all the contested, controversial, and significant descriptions of jurisdiction and access to the ICC. In every one of these critical votes, the United States voted in the minority with only a handful of other nation-states. The controversial, hard-fought articles of the ICC follow, showing the final vote on the merits by the conferees, with the articles numbered as they appear in the 1998 Rome Statute .

Part 2 (Jurisdiction, Admissibility, and Applicable Law) was centrally important, and very controversial, from the U.S. perspective. It contained sixteen articles (5–21), included after some bitter clashes between the United States and the majority of the states participating in the conference.

Article 5 of the ICC focused on the threshold for ICC jurisdiction: The ICC "shall be limited to the most serious crimes of concern to the international community as a whole (genocide, war crimes, crimes against humanity, and the crime of aggression [when it was defined at a subsequent time, but not sooner than 7 years after the Rome Statute comes into force])." At least 73 percent of the nations participating in the discussion—64 states—voted for automatic ICC jurisdiction for all three core crimes, whereas the United States and 20 others voted for automatic jurisdiction for crimes of genocide only with an (extremely unlikely) opt-in by an affected state for the other core crimes.

There was no disagreement on the definition of Genocide. Article 6 was taken from the 1948 Genocide Convention. Article 7 (Crimes Against Humanity) covers actions committed by either official or nongovernmental actors in either peacetime or time of armed conflict. Furthermore, crimes against humanity in the article authorized the ICC to prosecute forcible transfers of population, severe deprivation of physical liberty, rape, sexual slavery, enforced prostitution, forced pregnancy, and persecution on political, racial, national, ethnic, cultural, religious, gender, or other grounds that are universally recognized as impermissible under international law.

Article 8 (1), agreed upon by 80 percent (39) of the nations voting, states that there was ICC jurisdiction, "in particular," when war crimes were committed as part of a plan or conspiracy. Although it was a restriction on the jurisdiction of the prosecutor, it was seen as stronger than the minority view of jurisdiction. The losing position, argued by the United States and eight other nations, was that there was ICC jurisdiction "only" when war crimes were committed as part of a plan or conspiracy. Article 8(2) provides the ICC with jurisdiction over war crimes committed in both international and noninternational (internal) armed conflict.

Article 12(1) provides for automatic jurisdiction by the ICC over all three core crimes. (To obtain French agreement to the Rome Statute, a "transitional provision" (article 124) was added. It allows a nation party to the treaty to opt-out of court jurisdiction for alleged war crimes for a period of seven years following the "entry into force of the Statute for the Party concerned." However, Article 12(2) does not provide "universal jurisdiction" to accompany the automatic jurisdiction. Under 12(2), absent a referral to it by the UN Security Council, the ICC can take up a case only when submitted to it by a state party or initiated by the prosecutor when either the state on whose territory the crime was committed or the state of the accused's nationality is a state party or has accepted the ICC's jurisdiction over the crime on an ad hoc basis. (Article 12(2) is a limitation on the ICC until all states are parties to the statute, thereby making it universal.)

There emerged, as a result, the article 12 paradox. Even if the United States, for example, did not ratify the Rome Statute, its military and civilian forces were subject to ICC jurisdiction as long as the nation in which the alleged war crimes took place had ratified the statute and could not or would not bring to trial the soldiers charged with war crimes or other crimes of universal jurisdiction. But the opt-out in article 12 enables nation-states who had committed war crimes and who were state parties to the Rome Statute to not be exposed to ICC jurisdiction, at least for seven years, possibly for decades.

The controversial issue of whether the prosecutor's office had independent power was addressed in Article 15(1) of the Rome Statute. The U.S. position was convincingly rejected by 85 percent of the nations participating. By a vote of 63-13, the delegates adopted language that gave the prosecutor independent power, *proprio motu* ("on one's own motion," i.e., to investigate and initiate prosecutions), along with, as noted in article 13(b) and (c), referral of cases to the prosecutor's office by the Security Council or by a state party to the treaty. To dampen concern on the part of some states about the discretionary powers of the prosecutor initiating investigations *proprio motu,* articles 15(3–4) and 18 were grafted on to this part of the statute. The former requires the prosecutor to obtain judicial approval by the Chambers at an early stage of the ICC actions. Article 18 enables an "interested party" to challenge the admissibility of a case at an early stage in the ICC proceedings.

The Singapore compromise—allowing the Security Council to defer a case for one year—was included in the final Rome Statute as article 16. As finally adopted, it enabled the Security Council, when necessary for peacekeeping purposes, to halt ICC actions for one year: "No investigation or prosecution may be commenced or proceeded with under this statute for a period of 12 months after the Security Council, in a resolution adopted under Chapter VII of the Charter of the UN, has requested the Court to that effect; the request may be renewed by the Council under the same conditions." Fifty-three nations opted for the one-year deferral, whereas the U.S. and only four other nations voted for the unspecified-number-of-years deferral option.

These were the most controversial articles in the statute, all found in Part 2. The Rome Statute as adopted was only 66 pages long (almost 500 options in the draft treaty were resolved by the end of the conference). It contained the same 13 parts that constituted the PrepCom's working draft and had 128 articles, more than the working draft.

Kofi Annan, the UN Secretary-General, had a view light years distant from the critics. In his opening statement greeting the delegates and others, he said that

> there can be no global justice unless the worst of crimes —crimes against humanity—are subject to the law. In this age more than ever we recognize that the crime of genocide against one people truly is an assault on us all—a crime against humanity. The establishment of an ICC will ensure that humanity's response will be swift and will be just. (Annan 1998)

Justice was the central concept for those supporting the creation of the ICC. Without the reality of perpetrators of horrible crimes against persons indicted, shown in the dock, and without a trial, and punishment of those found guilty—either by a national court of justice or by the ICC if domestic law is not enforced—hatred between groups will fester, and there will be no realistic peace and rapprochement in that community after the fighting ends. Asked Sadako Ogata, the UN's High Commissioner for Refugees, "Is it fair and realistic to expect the survivors to forgive and to cooperate if there is not justice? In the absence of justice, private revenge may prevail, which will spread fear and undermine the possibility of reconciliation" (Ogata 1998).

ICTY Judge Gabrielle Kirk McDonald, one of the judges in the *Prosecutor v. Tadic* trial at The Hague, gave a speech to members of the U.S. Judge Advocate General's (JAG) School in Charlottesville, Virginia. Part of her talk focused on what she called the "Cycle of Impunity."

> The twentieth century is best described as one of split personality: aspiration and actuality. The reality is that this century has been the bloodiest period in history. As improvements in communications and weapons technology have increased, the frequency and barbarity of systematic uses of fundamental rights have likewise escalated, yet little has been done to address such abuses. . . . In the prospect of an ICC lies the promise of universal justice.

She continued:

> Impunity is not a new phenomenon. However, the crystallization of the cycle of impunity is very much a twentieth century concept: perpetrators of massive human rights violations have often been supported, rather than held accountable, by the international community. . . .

> With few, but notable exceptions, there has been no reckoning for the great majority of mass violations of human rights throughout this century; perpetrators have either not been identified, or have not been required to account for their crimes. The prevalence of such impunity has placed expediency above both principle and pragmatism.(McDonald 1998)

She closed her observations with a somber warning to the American JAG audience: "There will be no lasting peace without justice."

After fifty years (1948–1998), the global community finally structured a permanent international criminal court. There was, in the end, a great deal of unanimity on the fundamentals of a working court: jurisdiction; definition of the major crimes—genocide, crimes against humanity, and war crimes; an independent prosecutor's office that could initiate investigations about possible "grave violations" of international law; and the relationship of the court to the UN Security Council. In the end, only seven nations voted against the Rome Statute's adoption. In 2002, the Rome Treaty was ratified by the requisite minimum number of nations (60). The hard tasks lay ahead: selecting the prosecutor, appointing the prosecutor's staff, appointing the judges, and, most important, having the world community give its imprimatur to the actual operations of the ICC.

Conclusion

The ICC received more than the sixty required ratifications on April 11, 2002, and came into force on July 1, 2002. "A page in the history of humankind is being turned," said chief UN legal counsel Hans Corell (quoted in *New York Times,* April 12, 2002, p. 1A). In the end, the success of the ICC depends on the willingness of powerful nation-states, chief among them the United States, to support and to assist the ICC in these matters. Initially, there must be a commitment in domestic policy and law to act against persons living in their territory who were charged with committing these violent, universally condemned actions. If a nation-state will not or cannot provide a fair trial for the defendant, then ICC jurisdiction enables the independent prosecutor to initiate action in The Hague.

If it is to succeed, the ICC must reflect a balancing of international idealism with the realpolitik of the nation-state system. The one vehement critic of the ICC—the United States—thus far has refused to ratify the treaty. However, Philippe Kirsch, Canada's ambassador to Sweden and chairman of the commission responsible for preparing for the ICC's operations, said that once the ICC shows it will act in "a very judicial and nonpolitical way," the United States will accept the new court: "In my view, given the United States' tradition of commitment to international justice, it is a matter of time before there is some form of cooperation developing between the United States and the [ICC]."

References

Annan, Kofi. Speech in Rome, Italy, July 17, 1998. Available at www.un.org.

Bardakjian, K. *Hitler and the Armenian Genocide.* Cambridge, MA: Harvard University Press, 1985.

Bassiouni, M. Cherif. "From Versailles to Rwanda in Seventy Five Years: The Need to Establish a Permanent International Criminal Court." 10 *Harvard Human Rights Journal* (1997): 1–128.

Becker, Elizabeth. *When the War Was Over: The Voices of Cambodia's Revolution and Its People.* New York: Simon and Schuster, 1986.

Bell-Falkoff, Andrew. *Ethnic Cleansing.* New York: St. Martin's Press, 1996.

Campbell, John. *The Experience of World War II.* New York: Oxford University Press, 1989.

Chandler, David P. *The Tragedy of Cambodian History: Politics, War, and Revolution Since 1945.* New Haven, CT: Yale University Press, 1991.

Crnobrnja, Mihailo. *The Yugoslav Drama.* Quebec, Canada: McGill-Queens University Press, 1996.

Cushman, Thomas, and Stjepan G. Mestrovi, eds. *This Time We Knew: Western Responses to Genocide in Bosnia.* New York: New York University Press, 1996.

Dedijer, Vladimir. *The Yugoslav Auschwitz and the Vatican: The Croatian Massacre of the Serbs During World War Two.* Buffalo, NY: Prometheus Books, 1992.

DePaul, Kim, ed. *Children of Cambodia's Killing Fields: Memoirs by Survivors.* New Haven, CT: Yale University Press, 1998.

Dorsen, Norman, and Morton H. Halperin. "Justice After Genocide." *Washington Post,* May 13, 1998.

Gutman, Roy. *Witness to Genocide.* Shaftsbury, UK: Element Books, 1993.

Hilberg, Raul. *Perpetrators Victims Bystanders: The Jewish Catastrophe, 1933–1945.* New York: Harper Collins, 1992.

Kamm, Henry. *Cambodia: Report from a Stricken Land.* New York: Arcade Publishing, 1998.

Keane, Fergal. *Season of Blood: A Rwandan Journey.* New York: Viking Press, 1995.

Kiernan, Ben. "The Cambodian Genocide, 1975–1979." In *Century of Genocide,* ed. Samuel Totten. New York: Garland Publications, 1997.

———. *The Pol Pot Regime: Race, Power, and Genocide in Cambodia Under the Khmer Rouge, 1975–1979.* New Haven, CT: Yale University Press, 1996.

Kumar, Krishna, ed. *Rebuilding Societies After Civil War.* Boulder, CO: Lynne Rienner Publishers, 1997.

Kuper, Leo. *Genocide: Its Political Use in the Twentieth Century.* New Haven, CT: Yale University Press, 1981.

———. *The Prevention of Genocide.* New Haven, CT: Yale University Press, 1985.

Mass, Peter. *Love Thy Neighbor: A Story of War.* New York: A. A. Knopf, 1996.

McDonald, Gabrielle. Speech in Rome, Italy, July 17, 1998. Available at www.un.org.

Ogata, Sadako. Speech in Rome, Italy, July 17, 1998. Available at www.un.org.

Prunier, Gerard. *The Rwanda Crisis: History of a Genocide.* New York: Columbia University Press, 1995.

Rosenblatt, Roger. "Memories of Pol Pot." *Time,* August 18, 1998.

Sacirbey, Nedzib. "The Genesis of Genocide: Reflections on the Yugoslav Conflict." 3 *Brown Journal of World Affairs* (Winter/Spring 1996).

Silber, Laura, and Allan Little. *Yugoslavia: Death of a Nation.* New York: Penguin USA, 1996.

Stanley Foundation. "The UN Security Council and the ICC: How Should They Relate?" Arden House, NY: Stanley Foundation, February 20–22, 1998.

Stork, Joe. "The ICC in Focus." 3 *International Criminal Court* (1998).

Totten, Samuel, William S. Parsons, and Israel Charney, eds. *Century of Genocide.* New York: Garland Publications, 1997.

Vulliamy, Edward. *Seasons in Hell: Understanding Bosnia's War.* London: Simon and Schuster, 1994.

Weisburd, Mark A. *Use of Force: The Practice of States Since World War Two.* University Park: Pennsylvania State University Press, 1997.

Zimmerman, Warren. "The Demons of Kosovo." 52 *National Interest* (Spring 1998).

3

International Laws of War: A Chronology of Major Treaties and Events in Armed Conflicts that Triggered their Adoption, 1856–2002

From the mid–nineteenth century to today, the international community has codified the customary principles of armed conflicts and created new laws of war in response to events that shocked the collective moral conscience. Some of these conventions were created because of the insistence of private individuals such as Swiss national Henri Dumont in the 1850s or Vermont resident Jody Williams in the 1990s. Both extensively, successfully lobbied the world community for an international treaty to protect the wounded in the field or to end the use of antipersonnel landmines in armed conflicts. Interestingly, Dumont was the first recipient of the Nobel Prize for his efforts on behalf of the sick and wounded and the medical personnel who treated them. Williams was the recipient, along with her organization, the International Campaign to Ban Landmines (ICBL), of the 1997 Nobel Prize for work that led to the convening of the 1997 Ottawa Convention on the Prohibition, Use, Stockpiling, Production, and Transfer of Anti-Personnel Mines and on Their Destruction. (By the time of the 1997 Ottawa Convention, the ICBL had grown into a coalition of some 1,000 organizations in more than 75 nations.)

Other treaties became reality after nongovernmental organizations (NGOs) such as the International Committee of the Red Cross (ICRC) called for the convening of interested parties to address specific abominations that occurred during war, whether it was poison gas, the systematic rape of women, or some other horrible war crime. Other conventions were convened at the invitation of a nation's leader; for example, the 1907 Hague Convention met at the request of U.S. President Theodore Roosevelt. Finally, the United Nations has been the forum in which member states triggered actions that led to the creation of new international laws of war such as the 1948 Convention on the Prevention and Punishment of the Crime of Genocide.

In all these treaties and conventions there is the recognition that armed conflict is a reality of national and international life. However, after that acknowledgement, there is also the reality that war is not an unlimited event but that there are limits to the methods and the means of killing. Finally, that noncombatants—that is, civilians, wounded soldiers, soldiers hors de combat, and prisoners of war (POWs)—must be treated humanely and with dignity by the warring parties in an armed conflict. The treaty-drafters have evidenced great concern about the adverse effects of war on innocent victims. The statistics on this issue are grim: In 1900, about 90 percent of the dead and wounded in an armed conflict were combatants; in 1945, it was 50 percent; and in 2000, it was only 25 percent.

The laws of war establish the legitimate boundaries of actions in all armed conflicts, whether major wars or civil wars. Furthermore, as seen since the end of World War II, the world community has created tribunals of all types—national, hybrid, international—ad hoc and permanent to ensure that those who violate these international laws of war are brought to the bar of justice.

The chronology in this chapter enumerates the major characteristics of the international treaties that have created the international law of wars. Some of these laws (noted with asterisks) are reproduced in chapter 5.

Chronology

Paris, 1856 — Paris Declaration Respecting Maritime Law. A maritime convention met to address the status of neutral ships during wartime.

Battle of Solferino, Italy, 1859 — In one day, more than 40,000 French and Italian soldiers were killed or wounded and left to die on the battlefield.

1861–1865 — U.S. Civil War

Washington, D.C., 1863 — During the U.S. Civil War President Abraham Lincoln asked a Columbia University law professor, Francis Lieber, to draft a manual for the behavior of Union troops in the field. Promulgated as General Order No 100, Adjutant General's Office, on April 24, 1863, in Washington, D.C., it was distributed to every commander in the Union Army (and sent to Confederate leaders). It was followed by the belligerents and remains the core of the latest manual for the conduct of war by U.S. forces in the field. Lieber's code of behavior, entitled *Instructions for the Government of Armies of the United States in the Field,* had sections about the use of private property of the enemy, the protection of persons, "and especially of women, of religion, the arts and sciences, [and] the punishment of crimes against the inhabitants of hostile countries," deserters, POWs ("who shall be fed upon plain and wholesome food, whenever practicable, and treated with humanity"), partisan fighters, spies, captured messengers, abuse of the flag of truce, exchange of prisoners, parole, armistice, capitulation, and guidelines on "insurrection—Civil War—Rebellion." Lieber's *Instructions* became a model for other nations in the decades after it was originally published.

Geneva, August, 1864* — The Geneva Convention for the Amelioration of the Wounded and Sick of Armies in the Field, signed by twelve nations, created the International Committee of the Red Cross. It provided "inviolability" for medical staff and volunteers to care for wounded in the field, called for humane treatment of the wounded and POWs, and created an emblem for those who treated the wounded—a red cross on a white background, the reverse colors of the Swiss flag. By 1900, there were Red Cross societies in thirty-seven nations, including, in 1882, the United States.

St. Petersburg, Russia, 1868 — The St. Petersburg Declaration Renouncing the Use of Explosive Projectiles banned the use of explosive bullets in battle. The explosive bullets were prohibited because of the perceived need to "alleviate as much as possible the calamities of

St. Petersburg, Russia, 1868, *cont.*

war." The use of those bullets "uselessly aggravate the sufferings of disabled men [and are] contrary to the laws of humanity."

France, Germany, 1870–1871

Franco-Prussian War. War crimes committed against wounded belligerents on both sides led the ICRC to call for the creation of an international criminal court to adjudicate violations of the 1864 Geneva Convention.

The Hague, Netherlands, 1899*

Hague Declaration. Toward the end of the nineteenth century, many customary principles of war were codified at The Hague in 1899. The general thrust was to "serve the interests of humanity and the ever progressive needs of civilization" by "diminish[ing] the evils of war." This was to be accomplished by revising "the general laws and customs of war, either with a view to defining them with greater precision or to confining them within such limits as would mitigate their severity as far as possible." Another fundamental principle was born at these meetings: The individual, irrespective of nationality, had rights and duties as well as obligations under the laws of war. The first treaty of the modern era that addressed "the illegality of aggressive force [and its effects on civilians] was embodied in the 1899 Hague Declaration for the Pacific Settlement of International Disputes." Disarmament, and the need to provide arbitration and mediation for use as an alternative to war, were the foci of the conference. For the treaty-signers, international arbitration was "recognized . . . as the most effective, and at the same time, the most equitable, means of settling disputes which diplomacy has failed to settle."

The Hague, Netherlands, 1907*

The original 1899 Hague Declaration was amplfied at a 1907 meeting. It contained many separate conventions on different topics (including the laws and customs of war on land; the rights and duties of neutral powers and persons in case of war on land; the conversion of merchant ships into warships; the laying of automatic submarine contact mines; bombardment by naval forces in time of war; restrictions with regard to the exercise of the right of capture in naval war; and the rights and duties of neutral powers in naval war); a detailed annex codified existing and future restraints on waging war. The restrictions underscored the principle that the right of belligerents to fight war is not unlimited. It prohibited certain methods of fighting war, and the implicit assumption was that persons could be prosecuted for violating these new laws of war if they:

- bombarded undefended towns
- used poison and other weapons that caused "superfluous" injuries
- declared no quarter
- improperly used the flag of truce
- "wantonly" destroyed enemy cities, towns, or caused "devastation not justified by military necessity"
- "willfully damaged institutions dedicated to religion, charity and education, the arts and sciences, historic monuments and works of art and science"
- attacked or bombarded undefended towns, villages, or dwellings
- abused lawful authority over enemy civilians when occupying an enemy's territory
- mistreated POWs
- attacked soldiers who had laid down their arms
- used dum-dum bullets
- used projectiles containing asphyxiating gases "calculated to cause unnecessary suffering"
- used aerial bombs
- violated a nation's neutrality.

Both of the early Hague Conventions raised a new issue regarding the conduct of war between belligerents: "The duty owed by a belligerent occupant to citizens of the overrun nation." The

The Hague, Netherlands, 1907* *cont.*

"duty owed" to the citizens of the enemy nation by the occupier was that the occupier "shall take all the measures in his power to restore and ensure, as far as possible, public order and safety, while respecting, unless absolutely prevented, the law in force in the country." The 1907 treaty was silent regarding punishment of war crimes on the battlefield as well as collateral war crimes against unarmed civilians. There was no enforcement mechanism agreed to by the states that were party to the treaty, and only one of the articles addressed the consequence of violating the regulations. Article III stated, in its entirety, that "a belligerent party which violates the provisions of the said Regulations shall, if the case demands, be liable to pay compensation. It shall be responsible for all acts committed by persons forming part of its armed forces."

1914–1918

World War I. The world's first "total" war involved more than three dozen nations in armed conflict in Europe, the Middle East, Africa, and Asia. For the first time, new military tactics, technologies, and devices were introduced, including the machine gun, the tank, bombardment by airplanes, submarine warfare, trench warfare, barbed wire, new explosives, new cannon and mortars, and the use of poisonous gas. Conscription for military service was adopted by all belligerents, and entire civilian populations of the nations at war were mobilized to contribute to the war effort. Twenty-one million military personnel were injured; almost 10 million combatants were killed.

Versailles, France, 1919

The victors of World War I drew up the Versailles Treaty (as well as others), formally ending the war between the allies and the Central Powers. Germany (Treaty of Versailles, June 28, 1919); Austria (Treaty of Saint-Germaine-En-Laye, September 10, 1919); Bulgaria (Treaty of Neuilly-Sur-Seine, November 27, 1919); Hungary (Treaty of Trianon, June 4, 1920); and Turkey (Treaty of Sevres, August 10, 1920) were all forced to accept unforgiving peace terms, reflecting the deep hatred of Germany by the allies and the associated nations. The treaty included a war crimes tribunal to address charges that the Central Powers committed war crimes and otherwise violated the laws and customs of war. Sections 227–230 of the Treaty of Versailles mandated the establishment of an international war crimes tribunal. For the first time in history, these clauses established the principle that war crimes punishment of some sort was a proper conclusion of a war, rather than the traditional amnesty that followed earlier wars. Although not enforced, sections 227–230 were precedent-setting in international law. Section 227 "publicly arraign[ed] William II of Hohenzollern, formerly German Emperor, for a supreme offence against international morality and the sanctity of treaties." A special tribunal (consisting of five judges, one each from five victorious allied nations—the United States, Great Britain, France, Italy, and Japan) would have tried the accused, "assuring him the guarantees essential to the right of defense, . . . [and] to fix the punishment which it considers should be imposed." Germany and the other defeated Central Powers were required, in Section 228, to "recognize the right of the Allied and Associated Powers to bring before military tribunals persons accused of having committed acts in violation of the laws and customs of war. Such persons shall, if found guilty, be sentenced to punishments laid down by law." They were required to "hand over" to the victors "all persons accused of having committed an act in violation of the laws and customs of war." Section 229 outlined the due process guarantees accused war criminals would receive.

Finally, in Section 230, Germany and the other defeated nations were required to "furnish all documents and information of every kind, the production of which may be considered necessary to ensure the full knowledge of the incriminating acts, the discovery of offences and the just appreciation of responsibility."

Versailles, France, 1919	The League of Nations was created in article I of the Versailles Treaty. It ceased functioning in 1946, in part because the United States never joined the League.
The Hague, Netherlands, 1923	Hague Rules of Aerial Warfare. This treaty addressed several issues related to aerial warfare (markings, propaganda leaflets, terrorizing civilian populations, and attacking military targets). It was never adopted. The bombing provisions specifically addressed the terrorization of civilians: "Aerial bombing for the purpose or terrorizing the civilian population, of destroying or damaging private property not of a military character, or of injuring non-combatants is prohibited."
Geneva, Switzerland, 1925*	Geneva Protocol for the Prohibition of the Use in War of Asphyxiating, Poisonous or other Gases, and of Bacteriological Methods of Warfare. This treaty prohibited the first use—but not the possession—of poison gas and bacteriological methods of warfare.
Paris, France, 1928*	The Treaty of Paris (the Kellogg-Briand Pact for the Renunciation of War as an Instrument of National Policy) was ratified by nearly all nations prior to the start of World War II and was viewed as a customary principle binding the behavior of all civilized nations. There must be "a frank renunciation of war as an instrument of national policy made to the end that peaceful and friendly relations between their peoples may be perpetuated." All the major nations involved in World War I, including Germany and Japan, signed this treaty.
Geneva, Switzerland, 1929*	The Red Cross Convention Regarding the Amelioration of the Condition of Wounded and Sick of Armies in the Field; and the Geneva Convention on the Treatment of Prisoners of War. Both these conventions were later revised after World War II, when the better-known Geneva Conventions were created and ratified.

The Red Cross convention called for a cease-fire by belligerents in order to remove sick and wounded from the battlefield; the collection of the names of the wounded and the dead for transmission to the other side in an armed conflict; the improvement of sanitary conditions; and the protection of Red Cross doctors, nurses, and other staff, who were not to be harmed or captured by belligerent forces.

The POW convention prohibited reprisals and collective punishment for POWs. A POW was required to give only name, rank, and regimental number. After capture, the POW must be taken out of the war zone immediately—unless seriously wounded. The POW camp had to provide humane conditions for work and recreation. Food had to be the equivalent of what the armed forces of the enemy ate daily. Letters and packages had to be given to POWs. Escapes were to be punished, but not by death. At the conclusion of an armed conflict, all POWs must be repatriated.

London, 1936 [clarifying 1930 treaty]

London Process-Verbal Relating to the Rules of Submarine Warfare, Part IV, Treaty of London. This treaty dealt with actions by belligerent submarines against merchant shipping. It called for submarine commanders to "conform to the laws of International Law to which surface vessels are subject." This meant that a submarine "may not sink or render incapable of navigation a merchant vessel without first having placed passengers, crew, and ship's papers in a place of safety."

1935–1936

Fascist Italy, led by dictator Benito Mussolini, attacked Ethiopia, using planes to bomb civilian populations and undefended towns.

1936–1939

Spanish Civil War. Forces from some of the world's most powerful nations participated in this conflict between the republican forces and the Spanish military, led by General Francisco Franco. These included the Soviet Union (for the

1936–1939 *cont.*	republic), Nazi Germany, led by Adolf Hitler, and fascist Italy, led by Benito Mussolini. Nazi forces used dive-bombers to terrorize and bomb civilian populations and undefended towns and cities. Tactics that were later used in World War II were developed during this war. England, France, and the United States did not formally engage in hostilities, although volunteers from these and other nations fought for the republic.
1937	Japanese Armies invade China. Japanese airplanes were used to terrorize and kill civilians and destroy undefended towns and cities. This marks the beginning of World War II in the Pacific.
1938	Nazi Germany incorporated Sudetenland (Czechoslovakia) into the Third Reich. It is a move accepted by the United Kingdom and France. By 1939, the whole of Czechoslovakia is under the control of Nazi Germany.
Poland, 1939	World War II begins in Europe when Nazi Germany invades Poland, and Great Britain and France—treaty allies of Poland—declare war on Germany. Using innovative military techniques on land, at sea, and in the air, Nazi Germany quickly overwhelms nine European nations, including France. Only the United Kingdom continued the battle against Hitler. On December 7, 1941, Japan bombed Pearl Harbor, the U.S. naval base in Hawaii, killing almost 3,000 military and civilian personnel and destroying the U.S. battleship fleet sitting in the harbor. The following day, the United States declared war on Japan, and shortly thereafter Germany and Italy declared war on the United States. The major alliances were the Axis (Germany, Italy, and Japan) versus the Allies (chiefly, the United States, Great Britain, and the Soviet Union after it was invaded by erstwhile ally Germany in 1941). World War II was also a total war. Millions of civilians were killed by bombs dropped from airplanes on both sides of the battle lines. More civilians were

killed in World War II than were military combatants. Major cities devastated by aerial bombing included London, Berlin, Manchester, Nanking, Tokyo, and Dresden. During the war, the Nazis and Japan brutalized civilian populations, executing millions of civilians because of their race, religion, ethnicity, or national origin. Included groups were Jews, Gypsies, Poles, Russians, and Chinese. Six million European Jews alone were exterminated by Nazi Germany between 1939 and 1945. New events added to the lexicon of war and war crimes: concentration camps, killing centers, Xyklon gas, crematoria, gas chambers, crimes against humanity, and genocide. The Germans and the Japanese used millions of civilians as slave labor during the war (including Jews, Jehovah's Witnesses, communists, Poles, Russians, Gypsies, and Chinese). Sixty percent of these laborers died in less than six months, including 3 million Russian military POWs. The Nazis and the Japanese conducted horrible medical experiments on these groups of civilians and POWs during World War II.

San Francisco, May 1945 — Initial meeting of the United Nations.

London, August 1945 — London Charter. An accord is reached by the four Allies who fought Nazi Germany (the United States, United Kingdom, Soviet Union, and France). It established guidelines and procedures for the trial of major Nazi war criminals. The Allied Control Commission was established to govern occupied Germany after the war ended. An international military tribunal, the first in world history, was established and began work in November 1945 with almost two dozen major Nazi Germany political, governmental, and military leaders on the docket. These defendants were charged with one or more war crimes: waging an aggressive war; crimes against the peace; war crimes; crimes against humanity; and conspiracy to commit these crimes.

Nuremberg, Germany, 1945

An international military tribunal, consisting of one justice (and one alternate) from each of the Allied powers, began work in Nuremberg, Germany, to hear evidence and pass judgment in the trials of top Nazi leaders. It was the first such international criminal tribunal in history convened to hear cases against individuals accused of war crimes and crimes against humanity during wartime.

Tokyo, Japan, 1946

The International Military Tribunal–Far East was established by the supreme commander of Allied forces in the Pacific, U.S. General Douglas MacArthur, to hear evidence and pass judgment in the trials of major Japanese political, military, and economic leaders. The tribunal consisted of one jurist from each of the eleven Allied nations who fought against the Japanese Empire.

Nuremberg, Germany, 1946*

The Nuremberg Principles were enunciated and codified by the United Nations in 1946. These were the basic guidelines used by jurists at Nuremberg, Tokyo, and other places where war crimes trials of Nazis and Japanese military and governmental individuals took place. The principles are:

1. Individual criminal responsibility for war crimes;
2. Responsibility defined in customary international law;
3. "Head of State" and "sovereign immunity" are not valid defenses against charges;
4. "Superior Orders" is no defense "provided a moral choice was in fact possible";
5. Defendant has the "right to a fair trial on the facts and law";
6. Three categories of crimes were established: Crimes against the peace, that is, "planning, preparation, initiation or waging a war of aggression, or a war in violation of international treaties, agreements, or assurances, or participating in a common plan or conspiracy for

the accomplishment of any of the foregoing"; war crimes, that is, "violations of the laws and customs of war. Such violations shall include, but not be limited to, murder, ill-treatment or deportation to slave labor or for any purpose of civilian population of or in occupied territory, murder or ill-treatment of prisoners of war or persons on the seas, killing of hostages, plunder of public or private property, . . . or devastation not justified by military necessity"; and crimes against humanity, that is, "murder, extermination, enslavement, deportation, and other inhumane acts committed against any civilian population, before or during the war; or persecutions on political, racial or religious grounds in execution of or in connection with any crime within the jurisdiction of the Tribunal, whether or not in violation of the domestic law of the country where perpetrated."

7. Complicity in the commission of crimes enumerated in Principle 6 is a crime in international law;

New York, 1948*

The United Nations (UN) Convention on the Prevention and Punishment of the Crime of Genocide was adopted to prevent the horrors perpetrated by Nazi Germany against a religious group, the Jews. (The Nazis saw the Jews as a racial as well as a religious group.) The term "genocide" means the "destruction of a group." A Polish Jew, Raphael Lempkin, created the phrase in the 1930s (from *genos,* Greek for "race" or "tribe"; and *cide,* Latin for "murder"). For him, genocide meant a "coordinated plan of actions aimed at the destruction of essential foundations of the life of national groups, with the aim of annihilating the group." The international community, after realizing the extent of the Nazis' extermination program, readily adopted Lempkin's definition and incorporated it into the Genocide Convention. At the 1945 international military tribunal in Nuremberg, the prosecutor,

New York, 1948, *cont.*

Robert Jackson, charged the Nazi leaders with "crimes against humanity" using Lempkin's concept. Jackson said that the defendants "conduct[ed] a deliberate and systematic genocide, viz., the extermination of racial and national groups; against the civilian populations of certain occupied territories in order to destroy particular races and classes of people and national, racial or religious groups, particularly Jews, Poles, and Gypsies."

In the preamble to article I of part A, it was stated that genocide, "whether committed in time of peace or in time of war, is a crime under international law which the [contracting parties] undertake to prevent and to punish." This is a critical sentence, for it means that government officials can be charged with planning and/or committing genocide—even against their own citizens—either in peacetime or during war. The convention was embodied in UN Resolution No. 260(III) and had three parts. Part A contained the approved 1948 text; part B invited the world community to consider the possibility of creating a permanent international criminal court for the trial of persons charged—in the future—with genocide; and part C extended the applicability of the Genocide Convention to territories administered by nation-states. Articles II and III of part A are critical segments of the Genocide Convention. Article II defines "genocide" as "any of the following acts committed with intent to destroy, in whole or in part, a national, ethnical, racial or religious group," such as:

- "killing members of the group;
- causing serious bodily or mental harm to members of the group;
- deliberately inflicting on the group conditions of life calculated to bring about its physical destruction in whole or in part;
- imposing measures intended to prevent births within the group; [and]

- forcibly transferring children of the group to another group."

UN Resolution No. 96(I) of 1946 listed a somewhat different set of groups: racial, religious, political, and other groups. The resolution ratified in 1948 omitted any reference to "political" groups. Article III enumerated the actions that were punishable under the Genocide Convention:

- genocide;
- conspiracy to commit genocide;
- direct and public incitement to commit genocide;
- attempt to commit genocide; and
- complicity in genocide.

Most of the world's nations have ratified the 1948 Genocide Convention. It became one of the bases for charging military and governmental leaders with criminal acts at the International Criminal Tribunal for the Former Yugoslavia in 1993 and the International Criminal Tribunal for Rwanda in 1994.

Geneva, Switzerland, 1949*

The original 1929 Geneva Conventions were revised; collectively, the 1949 Geneva Conventions are the foundation stone of war crimes legislation. There are four of them: (I) Amelioration of the Condition of the Wounded and Sick in Armed Forces in the Field; (II) Wounded, Sick, and Shipwrecked Members of Armed Forces at Sea; (III) Relative to the Treatment of Prisoners of War; and (IV) Relative to the Protection of Civilian Persons in Time of War. After the concentration camps, killing centers, ill-treatment of POWs, and massive bombing of undefended cities during World War II, leading to millions of civilian deaths and the destruction of civilian and cultural property, the world community sought to strengthen the laws of war to prevent

Geneva, Switzerland, 1949, *cont.*

these events from happening again. The preamble noted that the convening of the 1949 meeting was "for the purpose of revising the 1929 Geneva Convention."

As the titles of the four conventions clearly suggest, the concern of the treaty-makers was more specific protection of the victims of war: the wounded (both on land and on the seas), hors de combat soldiers and sailors, POWs, and civilians on both sides of the battle. The ICRC was the principal NGO behind the convening of these meetings.

In 1977, two Geneva Protocols supplemented these four conventions (see below). The International Criminal Tribunal for the Former Yugoslavia (ICTY) and the International Criminal Tribunal for Rwanda (ICTR), as well as the Rome Statute's definition of "war crimes," are based on the four main Geneva Conventions.

The Hague, Netherlands, 1954

Hague Convention for the Protection of Cultural Property in the Event of Armed Conflict. In 1949, the United Nations began to discuss the issue of protection of cultural property during wartime. World War II had evidenced a great deal of theft and destruction of works of art and other cultural artifacts by Germany and Japan. By 1952, a UN committee drafted a convention on the protection, that is, "the safeguarding of and respect for," cultural heritage during wartime. In 1954, nation-states met at The Hague to adopt the convention. Article I defined cultural property to include, in part, "monuments of architecture, art, or history, whether religious or secular; manuscripts, books, and other objects of artistic, historical, or archeological interest; as well as scientific collections; . . . buildings, [and] centers containing a large amount of cultural property." Also included were regulations for carrying out the objectives of the treaty.

1945–1975

The first and second Indochina Wars between Vietnamese forces and France (1949–1954) and

United States (1963–1975, known as the Vietnam War).

New York, 1976

UN Convention on the Prohibition of Military or any Other Hostile Use of Environmental Modification Techniques. A prime factor in the creation of this treaty was the Americans' use of Agent Orange during the Vietnam War. This was a chemical defoliant dropped by air that destroyed forests in order to better spot and destroy the enemy. The preamble to the convention states, in part, that nations "desiring to prohibit effectively military or any other hostile use of environmental modification techniques in order to eliminate the dangers to mankind from such use,' agreed to take certain steps to bar such actions by a nation at war." The main focus was to eliminate the modification of the environment in war—for example, earthquakes, tsunamis, and changes in weather conditions—to kill and destroy combatants, civilians, and property. Article I limited all environmental modifying techniques that had "wide-spread, long-lasting, or severe effects" on water, clouds, earth, and so on. Article II defined the meaning of the idea "environmental modification techniques" as the "deliberate manipulation of natural processes—the dynamics, composition of the Earth, including its biota, lithosphere, hydrosphere and atmosphere, or of outer space."

Geneva, Switzerland, 1977*

Geneva Protocol I Additional to the Geneva Conventions of 12 August 1949 and Relating to the Protection of Victims of International Armed Conflicts; and Geneva Protocol II Additional to the Geneva Conventions of 12 August 1949 and Relating to the Protection of Victims of Non-International Armed Conflicts. By 1977, the world had seen, in Vietnam, Cambodia, and other areas of armed conflict, the proliferation of "noninternational armed conflicts," that is, civil wars. In addition, since the adoption of the 1949 Geneva Conventions, new techniques and instruments of

Geneva, Switzerland, 1977*, *cont.*

war had emerged and needed to be addressed by the world community. The two 1977 Geneva Protocols were ratified as supplements, not as replacements, for the 1949 conventions. General Protocol I embodies the customary principles and laws of war. It focused, among other subjects, on the protection of the wounded combatants and civilians. Under this protocol an international fact-finding commission can be established, competent to "enquire into any facts alleged to be a grave breach [of the laws of war] as defined in the [1949] Conventions and this Protocol, or other serious violations" and "to facilitate, through its good offices, the restoration of an attitude of respect for the [1949] Conventions and this Protocol." (In 1991, such a commission was established by the United Nations.)

Protocol II extends the protections of the laws of war to civil wars, an idea first proposed by the ICRC in 1912. The protocol extends (in article I) to all armed conflicts that "take place in the territory of a High Contracting Party between its armed forces and dissident armed forces or other organized armed groups which, under responsible command, exercise such control over a part of its territory as to enable them to carry out sustained and concerted military operations and to implement this Protocol." Article I excluded "riots, isolated and sporadic acts of violence, as not being armed conflicts."

Geneva, Switzerland, 1978*

Red Cross Fundamental Rules of International Humanitarian Law Applicable in Armed Conflicts. The ICRC and other NGOs, aware of the lack of clarity in war crimes definitions—because of the more than 550 articles in the four 1949 Geneva Conventions and the two 1977 Protocols—developed a brief document that attempted to summarize the essence of these hundreds of laws of war. In one page, the seven rules underscore the protection, fairness, and immunity due three sets of victims of war: POWs, belligerents hors do combat, and civilians. Rule 1:

"Persons hors de combat and those who do not take a direct part in the hostilities are entitled to respect for their lives and physical and moral integrity. They shall in all circumstances be protected and treated humanely without any adverse distinction." Rule 6: "Parties to a conflict and members of their armed forces do not have an unlimited choice of methods and means in warfare. It is prohibited to employ weapons or methods of warfare of a nature to cause unnecessary losses or excessive suffering." Rule 7 (focusing on civilians): "Parties to a conflict shall at all times distinguish between the civilian population and combatants in order to spare civilian population and property. Neither the civilian population as such nor civilian persons shall be the object of attack. Attacks shall be directed solely against military objectives."

New York, 1980

UN Conventions on Prohibitions or Restrictions on the Use of:

(I) Certain Conventional Weapons Which May Be Deemed to Be Excessively Injurious or to Have Indiscriminate Effects; Non-Detectable Fragments. The prohibited weapon was one that caused "superfluous injury or unnecessary suffering" by very small glass, wood and other fragments that cannot be detected by X-ray machines.

(II) Mines, Booby-traps, and Other Devices. Prohibited the indiscriminate use of such weapons, especially against civilians. Did not extend to civil wars.

(III) Incendiary Weapons. Given the devastation wrought by napalm (used indiscriminately by the United States during the Vietnam War), use of hydrocarbons, and other chemicals prohibited for use against civilians and civilian targets.

(IV) Blinding Laser Weapons (1995). Prohibited use of weapons that caused permanent blindness.

Amended Protocol II, 1996: Mines, Booby-Traps, and Other Devices	This amendment to Protocol II prohibited use of landmines in civil wars and in international armed conflicts. Definition of "landmines" broadened to include antipersonnel landmines developed since 1980.
Kuwait, 1991	OPERATION DESERT STORM, the U.S.-led Coalition victory against Iraq, which had invaded and occupied neighboring Kuwait in 1990.
1991–1995	Three wars in the former Yugoslavia between Serbia and Slovenia (1991); Croatia (1991–1995); and Bosnia-Herzegovina (1992–1995).
New York, 1993	UN Statute of International Criminal Tribunal for the Former Yugoslavia. Established by the United Nations and based at The Hague, Netherlands, the ICTY began work in 1995. The ICTY was the first ad hoc international criminal tribunal established since 1945–1946. It was created to deal with belligerents in the Bosnian wars who committed war crimes, crimes against humanity, and genocide. The UN statute established a prosecutor's office (responsible for bringing indictments against war criminals in Bosnia and Rwanda—see below), the staff office, and the tribunal—both trial and appeal courts. The jurisdiction of the ICTY was limited to the armed conflicts that took place in the former Yugoslavia in the 1990s, including the 1998 armed conflict between Yugoslavia and Serbia against ethnic Albanians in Kosovo province in 1998. It planned to continue its work throughout the first decade of the twenty-first century.
Rwanda, 1994	Civil war between Hutus and Tutsis in Rwanda, Africa. In less than three months of civil war, known as the Machete War, more than 800,000 Tutsis and moderate Hutus were massacred by the Hutus.
New York,	UN Statute of International Criminal Tribunal

1994	for Rwanda. Established by United Nations and based in Arusha, Tanzania, the ICTR began work in 1996 to conduct trials of those persons accused of planning, ordering, and committing war crimes, crimes against humanity, and genocide. It planned to continue its work through the first decade of the twenty-first century.
San Remo, Italy, 1994	*San Remo Manual on International Law Applicable to Armed Conflicts at Sea.* This manual, like the 1978 *Red Cross Fundamental Rules,* is not itself a treaty but a summary of the major conventions dealing with armed conflicts at sea. There had been no restatement or condensed summary of these laws of war since 1913. The introductory note states, in part, that "the purpose of the Manual is to provide a *contemporary restatemen*t of international law applicable to armed conflicts at sea. The Manual includes a few provisions which might be considered progressive developments in the law but most of its provisions are considered to state the law which is currently applicable."
New York, 1994	UN Convention on the Safety of UN and Associated Personnel. This treaty placed UN personnel, police, administration, and military on peacekeeping operations in the category of "protected persons," that is, ministers, medical personnel, POWs, wounded, soldiers hors de combat, and civilians. It was an effort to prevent attacks against UN personnel engaged in legitimate international peacekeeping missions.
Ottawa, Canada, 1997*	Ottawa Convention on the Prohibition, Use, Stockpiling, Production, and Transfer of Anti-Personal Mines and on Their Destruction. This treaty was adopted in response to the ugly reality of the indiscriminate use of antipersonnel landmines. These weapons have maimed and killed millions of civilians, especially children, caught up in civil or regional wars. Because there was little removal of landmines following the

Ottawa, Canada, 1997* *cont.*

end of conflict, deaths and injuries continued. Discrimination is a hallmark principle in the international laws of war. In 1996, a small group of nation-states, assisted by the ICBL, persuaded the United Nations to hold a conference that would ban the production, sale, and use of antipersonnel landmines. The preamble stated the purpose of the treaty: To "put an end to the suffering and the casualties caused by anti-personnel mines, that kill and maim hundreds of people every week, mostly innocent and defenseless civilians and especially children." In Article I, the general obligation of the state parties to the treaty were starkly announced: "Each State Party undertakes never under any circumstances: (a) to use anti-personnel mines, (b) To develop, produce, otherwise acquire, stockpile, retain or transfer to anyone, directly or indirectly, anti-personnel mines, (c) to assist, encourage, or induce, in any way anyone to engage in any activity prohibited to a State Party under this Convention." By 2000, almost 100 nations signed the treaty. The United States, however, refused to ratify the Ottawa Convention due to its bilateral military treaties with other nations, for example, South Korea, and the fact that antipersonnel landmines were an essential part of the defense mechanisms employed to deter aggression.

Rome, 1998*

Rome Statute of the International Criminal Court. After nine years of planning and drafting proposed statutes that would create a permanent international criminal court with an independent prosecutor's office and with jurisdiction to hear cases involving persons accused of war crimes, crimes against humanity, and genocide, more than 125 nations met in Rome to discuss and ratify the statute. After ratification, there was the requisite sixty (60) signatures needed to implement the International Criminal Court (ICC). These were received by spring 2002.

Kosovo, Serbian Republic, 1998–1999	Yugoslav Serb armed conflict with ethnic Albanians in the Kosovo War and North Atlantic Treaty Organization intervention, in the air and on the ground, to end the armed conflict.
Afghanistan, 2001–	OPERATION ENDURING FREEDOM, the U.S.-led military action against the Taliban government and Al-Qaeda terrorists.
The Hague, Netherlands, 2002	The ICC began operations in July 2002.

Conclusion

There as yet has been no international treaty that expressly prohibits the use of nuclear weapons as tactical instruments of war. There has, however, been discussion whether the use of such weapons is an example of the customary principle prohibiting unnecessary suffering.

References

Bassiouni, M. Cherif. *Crimes Against Humanity in International Criminal Law.* Nijhoff: Dortrecht, 1992.

Best, Geoffrey. *War and Law Since 1945.* Clarendon, UK: Oxford University Press, 1994.

Friedman, Leon. *The Laws of War: A Documentary History.* 2 vols. New York: Random House, 1972.

Hilberg, Raul. *The Destruction of European Jewry.* New York: Holmes and Meier, 1968.

Kuper, Leo. *The Prevention of Genocide.* New Haven, CT: Yale University Press, 1985.

Reisman, W. Michael, and Chris T. Antoniou. *The Laws of War: A Comprehensive Collection of Primary Documents on International Laws Governing Armed Conflict.* New York: Vintage, 1994.

Roberts, Adam, and Richard Guelff. *Documents on the Laws of War.* 3rd ed. New York: Oxford University Press, 2001.

Scott, James B. *The Hague Conventions and Declarations of 1899 and 1907.* 3rd ed. New York: Oxford University Press, 1918.

Smith, Bradley F. *The Road to Nuremberg.* New York: Basic Books, 1981.

Taylor, Telford. *The Anatomy of the Nuremberg Trials: A Personal Memoir.* New York: Knopf, 1992.

4

People and Events

Kofi Annan (1938–)

Kofi Annan of Ghana is the seventh Secretary-General of the United Nations. The first Secretary-General to be elected from the ranks of United Nations (UN) staff, he began his first term on January 1, 1997. On June 29, 2001, acting on a recommendation by the Security Council, the General Assembly appointed him by acclamation to a second term of office, beginning on January 1, 2002, and ending on December 31, 2006. Annan served as assistant Secretary-General for peacekeeping operations (March 1992–February 1993) and then as under Secretary–General (March 1993-December 1996). His tenure as under Secretary-General coincided with unprecedented growth in the size and scope of UN peacekeeping operations, with a total deployment, at its peak in 1995, of almost 70,000 military and civilian personnel from 77 countries. From November 1995 to March 1996, following the Dayton Peace Accords that ended the war in Bosnia-Herzegovina, Annan served as special representative of the Secretary-General to the former Yugoslavia, overseeing the transition in Bosnia-Herzegovina from the United Nations Protection Force to the multinational Implementation Force led by the North Atlantic Treaty Organization (NATO). On December 10, 2001, the Secretary-General and United Nations received the Nobel Prize. In conferring the prize, the Nobel Committee said Annan "had been pre-eminent in bringing new life to the Organization." In also conferring the prize on the world body, the committee said that it wished "to proclaim that the only negotiable road to global peace and cooperation goes by way of the United Nations." The Secretary-General is fluent in English, French, and several African languages. He is married to Nane Annan, of Sweden, a lawyer and artist who has a great interest in understanding the work of the United Nations in the field. Two issues of particular concern to her are HIV/AIDS and education for women. She has also written a book for children about the United Nations. The Annans have three children. (United Nations Department of Public Information, 2000–2002, www.un.org)

Balkan Wars, 1991–1995

After the fall of international communism in 1989, Yugoslavia's communist government struggled unsuccessfully to cope with a plunging economy and the reemergence of local nationalism. Yugoslavia's split began in May 1991, when Croatia and Slovenia declared their independence from the Serbian-dominated central government in Belgrade. To keep Bosnia-Herzegovina from seceding, Serbia offered to redraw territorial boundaries. But the Muslim president of Bosnia, Alija Izetbegovic, rejected the Serbian offer because he felt it did not give real power to the Muslims. He held a referendum on independence for Bosnia-Herzegovina. Bosnian Serbs boycotted the referendum, but 90 percent of those who did vote opted for Bosnian independence. On March 3, 1992, Izetbegovic proclaimed Bosnia-Herzegovina an independent republic. Bosnian Serbs rebelled, and an armed struggle broke out to determine which ethnic group would control the country. Bosnia-Herzegovina was composed of 40 percent Muslims, 30 percent Serbs, and 18 percent Croats. Although Bosnia's Muslims were in the majority with 2 million people, Bosnia's Serbian minority was better armed, receiving support from the neighboring Serbian army. Serbian militias, backed by the Serbian military, took control of two-thirds of Bosnia. Afterward, the Bosnian Serbs launched a reign of terror against the country's Muslim population. Enforcing a policy of ethnic cleansing, Bosnian Serbs set out to purify Bosnia by expelling Bosnian Muslims from the country. Bosnian Serb forces drove Muslims from their homes, subjecting them to systematic rape, confinement in concentration camps, and genocide.

Although some atrocities also occurred in Croatian-held and Muslim-held areas, international alarm was aroused mainly by pictures of starving concentration camp inmates and civilian casualties in Sarajevo as its Muslim population was besieged by the Serbian army in March 1992. Serbian artillery bombarded city streets and marketplaces daily. Finally, a NATO ultimatum brought about a cease-fire and the withdrawal of Serbian artillery in 1994. After a prolonged period of indecision, the world community took action to restore Bosnia's integrity. Peace negotiations held at Wright-Patterson Air Force Base in Dayton, Ohio, in late 1995 included presidents Milosevic of Serbia, Izetbegovic of Bosnia and Franjo Tudjman of Croatia. The three agreed on a government structure for Bosnia—a six-member council consisting of two Muslims, two Serbs, and two Croats headed by two cochairs to function as prime ministers.

Government ministries would also be divided among Serbs, Croats, and Muslims. In March 1996, the government of Bosnia-Herzegovina was given back control of the suburbs surrounding Sarajevo. Under the peace treaty, the capital area was to be in the hands of the Muslim-dominated government.

The UN international war crimes tribunal met the same month in The Hague, questioning Serbian soldiers about war crimes and issuing arrest warrants for Bosnian Serb officers. Serbians have refused to hand over officers charged with war crimes, instead regarding them as heroes. The first national postwar elections were held in Bosnia in September 1996 under the supervision of NATO troops. Bosnia's multiethnic parliament met for the first time in January 1997 and appointed a cabinet.

Cherif Bassiouni (December 8, 1937–)

Professor of law, DePaul University, Chicago, nominated for the Nobel Prize in 1999. Expert on international laws and customs of war, he is former chairman of the UN Commission of Experts Established pursuant to UN Security Council Resolution No. 780 (1992), charged with collecting war crimes evidence in the former Yugoslavia. Bassiouni, of Egypt, president of the International Institute of Higher Studies in Criminal Sciences in Siracusa, Italy, was also elected chairman of the drafting committee of the Diplomatic Conference on the Establishment of an International Criminal Court.

Winston Churchill (1874–1965)

Sir Winston Leonard Spencer Churchill was a British historian, orator, and politician; president of the Board of Trade, 1908–1910; British home secretary, 1910–1911; British first lord of the admiralty, 1911–1915, 1939–1940; oversaw naval buildup before and during World War I; initiated defense of Antwerp, 1914, unsuccessful Dardanelles campaign, 1915; fought in France, 1916; British munitions minister, 1917; British war secretary, 1919–1921; British air secretary, 1919–1921; British colonial secretary, 1921–1922; British chancellor of the exchequer, 1924–1929; restored gold standard; warned of growing menace of Nazi Germany; condemned Munich Agreement, 1938; leader of Conservative Party, 1940–1955; British prime minister, 1940–1945, 1951–1955; British defense secretary, 1940–1945, 1951–1952; oversaw British strategy during most of World War II; pledged support for Soviets after Germany launched assault on Soviet Union 1941; with Franklin Roosevelt, negotiated Atlantic Charter, 1941, establishing joint British-U.S. policy goals; held war conferences with Franklin Roosevelt at Washington, D.C., 1942, 1943, and Casablanca, 1943, with Franklin Roosevelt and Chiang Kai-shek at Cairo, 1943, with Franklin Roosevelt and Joseph Stalin at Tehran, 1943, and Yalta, 1945, with Harry Truman and Joseph Stalin at Potsdam, 1945; in speech at Fulton, Missouri, 1946, enunciated start of Cold War, with Britain and the United States leading opposition to Soviet communism, and coined phrase "iron curtain"; promoted European federation; wrote six-volume *The World Crisis,* 1923–1931, six-volume *Marlborough: His Life and Times,* 1933–1938, six-volume *The Second World War,* 1948–1954, four-volume *A History of the English-speaking Peoples,* 1956–1958; Nobel Prize in Literature, 1953; made honorary U.S. citizen, 1963. (National Library of Scotland and Churchill Archives, 2002)

Dayton Peace Accord of 1995

Peace agreement between the Bosnians, Croats, and Serbs signed in Paris, ending a war that engulfed the Balkans for more than three years, claimed more than 400,000 lives, and made 5 million people homeless. "Bosnia must find a way, with God's grace, to lay down the hatreds, to give up the revenge, to go forward together," said President Clinton.

Following are the key provisions of the Dayton peace plan for Bosnia announced by U.S. President Bill Clinton:

- Preserve Bosnia as a single state within its present borders. The state would be made up of two parts: a Bosnian-Croat federation and a Bosnian Serb republic, with a "fair distribution of land between the two."
- The capital city of Sarajevo will remain united. It is to have an "effective" central government, including a na-

tional parliament, the presidency, and a constitutional court with responsibility for foreign policy, foreign trade, monetary policy, citizenship, immigration, and other important functions.

- The presidency and the parliament will be chosen through free, democratic elections held under international supervision.
- Refugees will be allowed to return to their homes. People will be able to move freely throughout Bosnia, and the human rights "of every Bosnian citizen" will be monitored by an independent commission and an internationally trained civilian police force.
- Individuals charged with war crimes will be excluded from political life.
- A "strong international force" should supervise the separation of forces to give them confidence that each side will live up to their agreements.

Clinton said that "only NATO can do that job and the United States, as NATO's leader, must play an essential role in this mission."

Henri Dunant (1828–1910)

A Swiss businessman, visited the battlefield at Solferino, Italy, where he saw 40,000 dead and wounded. Appalled at the slaughter of so many and that so few persons were trying to care for the wounded, he used his own money to buy medical supplies. At home in Geneva, he wrote a book, *A Memory of Solferino*, 1862, about his experience on the battlefield. In it, he asked whether it would be "possible in time of peace and quiet to form relief societies for the purpose of having care given to the wounded in wartime by zealous, devoted, and thoroughly qualified volunteers?" The book was widely read and had an impact on its readers. At the call of another Swiss humanist, Gustave Moynier, president of Geneva's Welfare Society, sixteen European nations met in August, 1864, and twelve signed the Geneva Convention for the Amelioration of the Wounded and Sick of Armies in the Field. The treaty created International Committee of the Red Cross.

Richard J. Goldstone (1938–)

Richard J Goldstone was born on October 26, 1938. After graduating from the University of the Witwatersrand with a B.A. L.L.B.

cum laude in 1962, he practiced as an advocate at the Johannesburg bar. In 1989, he was appointed judge of the appellate division of the supreme court of South Africa; since July 1994, he has been a justice of the constitutional court. From 1991 to 1994, he served as chair of the Commission of Inquiry regarding Public Violence and Intimidation, which came to be known as the Goldstone Commission. From August 15, 1994, to September 1996 he served as chief prosecutor of the UN International Criminal Tribunals for the Former Yugoslavia and Rwanda. From August 1999 until December 2001, he was the chair of the International Independent Inquiry on Kosovo. In December 2001, he was appointed chair of the International Task Force on Terrorism.

Adolf Hitler (1889–1945)

Austrian-born Nazi dictator, orator, and politician; immigrated to Bavaria, 1913; fought in Bavarian regiment in World War I, 1914–1918, receiving Iron Cross, First Class, 1918; joined German Workers' Party in Munich, 1919; placed in charge of propaganda for German Workers' Party, 1920 (name changed to Nationalsozialistische Deutsche Arbeitpartei, 1920—the Nazi German Workers' Party); named president of Nazi Party 1921, with dictatorial power over party apparatus; gained support of Erich Ludendorff; using Erich Ludendorff as figurehead, led unsuccessful attempt to overthrow Bavarian government (Beer Hall Putsch), 1923, in Munich; arrested and sentenced to five years in prison; imprisoned 1923–1924 in Landsberg fortress before being prematurely paroled in 1924; while in prison, wrote *Mein Kampf* (My Struggle; dictated to Rudolf Hess); resumed Nazi organizational and propagandist activities, gaining many converts due largely to worsening economy and rising nationalism; candidate for president of Germany, 1932, but defeated by Paul von Hindenburg; helped secure lifting of ban on Nazi Storm Troops, 1932, leading to period of increased street skirmishes with opposition groups; offered chancellorship after resignation of Franz von Papen but declined upon failing to receive guarantee of full power, 1932; after resignation of Kurt von Schleicher, appointed chancellor by Paul von Hindenburg, 1933; chancellor of Germany, 1933–1945; gained control over Reichstag through Nazi-Nationalist majority in 1933 election; was granted dictatorial powers, lasting through 1937, as result of Enabling Act passed by Reichstag, 1933; declared national boycott of Jewish-owned businesses, 1933; oversaw passage of Civil Service Law, 1933, enabling dismissal of non-Aryan public officials; declared Nazi Party to be sole official political party, 1933; withdrew Germany from League of Nations, 1933; established summary People's Court, 1934, to try cases of treason; instigated Great Blood Purge, 1934, executing seventy-four people, including senior party officials, for alleged plot against Hitler regime; upon death of Paul von Hindenburg in 1934, received title of president (confirmed by plebiscite), assumed title of Führer, and gained dictatorial powers on permanent basis; following favorable plebiscite in Saar Basin, reincorporated Saar region of France into Germany, 1935; repudiated disarmament clauses of Versailles Treaty and reinstituted compulsory military service, 1935; instituted Nuremberg Laws, 1935, depriving Jews of civil rights and banning intermarriage between Jews and Gentiles; repudiated Locarno Pacts and reoccupied Rhineland 1936; with Galeazzo Ciano, negotiated formation of Berlin-Rome Axis, 1936; concluded pact with Japan, 1936; recognized Francisco Franco regime as government of Spain, 1936; invaded and annexed Austria, 1938 (Anschluss); in response to separatist agitation by ethnic Germans in Sudetenland region of Czechoslovakia, annexed Sudetenland, 1938, annexation recognized by major powers in Munich Pact of 1938; German defense minister, 1938–1945, intending to exert direct control over military operations; annexed Bohemia and Moravia, 1939, dissolving Czechoslovakia but leaving Slovakia nominally independent; negotiated nonaggression pact with Russia, 1939; invaded Poland, 1939, starting World War II; invaded Norway and Denmark, followed by Belgium, Luxembourg, and Netherlands, all in 1940; occupied Paris and most of France, 1940, concluding armistice with Henri Petain, 1940; with Italy and Japan, concluded Tripartite Pact, 1940; invaded Yugoslavia, 1941; despite nonaggression pact with Josef Stalin, launched surprise invasion of Russia, 1941; continued to exercise direct supervision of military operations, despite lack of strategic ability, leading to failure of Russia campaign and downturning of German fortunes; survived assassination attempt, 1944, led by German officers hoping to place competent military leadership in control and save Germany from total defeat; facing imminent defeat and Russian occupation of Berlin, committed suicide in bunker in Berlin, days before Germany's unconditional surrender; throughout chancellorship, directed systematic oppression and extermination (Holocaust) of ethnic, religious, and social minorities, especially Jews; as direct instigator of Holocaust and World War II, often cited as ultimate embodiment of evil.

International Military Tribunal, Nuremberg, Germany, 1945

For the first time in recorded history, the international community created and implemented a set of protocols to indict, try, and sentence individuals who were found guilty of violating the laws and customs of war.

Robert H. Jackson (1892–1954)

Associate justice of the U.S. Supreme Court (1941–1954). Born in Spring Creek, Pennsylvania. Despite the fact that he did not have a law degree, he was admitted to the bar in 1913 after a brief period of study at Albany law school. In 1934, he was appointed general counsel of the Bureau of Internal Revenue. From 1936 to 1938, he served as assistant U.S. Attorney General in charge of the antitrust division. A strong advocate of New Deal policies, Jackson became (in 1938) U.S. Solicitor General. In 1940, he became U.S. Attorney General, and in 1941 President Franklin D. Roosevelt appointed him to the Supreme Court. He went on leave (1945–1946) from the bench to be U.S. chief counsel at the Nuremberg war crimes trial. His feud with Justice Hugo L. Black probably eliminated him from consideration for chief justice when Harlan Stone died. His best-known decision was *West Virginia State Board of Education v. Barnette* (1943), which struck down statutes that made saluting the flag mandatory for school children, thereby significantly expanding the scope of free speech laid out in the First Amendment of the U.S. Constitution. Known for his eloquent literary style, Jackson defended freedom of religion with particular distinction. He wrote *The Struggle for Judicial Supremacy* (1940), *The Case Against the Nazi War Criminals* (1945), and *The Supreme Court in the American System of Government* (1955).

Radovan Karadzic (1945–)

Former Bosnian Serb leader Radovan Karadzic is one of the most wanted men in the world. Charged with leading the slaughter of thousands of Bosnian Muslims and Croats, he has twice been indicted by the United Nations war crimes tribunal in The Hague. The United Nations says his murder squads killed up to 6,000 Muslims at Srebrenica in July 1995 "in order to kill, terrorize and demoralize the Bosnian Muslim and Bosnian Croat population." He was also charged over the shelling of Sarajevo and the use of 284 UN peacekeepers as human shields in May and June 1995.

After the Dayton accord that ended the Bosnian war, the former nationalist president went into hiding—possibly in the mountainous southeastern area of the Serb-controlled part of Bosnia and protected by paramilitaries. Radovan Karadzic, a former consultant psychiatrist at the Kosovo Hospital in Sarajevo, has denied the charges against him and refused to recognize the legitimacy of the UN tribunal. "If The Hague was a real juridical body I would be ready to go there to testify or do so on television, but it is a political body that has been created to blame the Serbs," he told the *Times* (U.K.) newspaper in February 1996.

Karadzic's businessman son has lived in Belgrade for some years, and his daughter is reportedly looking for a buyer for her TV and radio station, Astra, which is based in Pale, the ski resort town near Sarajevo. His wife, Ljiljana Karadzic, who heads the Red Cross in the Bosnian Serb republic, attended celebrations in Pale in July 1999 to mark the tenth anniversary of the founding of her husband's Serbian Democratic Party. Karadzic was born in a stable in Montenegro, where his mother, Jovankas, still lives. His father, Vuk, has been dead for many years. Jovankas Karadzic has described her son as loyal and a hard worker who used to help her in the home and in the field. She said he was a serious boy who was respectful toward the elderly and helped his school friends with their homework.

Raphael Lemkin (1901–1959)

Genocide is distinguishable from all other crimes by the motivation behind it. Toward the end of World War II, when the full horror of the Nazi extermination program and concentration camps became public knowledge, Winston Churchill stated that the world was being brought face to face with "a crime that has no name."

History was of little use in finding a recognized word to fit the nature of the crime that Nazi Germany, a modern, industrialized state, had engaged in. There simply were no precedents in regard to either the nature or the degree of the crime. Raphael Lemkin, the Polish-born adviser to the U.S. War Department, saw that the world was being confronted with a totally unprecedented phenomena and that "new conceptions require new terminology." In his book *Axis Rule in Occupied Europe* (1944), he coined the word "genocide," constructed in contradiction to the accepted rules of etymology, from the Greek *genos* ("race" or "tribe") and the Latin suffix *cide* ("to murder"). According to

Lemkin, genocide signifies "the destruction of a nation or of an ethnic group and implies the existence of a coordinated plan, aimed at total extermination, to be put into effect against individuals chosen as victims purely, simply and exclusively because they are members of the target group." (Biography, American Jewish Archives, 2002)

Francis Lieber (1800–1872)

Columbia University law professor who, at the request of President Abraham Lincoln, drafted a manual for the behavior of Union troops in the field during the Civil War. Promulgated as General Order No. 100, Adjutant General's Office, on April 24, 1863, in Washington, D.C., it was distributed to every commander in the Union Army (and sent to Confederate leaders), was followed by the belligerents, and remains the core of latest manual for the conduct of war by U.S. forces in the field.

Feodor Martens (1845–1909)

A Russian jurist attending the 1907 Hague conference, he introduced a general statement of principle in the treaty. Concerned that the treaty could not cover "all of the circumstances which arise in [war]," the so-called Martens clause was added to the preamble of the 1907 treaty:

> Until a more complete code of the laws of war has been issued, the High Contracting Parties deem it expedient to declare that, in cases not included in the Regulations adopted by them, the inhabitants and the belligerents remain under the protection and the rule of the principles of the laws of nations, as they result from the usages established among civilized peoples, from the laws of humanity, and the dictates of the public conscience.

Slobodan Milosevic (1941–)

Former president of Serbian Republic, 1990–1997, and president of Yugoslavia, from 1997 until his defeat in 2000. Extradited to The Hague in 2001 for trial before the International Criminal Tribunal for the Former Yugoslavia, he was the first sitting head of state to be indicted for war crimes, crimes against humanity, and genocide while still in power.

A native of the Serbian town of Pozarevac, Milosevic was born on August 29, 1941, to an orthodox priest and a teacher. He graduated from Belgrade University with a degree in law and climbed the political ladder as a communist technocrat. Milosevic has headed Yugoslavia's state-run gas-extraction company and the country's state-run bank, the United Bank of Belgrade. He served as leader of the Belgrade Communist Party from 1978 to 1982 and was named head of the Serbian Communist Party in 1987. Milosevic attained international stature in the 1980s during his country's ethnic conflicts. The strife resulted from a breakdown of the nation-building of Marshal Josip Broz Tito, the wartime guerrilla leader who ruled Yugoslavia from 1945 until his death in 1980. Eventually, the communist governments of Eastern Europe collapsed, and the fall of the Soviet Union weakened the glue that had held together the diverse, mutually antagonistic ethnic groups of the former Soviet bloc. The Serbian desire for a reunified homeland manifested itself in a resurgent nationalistic movement. Slobodan Milosevic rode that nationalism to power.

Milosevic was a minor political figure in 1987 when an incident occurred that thrust him into prominence. On April 24, 1987, Milosevic was summoned to help calm a riotous crowd of Serbs outside the town hall in Kosovo Polje. The Serbs were claiming mistreatment by the Albanian majority and were barred from entering the town hall by baton-wielding police. Milosevic silenced the Serbian crowd, telling them "no one will ever beat you again," and invited them into the hall to voice their grievances to the Communist Party delegates. Afterward, Milosevic shaped the issues of alleged Albanian mistreatment of Serbs and a widespread sense of economic deprivation into concrete political goals. In 1989, he inspired violent Serbian demonstrations that drove the constitutionally elected leaders of both Vojvodina and Kosovo out of office. Milosevic had begun building a Greater Serbia. Milosevic's overwhelming popularity among his people has been attributed to his devotion to Serbian unification. Revered as a savior by some, he is called the "butcher of the Balkans" by others.

Ratko Mladic (1943–)

A UN tribunal charged Mladic and Radovan Karadzic with, among other things, furthering the internment of thousands of non-Serbs in concentration camps, where the prisoners were subjected to inhumane conditions and many died. Also charged with the responsibility for shelling of Sarajevo, as well as the smaller Bosnian towns of Tuzla and Srebrenica, "in order to kill, terrorize and demoralize the Bosnian Muslim and Bosnian Croat civilian population." Also blamed for abetting the "systematic" campaign of sniping at civilians in Sarajevo and for the seizure and use as human shields of 284 UN peacekeepers in May and June 1995. He remains at large, living in Serbia.

Henry Morgenthau Jr. (1891–1967)

Henry Morgenthau Jr. was born on May 11, 1891, in New York City. He was the son of Henry and Josephine (Sykes) Morgenthau. He married Elinor Fatman in 1916 and had three children. Two years after her death in 1949, he married Marcelle Puthon Hirsch of New York. He was nominated by President Franklin D. Roosevelt to be secretary of the treasury. He served from January 1, 1934, until July 22, 1945. During his term, Morgenthau is credited with exercising a stabilizing effect on administration monetary policies. In that time, through taxation and loans, he raised $450 billion for government programs and for war purposes. In 1944, he proposed the Morgenthau Plan, under which postwar Germany would be stripped of its industry and converted into an agricultural nation. At the Bretton Woods conference in 1944, Morgenthau assumed a leading role in establishing postwar economic policies and currency stabilization. That had been one of his prime goals since Depression days.

In July 1945, three months after the death of President Roosevelt, Morgenthau resigned as secretary but remained in office until President Harry Truman's return from the Big Three conference in Berlin. Henry Morgenthau Jr. died on February 6, 1967, in Poughkeepsie, New York.

Nazi Holocaust, 1939–1945

In January 1933, after a bitter ten-year political struggle, Adolf Hitler came to power in Germany. During his rise to power, Hitler had repeatedly blamed the Jews for Germany's defeat in World War I and subsequent economic hardships. Hitler also put forward racial theories asserting that Germans with fair skin, blond hair, and blue eyes were the supreme form of humanity—the master race. The Jews, according to Hitler, were the racial opposite and were actively engaged in an international conspiracy to keep this master race from assuming its rightful position as rulers of the world. Jews at this time comprised only about 1 percent of Germany's population of 55 million persons. They had lived in Germany for centuries, fought bravely for the Fatherland in its wars, and prospered in numerous professions.

But they were gradually shut out of German society by the Nazis through a never-ending series of laws and decrees, culminating in the Nuremberg Laws of 1935, which deprived them of their German citizenship and forbade intermarriage with non-Jews. They were removed from schools, banned from the professions, excluded from military service, and were even forbidden to share a park bench with a non-Jew. At the same time, a carefully orchestrated smear campaign under the direction of Propaganda Minister Joseph Goebbels portrayed Jews as enemies of the German people. Daily anti-Semitic slurs appeared in Nazi newspapers, on posters, in movies, on radio, in speeches by Hitler and top Nazis, and in classrooms. As a result, state-sanctioned anti-Semitism became the norm throughout Germany. The Jews lost everything, including their homes and businesses, with no protest or public outcry from non-Jewish Germans.

The actual beginning of the Holocaust was the Night of Broken Glass (Kristallnacht). It occurred on November 9–10, 1938, after 17-year-old Herschel Grynszpan shot and killed Ernst vom Rath, a German embassy official in Paris, in retaliation for the harsh treatment his Jewish parents had received from Nazis. Spurred on by Goebbels, Nazis used the death of vom Rath as an excuse to conduct the first state-run pogrom against Jews. Ninety Jews were killed, 500 synagogues were burned, and most Jewish shops had their windows smashed. The first mass arrest of Jews also occurred as more than 25,000 men were hauled off to concentration camps. As a kind of cynical joke, the Nazis then fined the Jews 1 billion marks for the destruction that the Nazis themselves had caused during Kristallnacht. On the eve of World War II, Führer (supreme leader) Adolf Hitler publicly threatened the Jews of Europe during a speech in Berlin: "In the course of my life I have very often been a prophet, and have usually been ridiculed for it. During the time of my struggle for power it was in the first instance only the Jewish race that received my prophecies with laughter when I said that I would one day take over the leadership of the State, and with it that of the whole nation, and that I would then among other things settle the Jewish problem. Their laughter was uproarious, but I think that for some time now they have been laughing on the other side of their face.

Today I will once more be a prophet: if the international Jewish financiers in and outside Europe should succeed in plunging the nations once more into a world war, then the result will not be the Bolshevizing of the earth, and thus the victory of Jewry, but the annihilation of the Jewish race in Europe!" On April 30, 1945, surrounded by the Soviet army in Berlin, Adolf Hitler committed suicide, and the Third Reich soon collapsed. By now, most of Europe's Jews had been killed. Four million had been gassed in the death camps while another 2 million had been shot dead or died in the ghettos.

The victorious Allies (Great Britain, the United States, and the Soviet Union) then began the daunting task of sorting through the carnage to determine exactly who was responsible. Seven months later, the Nuremberg war crimes trials began, with 22 surviving top Nazis charged with crimes against humanity. During the trial, a now-repentant Hans Frank, the former Nazi governor of Poland declared: "A thousand years will pass and the guilt of the Germany will not be erased."

Florence Nightingale (1820–1910)

In 1854, Florence Nightingale took thirty-eight women to Turkey to nurse wounded and sick British soldiers in the Crimean War. This was the first time the government had allowed women to do this. Almost all modern nursing systems and techniques we know today can be traced back to her. She suffered from post-traumatic stress disorder for the rest of her life. She became not only the first modern war nurse and nurse commander but also its first documented psychological casualty. Written by the field's brilliant first theorist-researcher and first published in 1859, *Notes on Nursing: What It Is and What It Is Not* is regarded as nursing's first textbook.

Pol Pot (1925–1998)

Prime minister of Cambodia (1975–1979). Pol Pot was born in 1925 (as Saloth Sar) into a farming family in central Cambodia, which was then part of French Indochina. In 1949, at age 20, he traveled to Paris on a scholarship to study radio electronics but became absorbed in Marxism and neglected his studies. He returned to Cambodia in 1953 and joined the underground communist movement. The following year, Cambodia achieved full independence from France and was then ruled by a royal monarchy. By 1962, Pol Pot had become leader of the Cambodian Communist Party and was forced to flee into the jungle to escape the wrath of Prince Norodom Sihanouk, leader of Cambodia. In the jungle, Pol Pot formed an armed resistance movement that became known as the Khmer Rouge (Red Cambodians) and waged a guerrilla war against Sihanouk's government. In 1970, Prince Sihanouk was ousted, not by Pol Pot but due to a U.S.-backed right-wing military coup. An embittered Sihanouk retaliated by joining with Pol Pot, his former enemy, in opposing Cambodia's new military government. That same year, the United States invaded Cambodia to expel the North Vietnamese from their border encampments but instead drove them deeper into Cambodia, where they allied themselves with the Khmer Rouge. From 1969 until 1973, the United States intermittently bombed North Vietnamese sanctuaries in eastern Cambodia, killing up to 150,000 Cambodian peasants. As a result, peasants fled the countryside by the hundreds of thousands and settled in Cambodia's capital city, Phnom Penh. All of these events resulted in economic and military destabilization in Cambodia and a surge of popular support for Pol Pot. By 1975, the United States had withdrawn its troops from Vietnam. Cambodia's government, plagued by corruption and incompetence, also lost its U.S. military support. Taking advantage of the opportunity, Pol Pot's Khmer Rouge army, consisting of teenage peasant guerrillas, marched into Phnom Penh and on April 17 effectively seized control of Cambodia. Once in power, Pol Pot began a radical experiment to create an agrarian utopia inspired in part by Mao Tse-tung's Cultural Revolution, which he had witnessed firsthand during a visit to communist China. Mao's Great Leap Forward economic program included forced evacuations of Chinese cities and the purging of class enemies. Pol Pot would now attempt his own Super Great Leap Forward in Cambodia, which he renamed the Democratic Republic of Kampuchea. He began by declaring, "This is Year Zero" and that society was about to be "purified." Capitalism, Western culture, city life, religion, and all foreign influences were to be extinguished in favor of an extreme form of peasant communism. All foreigners were thus expelled, embassies were closed, and any foreign economic or medical assistance was refused. The use of foreign languages was banned. Newspapers and TV stations were shut down, radios and bicycles confiscated, and mail and telephone usage curtailed. Money was forbidden. All businesses were shuttered, religion banned, education halted, health care eliminated, and parental authority revoked. Thus, Cambodia was sealed off from the outside world. All of Cambodia's cities were then forcibly evacuated. At Phnom Penh, 2 million inhabitants were evacuated on foot into the countryside at gunpoint. As many as 20,000 died along the way. Millions of Cambodians accustomed to city life were now forced into slave labor in Pol Pot's killing fields, where they soon began dying from overwork, malnutrition, and disease, barely surviving on a diet of one tin of rice (180 grams) per person every two days. Workdays in the fields began around 4 A.M. and lasted until 10 P.M., with only two rest periods allowed during the 18-hour day, all under the armed supervision of young Khmer Rouge soldiers eager to kill anyone for the slightest infraction. Starving people were forbidden to eat the fruits and rice they were harvesting. After the rice crop was harvested, Khmer Rouge trucks would arrive and confiscate the entire crop. Ten to fifteen families lived together, with a chairman at the head of each group. All work decisions were made by the armed supervisors with no participation from the workers, who were told "whether you live or die is not of great significance." Every tenth day was a day of rest. There were also three days off during the Khmer New Year festival. Throughout Cambodia, deadly purges were conducted to eliminate remnants of the old society—the educated, the wealthy, Buddhist monks, police, doctors, lawyers, teachers, and former government officials. Former soldiers were killed along with their wives and children. Anyone suspected of disloyalty to Pol Pot, including eventually many Khmer Rouge leaders, was shot or bludgeoned with an ax.

"What is rotten must be removed," a Khmer Rouge slogan proclaimed. In the villages, unsupervised gatherings of more than two persons were forbidden. Young people were taken from their parents and placed in communals. They were later married in collective ceremonies involving hundreds of often unwilling couples. Up to 20,000 persons were tortured into giving false confessions at Tuol Sleng, a school in Phnom Penh that had been converted into a jail. Elsewhere, suspects were often shot on the spot before any questioning. Ethnic groups were attacked, including the three largest minorities: the Vietnamese, Chinese, and Cham Muslims, along with twenty other smaller groups. Fifty percent of the estimated 425,000 Chinese living in Cambodia in 1975 perished. The Khmer Rouge also forced Muslims to eat pork and shot those who refused. On December 25, 1978, Vietnam launched a full-scale invasion of Cambodia seeking to end Khmer Rouge border attacks. On January 7, 1979, Phnom Penh fell and Pol Pot was deposed. The Vietnamese then installed a puppet government consisting of Khmer Rouge defectors. Pol Pot retreated into Thailand with the remnants of his Khmer Rouge army and began a guerrilla war against a succession of Cambodian governments lasting for the next seventeen years. After a series of internal power struggles in the 1990s, he finally lost control of the Khmer Rouge.

In April 1998, 73-year-old Pol Pot died of an apparent heart attack following his arrest, before he could be brought to trial by an international tribunal for the events of 1975–1979. The attempt by Pol Pot to form a communist peasant farming society resulted in the deaths of 25 percent of the country's population from starvation, overwork, and murder.

Franklin D. Roosevelt (1882–1945)

Assuming the presidency at the depth of the Great Depression, Franklin D. Roosevelt helped Americans regain faith in themselves. He brought hope, as he promised prompt, vigorous action, asserting in his inaugural address, "The only thing we have to fear is fear itself." Born in 1882 in Hyde Park, New York—now a national historic site—he attended Harvard University and Columbia Law School. On St. Patrick's Day 1905, he married Eleanor Roosevelt, niece of a former president, Theodore Roosevelt. Following the example of his fifth cousin Theodore Roosevelt, whom he greatly admired, Franklin D. Roosevelt entered public service through politics, but as a Democrat. He won election to the New York state senate in 1910. President Woodrow Wilson appointed him assistant secretary of the navy, and he was the Democratic nominee for vice president in 1920. In the summer of 1921, when he was 39, disaster hit when he was stricken with poliomyelitis. Demonstrating indomitable courage, he fought to regain the use of his legs, particularly through swimming. At the 1924 Democratic Convention, he dramatically appeared on crutches to nominate Alfred E. Smith as "the Happy Warrior." In 1928, Roosevelt became governor of New York. He was elected president in November 1932 to the first of four terms. By March there were 13 million unemployed, and almost every bank was closed. In his first hundred days, he proposed, and Congress enacted, a sweeping program to bring recovery to business and agriculture, relief to the unemployed and to those in danger of losing farms and homes, and reform, especially through the establishment of the Tennessee Valley Authority. By

1935, the nation had achieved some measure of recovery, but businessmen and bankers were turning more and more against Roosevelt's New Deal program. They feared his experiments, were appalled because he had taken the nation off the gold standard and allowed deficits in the budget, and disliked the concessions to labor. Roosevelt responded with a new program of reform: Social Security, heavier taxes on the wealthy, new controls over banks and public utilities, and an enormous work relief program for the unemployed. In 1936, he was reelected by a wide margin. Feeling he was armed with a popular mandate, he sought legislation to enlarge the U.S. Supreme Court, which had been invalidating key New Deal measures. Roosevelt lost the Supreme Court packing battle, but a revolution in constitutional law took place. Thereafter the government could legally regulate the economy. Roosevelt had pledged the United States to the "good neighbor" policy, transforming the Monroe Doctrine from a unilateral American manifesto into arrangements for mutual action against aggressors. He also sought, through neutrality legislation, to keep the United States out of the war in Europe even while strengthening nations that were threatened or attacked. When France fell and England came under siege in 1940, he began to send Great Britain all possible aid short of actual military involvement. When the Japanese attacked Pearl Harbor on December 7, 1941, Roosevelt directed organization of the nation's manpower and resources for global war. Feeling that the future peace of the world would depend upon relations between the United States and Russia, he devoted much thought to the planning of the United Nations, in which, he hoped, international difficulties could be settled. As the war drew to a close, Roosevelt's health deteriorated, and on April 12, 1945, while at Warm Springs, Georgia, he died of a cerebral hemorrhage.

Rwanda Civil War, 1994

Beginning on April 6, 1994, and for the next hundred days, up to 800,000 Tutsis were killed by Hutu militia using clubs and machetes, with as many as 10,000 killed each day. Rwanda is one of the smallest countries in Central Africa, with just 7 million people, and comprises two main ethnic groups, the Hutus and the Tutsis. Although the Hutus account for 90 percent of the population, in the past the Tutsi minority was considered the aristocracy of Rwanda and dominated Hutu peasants for decades, especially while Rwanda was under Belgian colonial rule. Following independence from Belgium in 1962, the Hutu majority seized power and reversed the roles, oppressing the Tutsis through systematic discrimination and acts of violence. As a result, more than 200,000 Tutsis fled to neighboring countries and formed a rebel guerrilla army, the Rwandan Patriotic Front. In 1990, this rebel army invaded Rwanda and forced Hutu President Juvenal Habyalimana into signing an accord that mandated that the Hutus and Tutsis would share power. Ethnic tensions in Rwanda were significantly heightened in October 1993 upon the assassination of Melchior Ndadaye, the first popularly elected Hutu president of neighboring Burundi.

A UN peacekeeping force of 2,500 multinational soldiers was then dispatched to Rwanda to preserve the fragile cease-fire between the Hutu government and the Tutsi rebels. Peace was threatened by Hutu extremists who were violently opposed to sharing any power with the Tutsis. Among these extremists were those who desired nothing less than the actual extermination of the Tutsis. It was later revealed that they had even drawn up lists of prominent Tutsis and moderate Hutu politicians to kill should the opportunity arise. In April 1994, amid ever-increasing prospects of violence, Rwandan President Habyalimana and Burundi's new President, Cyprien Ntaryamira, held several peace meetings with Tutsi rebels. On April 6, while returning from a meeting in Tanzania, a small jet carrying the two presidents was shot down by ground-fired missiles as it approached the airport at Kigali. Immediately after their deaths, Rwanda plunged into political violence as Hutu extremists began targeting prominent opposition figures who were on their death lists, including moderate Hutu politicians and Tutsi leaders. The killings then spread throughout the countryside as Hutu militia, armed with machetes, clubs, guns, and grenades, began indiscriminately killing Tutsi civilians. All individuals in Rwanda carried identification cards specifying their ethnic background, a practice left over from colonial days. These "tribal cards" now meant the difference between life and death. Amid the onslaught, the small UN peacekeeping force was overwhelmed as terrified Tutsi families and moderate politicians sought protection. Among the peacekeepers were ten soldiers from Belgium who were captured by the Hutus, tortured, and murdered. As a result, the United States, France, Belgium, and Italy all began evacuating their own personnel from Rwanda. However, no effort was made to evacuate Tutsi civilians or Hutu moderates. Instead, they were left behind entirely at the mercy of the avenging Hutu. Back at UN Headquarters in New York, the killings were initially categorized as a breakdown in the cease-fire between the Tutsis and Hutus. Throughout the massacre, both the United Nations and the United States carefully refrained from labeling the killings as genocide, which would have necessitated some kind of emergency intervention. On April 21, the Red Cross estimated that hundreds of thousands of Tutsis had already been massacred since April 6—an extraordinary rate of killing. The UN Security Council responded to the worsening crisis by voting unanimously to abandon Rwanda. The remainder of UN peacekeeping troops were pulled out, leaving behind a only tiny force of about 200 soldiers for the entire country.

The Hutus, now without opposition from the world community, engaged in genocidal mania, clubbing and hacking to death defenseless Tutsi families with machetes everywhere they were found. The Rwandan state radio, controlled by Hutu extremists, further encouraged the killings by broadcasting nonstop hate propaganda and even pinpointed the locations of Tutsis in hiding. The killers were aided by members of the Hutu professional class, including journalists, doctors, and educators, along with unemployed Hutu youths and peasants who killed Tutsis just to steal their property. Many Tutsis took refuge in churches and mission compounds. These places became the scenes of some of the worst massacres. In one case, at Musha, 1,200 Tutsis who had sought refuge were killed beginning at 8 A.M. lasting until the evening. Hospitals also became prime targets as wounded survivors were sought out and then killed. In some local villages, militiamen forced Hutus to kill their Tutsi neighbors or face a death sentence for themselves and their entire families. They also forced Tutsis to kill members of their own families. By mid-May, an estimated 500,000 Tutsis had been slaughtered. Bodies were now commonly seen floating down the Kigara River into Lake Victoria. Confronted with international TV news reports depicting genocide, the UN Security Council voted to send up to 5,000 soldiers to Rwanda. However, the Security Council failed to establish any timetable and thus never sent the troops in time to stop the massacres. The killings ended only after armed Tutsi rebels, invading from neighboring countries, managed to defeat the Hutus and halt the genocide in July 1994. By then, more than one-tenth of the population, an estimated 800,000 persons, had been killed.

Josef Stalin (1879–1953)

Born Iosif Vissarionovich Dzhugashvili, Stalin was a Soviet dictator and communist politician; secretary-general of the Soviet Communist Party, 1924–1953; de facto dictator of Soviet Union, 1929–1953; concluded nonaggression pact with Nazi Germany, 1939; premier of Soviet Union, 1941–1953; Soviet defense minister, 1941–1947.

Josip Broz Tito (1892–1980)

Yugoslavian dictator from end of World War II until his death in 1980. Joined Communist Party in the 1920s. Leader of partisan forces against Nazi Germany in World War II. After war's end, founded the Socialist Federal Republic of Yugoslavia. Tito was dedicated to a global communist ideal that transcended nationalism. Individual ethnic nationalism was suppressed. Tito also shrewdly recognized the threat to Yugoslavian unity posed by a strong Serbia, the largest of the country's republics. When piecing together post–World War II Yugoslavia, Tito deliberately divided Serbia into two noncontiguous provinces—Vojvodina in the north, and Kosovo in the south—to reduce the republic's power. The resulting gerrymandering left one-third of the Serbian population outside their own province and an Albanian majority firmly in place. He was able to effectively stifle the republic's many ethnic and religious rivalries during his reign. When he died, there was no one who could keep the federation together, and by 1991 the federation began its dissolution when Slovenia and Croatia broke away and declared their independence.

Jody Williams (1950–)

Jody Williams was born in Vermont in 1950. From early on in life, she realized the importance of looking after others. This developed partly in response to witnessing the problems of her disabled brother, who was picked on by other school children. Her understanding of the problems that affect many people in the world was enhanced when she took on a job teaching English as a second language in Mexico. It exposed her directly to the poverty that many people in the world experience.

At Johns Hopkins University, she completed a master's degree in international relations in 1984. In 1991, she began working for the Vietnam Veterans of America Foundation and was the founding coordinator of the International Campaign to Ban Landmines (ICBL), which was launched by six nongovernmental organizations (NGOs) in October 1992. The commitment has grown to more than 1,000 NGOs in more than sixty countries. Like many other such campaigns, success did not come overnight. It took six years to build the momentum needed for the weapons to be banned. Many others would have given up hope. Like civil rights, this campaign was one that would need strength and a commitment to the final aim—in this case, eliminating these dreadful weapons. Landmines, unlike conventional weapons, stay around once the war is over; they are indiscriminate in who they target. It has been argued that the reason for their prolific use is that they are cheap to manufacture and spread around. Their detection and removal, however, are nowhere near as easy. It has long been argued that the only way to effectively deal with the problem of landmines that target people is to ban their use completely. A Nobel Prize was awarded to Williams in 1997 to the ICBL and its American coordinator, Williams. That year's choice for the peace prize was expected to give a political boost to the antilandmine campaign. Francis Sejersted, chairman of the Norwegian Nobel Committee, said: "There are those among us who are unswerving in their faith that things can be done to make our world a better, safer, and more humane place and who also, even when the tasks appear overwhelming, have the courage to tackle them."

5

Major Treaties and Reports

The materials in this chapter outline the evolutionary development of the written laws of war as reflected in the international treaties and conventions that emerged toward the end of the nineteenth century. They all focus on protection of belligerents, the sick and wounded on the field of battle—whether on land or at sea—those captured during battles and their treatment as prisoners of war, and, especially in the twentieth century, the protection of innocents in war and during occupation of their homeland. The relevant text is reproduced verbatim in whole or in part; some reformatting has been introduced to clarify the documents' organization.

Major Treaties (Excerpts)

Geneva Convention for the Amelioration of the Wounded and Sick of Armies in the Field, 1864

This treaty, signed in Geneva, Switzerland, was the first international treaty to direct the attention of the international community to the plight of the wounded soldiers in the field who were typically left to die of their injuries. The convention members were invited by the world's first major nongovernmental organization (NGO), the International Committee of the Red Cross.

Convention for the Amelioration of the Condition of the Wounded in Armies in the Field [Red Cross Convention] (August 22, 1864)

ARTICLE 1

Ambulances and military hospitals shall be acknowledged to be neuter, and, as such, shall be protected and respected by belligerents so long as any sick or wounded may be therein.

Such neutrality shall cease if the ambulances or hospitals should be held by a military force.

ARTICLE 2

Persons employed in hospitals and ambulances, comprising the staff for superintendence, medical service, administration, transport of wounded, as well as chaplains, shall participate in the benefit of neutrality, whilst so employed, and so long as there remain any wounded to bring in or to succor.

ARTICLE 3

The persons designated in the preceding article may, even after occupation by the enemy, continue to fulfil their duties in the hospital or ambulance which they serve, or may withdraw in order to rejoin the corps to which they belong.

Under such circumstances, when these persons shall cease from their functions, they shall be delivered by the occupying army to the outposts of the enemy.

ARTICLE 4

As the equipment of military hospitals remains subject to the laws of war, persons attached to such hospitals cannot, in withdrawing, carry away any articles but such as are their private property.

Under the same circumstances an ambulance shall, on the contrary, retain its equipment.

ARTICLE 5

Inhabitants of the country who may bring help to the wounded shall be respected, and shall remain free. The generals of the belligerent Powers shall make it their care to inform the inhabitants of the appeal addressed to their humanity, and of the neutrality which will be the consequence of it.

Any wounded man entertained and taken care of in a house shall be considered as a protection thereto. Any inhabitant who shall have entertained wounded men in his house shall be exempted from the quartering of troops, as well as from a part of the contributions of war which may be imposed.

ARTICLE 6

Wounded or sick soldiers shall be entertained and taken care of, to whatever nation they may belong.

Commanders-in-chief shall have the power to deliver immediately to the outposts of the enemy soldiers who have been wounded in an engagement, when circumstances permit this to be done, and with the consent of both parties.

Those who are recognized, after their wounds are healed, as incapable of serving, shall be sent back to their country.

The others may also be sent back, on condition of not again bearing arms during the continuance of the war.

Evacuations, together with the persons under whose directions they take place, shall be protected by an absolute neutrality.

ARTICLE 7

A distinctive and uniform flag shall be adopted for hospitals, ambulances and evacuations. It must, on every occasion, be accompanied by the national flag. An arm-badge (brassard) shall also be allowed for individuals neutralized, but the delivery thereof shall be left to military authority.

The flag and the arm-badge shall bear a red cross on a white ground.

ARTICLE 8

The details of execution of the present convention shall be regulated by the commanders-in-chief of belligerent armies, according to the instructions of their respective governments, and in conformity with the general principles laid down in this convention.

ARTICLE 9

The high contracting Powers have agreed to communicate the present convention to those Governments which have not found it convenient to send plenipotentiaries to the International Conference at Geneva, with an invitation to accede thereto; the protocol is for that purpose left open.

ARTICLE 10

The present convention shall be ratified, and the ratifications shall be exchanged at Berne, in four months, or sooner, if possible.

In faith whereof the respective Plenipotentiaries have signed it and have affixed their seals thereto.

Done at Geneva, the twenty-second day of the month of August of the year one thousand eight hundred and Sixty-four.

Hague Declaration, II, IV, Final Act, 1899

Czar Nicholas II of Russia invited all nations to attend a convention at The Hague, Netherlands, in order to discuss limitations on armaments. Twenty-six nations sent delegates. Paradoxically, they did not agree on arms limits but did agree on three conventions dealing with the peaceful settlement of disputes, the laws and customs of war on land, and the protection of the wounded and the sick on land and at sea.

The Hague Peace Convention was the first treaty to codify the heretofore customary principles that governed land warfare. Feodor Martens's watershed clause, italicized below, appeared for the first time in an international treaty.

Convention with Respect to the Laws and Customs of War on Land [Hague II] (July 29, 1899)

Entry into Force: 4 September 1900

His Majesty the Emperor of Germany, King of Prussia; [etc.]:

Considering that, while seeking means to preserve peace and prevent armed conflicts among nations, it is likewise necessary to have regard to cases where an appeal to arms may be caused by events which their solicitude could not avert;

Animated by the desire to serve, even in this extreme hypothesis, the interest of humanity and the ever increasing requirements of civilization;

Thinking it important, with this object, to revise the laws and general customs of war, either with the view of defining them more precisely, or of laying down certain limits for the purpose of modifying their severity as far as possible;

Inspired by these views which are enjoined at the present day, as they were twenty-five years ago at the time of the Brussels Conference in 1874, by a wise and generous foresight;

Have, in this spirit, adopted a great number of provisions, the object of which is to define and govern the usages of war on land.

In view of the High Contracting Parties, these provisions, the wording of which has been inspired by the desire to diminish the evils of war so far as military necessities permit, are destined to serve as general rules of conduct for belligerents in their relations with each other and with populations.

It has not, however, been possible to agree forthwith on provisions embracing all the circumstances which occur in practice.

On the other hand, it could not be intended by the High Contracting Parties that the cases not provided for should, for want of a written provision, be left to the arbitrary judgment of the military Commanders.

Until a more complete code of the laws of war is issued, the High Contracting Parties think it right to declare that in cases not included in the Regulations adopted by them, populations and belligerents remain under the protection and empire of the principles of international law, as they result from the usages established between civilized nations, from the laws of humanity, and the requirements of the public conscience;

. . .

Article 1

The High Contracting Parties shall issue instructions to their armed land forces, which shall be in conformity with the "Regulations respecting the Laws and Customs of War on Land" annexed to the present Convention.

Article 2

The provisions contained in the Regulations mentioned in Article 1 are only binding on the Contracting Powers, in case of war between two or more of them.

These provisions shall cease to be binding from the time when, in a war between Contracting Powers, a non-Contracting Power joins one of the belligerents.

. . .

Annex to the Convention: Regulations Respecting the Laws and Customs of War on Land

SECTION I.—ON BELLIGERENTS

CHAPTER I.—On the Qualifications of Belligerents

Article 1

The laws, rights, and duties of war apply not only to armies, but also to militia and volunteer corps, fulfilling the following conditions:

To be commanded by a person responsible for his subordinates;

To have a fixed distinctive emblem recognizable at a distance;

To carry arms openly; and

To conduct their operations in accordance with the laws and customs of war.

In countries where militia or volunteer corps constitute the army, or form part of it, they are included under the denomination "army."

Article 2

The population of a territory which has not been occupied who, on the enemy's approach, spontaneously take up arms to resist the invading troops without having time to organize themselves in accordance with Article 1, shall be regarded a belligerent, if they respect the laws and customs of war.

Article 3

The armed forces of the belligerent parties may consist of combatants and non-combatants. In case of capture by the enemy both have a right to be treated as prisoners of war.

CHAPTER II.—On Prisoners of War

Article 4

Prisoners of war are in the power of the hostile Government, but not in that of the individuals or corps who captured them.

They must be humanely treated.

All their personal belongings, except arms, horses, and military papers remain their property.

Article 5

Prisoners of war may be interned in a town, fortress, camp, or any other locality, and bound not to go beyond certain fixed limits; but they can only be confined as an indispensable measure of safety.

Article 6

The State may utilize the labor of prisoners of war according to their rank and aptitude. Their tasks shall not be excessive, and shall have nothing to do with the military operations.

Prisoners may be authorized to work for the Public Service, for private persons, or on their own account.

Work done for the State shall be paid for according to the tariffs in force for soldiers of the national army employed on similar tasks.

When the work is for other branches of the Public Service or for private persons, the conditions shall be settled in agreement with the military authorities.

The wages of the prisoners shall go towards improving

their position, and the balance shall be paid them at the time of their release, after deducting the cost of their maintenance.

Article 7

The Government into whose hands prisoners of war have fallen is bound to maintain them.

Failing a special agreement between the belligerents, prisoners of war shall be treated as regards food, quarters, and clothing, on the same footing as the troops of the Government which has captured them.

Article 8

Prisoners of war shall be subject to the laws, regulations, and orders in force in the army of the State into whose hands they have fallen.

Any act of insubordination warrants the adoption, as regards them, of such measures of severity as may be necessary.

Escaped prisoners, recaptured before they have succeeded in rejoining their army, or before quitting the territory occupied by the army that captured them, are liable to disciplinary punishment.

Prisoners who, after succeeding in escaping are again taken prisoners, are not liable to any punishment for the previous flight.

Article 9

Every prisoner of war, if questioned, is bound to declare his true name and rank, and if he disregards this rule, he is liable to a curtailment of the advantages accorded to the prisoners of war of his class.

Article 10

Prisoners of war may be set at liberty on parole if the laws of their country authorize it, and, in such a case, they are bound, on their personal honor, scrupulously to fulfill, both as regards their own Government and the Government by whom they were made prisoners, the engagements they have contracted.

In such cases, their own Government shall not require of nor accept from them any service incompatible with the parole given.

Article 11

A prisoner of war can not be forced to accept his liberty on parole; similarly the hostile Government is not obliged to assent to the prisoner's request to be set at liberty on parole.

Article 12

Any prisoner of war, who is liberated on parole and recaptured, bearing arms against the Government to whom he had pledged his honor, or against the allies of that Government, forfeits his right to be treated as a prisoner of war, and can be brought before the Courts.

Article 13

Individuals who follow an army without directly belonging to it, such as newspaper correspondents and reporters, sutlers, contractors, who fall into the enemy's hands, and whom the latter think fit to detain, have a right to be treated as prisoners of war, provided they can produce a certificate from the military authorities of the army they were accompanying.

Article 14

A Bureau for information relative to prisoners of war is instituted, on the commencement of hostilities, in each of the belligerent States, and, when necessary, in the neutral countries on whose territory belligerents have been received. This Bureau is intended to answer all inquiries about prisoners of war, and is furnished by the various services concerned with all the necessary information to enable it to keep an individual return for each prisoner of war. It is kept informed of interments and changes, as well as of admissions into hospital and deaths.

It is also the duty of the Information Bureau to receive and collect all objects of personal use, valuables, letters, etc., found on the battlefields or left by prisoners who have died in hospital or ambulance, and to transmit them to those interested.

Article 15

Relief Societies for prisoners of war, which are regularly constituted in accordance with the law of the country with the object of serving as the intermediary for charity, shall receive from the belligerents for themselves and their duly accredited agents every facility, within the bounds of military requirements and Administrative Regulations, for the effective accomplishment of their humane task. Delegates of these Societies may be admitted to the places of interment for the distribution of relief, as also to the halting places of repatriated prisoners, if furnished with a personal permit by the military authorities, and on giving an engagement in writing to comply with all their Regulations for order and police.

Article 16

The Information Bureau shall have the privilege of free postage.

Letters, money orders, and valuables, as well as postal

parcels destined for the prisoners of war or dispatched by them, shall be free of all postal duties both in the countries of origin and destination, as well as in those they pass through.

Gifts and relief in kind for prisoners of war shall be admitted free of all duties of entry and others, as well as of payments for carriage by the Government railways.

Article 17

Officers taken prisoners may receive, if necessary, the full pay allowed them in this position by their country's regulations, the amount to be repaid by their Government.

Article 18

Prisoners of war shall enjoy every latitude in the exercise of their religion, including attendance at their own church services, provided only they comply with the regulations for order and police issued by the military authorities.

Article 19

The wills of prisoners of war are received or drawn up on the same conditions as for soldiers of the National Army.

The same rules shall be observed regarding death certificates, as well as for the burial of prisoners of war, due regard being paid to their grade and rank.

Article 20

After the conclusion of peace, the repatriation of prisoners of war shall take place as speedily as possible.

CHAPTER III.—On the Sick and Wounded

Article 21

The obligations of belligerents with regard to the sick and wounded are governed by the Geneva Convention of the 22nd August, 1864, subject to any modifications which may be introduced into it.

SECTION II.—ON HOSTILITIES

CHAPTER I.—On means of injuring the Enemy, Sieges, and Bombardments

Article 22

The right of belligerents to adopt means of injuring the enemy is not unlimited.

Article 23

Besides the prohibitions provided by special Conventions, it is especially prohibited:—

To employ poison or poisoned arms;

To kill or wound treacherously individuals belonging to the

hostile nation or army;

To kill or wound an enemy who, having laid down arms, or having no longer means of defence, has surrendered at discretion;

To declare that no quarter will be given;

To employ arms, projectiles, or material of a nature to cause superfluous injury;

To make improper use of a flag of truce, the national flag, or military ensigns and the enemy's uniform, as well as the distinctive badges of the Geneva Convention;

To destroy or seize the enemy's property, unless such destruction or seizure be imperatively demanded by the necessities of war.

Article 24

Ruses of war and the employment of methods necessary to obtain information about the enemy and the country, are considered allowable.

Article 25

The attack or bombardment of towns, villages, habitations or buildings which are not defended, is prohibited.

Article 26

The Commander of an attacking force, before commencing a bombardment, except in the case of an assault, should do all he can to warn the authorities.

Article 27

In sieges and bombardments all necessary steps should be taken to spare as far as possible edifices devoted to religion, art, science, and charity, hospitals, and places where the sick and wounded are collected, provided they are not used at the same time for military purposes.

The besieged should indicate these buildings or places by some particular and visible signs, which should previously be notified to the assailants.

Article 28

The pillage of a town or place, even when taken by assault, is prohibited.

CHAPTER II.—On Spies

Article 29

An individual can only be considered a spy if, acting clandestinely, or on false pretences, he obtains, or seeks to obtain information in the zone of operations of a belligerent, with the intention of communicating it to the hostile party.

Thus, soldiers not in disguise who have penetrated into the zone of operations of a hostile army to obtain information are not considered spies. Similarly, the following are not considered spies: soldiers or civilians, carrying out their mission openly, charged with the delivery of despatches destined either for their own army or for that of the enemy. To this class belong likewise individuals sent in balloons to deliver despatches, and generally to maintain communication between the various parts of an army or a territory.

Article 30

A spy taken in the act cannot be punished without previous trial.

Article 31

A spy who, after rejoining the army to which he belongs, is subsequently captured by the enemy, is treated as a prisoner of war, and incurs no responsibility for his previous acts of espionage.

. . .

SECTION III.—ON MILITARY AUTHORITY OVER HOSTILE TERRITORY

Article 42

Territory is considered occupied when it is actually placed under the authority of the hostile army.

The occupation applies only to the territory where such authority is established, and in a position to assert itself.

Article 43

The authority of the legitimate power having actually passed into the hands of the occupant, the latter shall take all steps in his power to re-establish and insure, as far as possible, public order and safety, while respecting, unless absolutely prevented, the laws in force in the country.

Article 44

Any compulsion of the population of occupied territory to take part in military operations against its own country is prohibited.

Article 45

Any pressure on the population of occupied territory to take the oath to the hostile Power is prohibited.

Article 46

Family honors and rights, individual lives and private property, as well as religious convictions and liberty, must be respected.

Private property cannot be confiscated.

Article 47

Pillage is formally prohibited.

Article 48

If, in the territory occupied, the occupant collects the taxes, dues, and tolls imposed for the benefit of the State, he shall do it, as far as possible, in accordance with the rules in existence and the assessment in force, and will in consequence be bound to defray the expenses of the administration of the occupied territory on the same scale as that by which the legitimate Government was bound.

Article 49

If, besides the taxes mentioned in the preceding Article, the occupant levies other money taxes in the occupied territory, this can only be for military necessities or the administration of such territory.

Article 50

No general penalty, pecuniary or otherwise, can be inflicted on the population on account of the acts of individuals for which it cannot be regarded as collectively responsible.

Article 51

No tax shall be collected except under a written order and on the responsibility of a Commander-in-Chief.

This collection shall only take place, as far as possible, in accordance with the rules in existence and the assessment of taxes in force.

For every payment a receipt shall be given to the taxpayer.

Article 52

Neither requisitions in kind nor services can be demanded from communes or inhabitants except for the necessities of the army of occupation. They must be in proportion to the resources of the country, and of such a nature as not to involve the population in the obligation of taking part in military operations against their country.

These requisitions and services shall only be demanded on the authority of the Commander in the locality occupied.

The contributions in kind shall, as far as possible, be paid for in ready money; if not, their receipt shall be acknowledged.

. . .

Article 60

The Geneva Convention applies to sick and wounded interned in neutral territory.

Hague Convention III, 1907

In 1904, U.S. President Theodore Roosevelt invited all nations to send representatives to The Hague to examine issues relating to war that had not been fully addressed at the 1899 meeting. In 1906, after the end of Russia's war with Japan, Czar Nicholas II of Russia invited nation-states to attend the Second Hague Peace Conference. Forty-four nations sent representatives. Again, there was no agreement on arms limitations. However, there was the adoption of thirteen conventions. The preamble to the 1907 treaty retained the Martens clause, italicized in the excerpt reprinted below.

Convention Respecting the Laws and Customs of War on Land, October 18, 1907

Seeing that, while seeking means to preserve peace and prevent armed conflicts between nations, it is likewise necessary to bear in mind the case where the appeal to arms has been brought about by events which their care was unable to avert;

Animated by the desire to serve, even in this extreme case, the interests of humanity and the ever progressive needs of civilization;

Thinking it important, with this object, to revise the general laws and customs of war, either with a view to defining them with greater precision or to confining them within such limits as would mitigate their severity as far as possible;

Have deemed it necessary to complete and explain in certain particulars the work of the First Peace Conference, which, following on the Brussels Conference of 1874, and inspired by the ideas dictated by a wise and generous forethought, adopted provisions intended to define and govern the usages of war on land.

According to the views of the High Contracting Parties, these provisions, the wording of which has been inspired by the desire to diminish the evils of war, as far as military requirements permit, are intended to serve as a general rule of conduct for the belligerents in their mutual relations and in their relations with the inhabitants.

It has not, however, been found possible at present to concert regulations covering all the circumstances which arise in practice;

On the other hand, the High Contracting Parties clearly do not intend that unforeseen cases should, in the absence of a written undertaking, be left to the arbitrary judgment of military commanders.

Until a more complete code of the laws of war has been issued, the High Contracting Parties deem it expedient to declare that, in cases not included in the Regulations adopted by them, the inhabitants and the belligerents remain under the protection and the rule of the principles of the law of nations, as they result from the usages established among civilized peoples, from the laws of humanity, and the dictates of the public conscience.

. . . .

Article 1.

The Contracting Powers shall issue instructions to their armed land forces which shall be in conformity with the Regulations respecting the laws and customs of war on land, annexed to the present Convention.

Art. 2.

The provisions contained in the Regulations referred to in Article 1, as well as in the present Convention, do not apply except between Contracting Powers, and then only if all the belligerents are parties to the Convention.

Art. 3.

A belligerent party which violates the provisions of the said Regulations shall, if the case demands, be liable to pay compensation.

It shall be responsible for all acts committed by persons forming part of its armed forces.

Art. 4.

The present Convention, duly ratified, shall as between the Contracting Powers, be substituted for the Convention of 29 July 1899, respecting the laws and customs of war on land.

The Convention of 1899 remains in force as between the Powers which signed it, and which do not also ratify the present Convention.

Art. 5.

The present Convention shall be ratified as soon as possible. The ratifications shall be deposited at The Hague.

The first deposit of ratifications shall be recorded in a procès-verbal signed by the Representatives of the Powers which take part therein and by the Netherlands Minister for Foreign Affairs.

The subsequent deposits of ratifications shall be made by means of a written notification, addressed to the Netherlands Government and accompanied by the instrument of ratification.

A duly certified copy of the procès-verbal relative to the first deposit of ratifications, of the notifications mentioned in the preceding paragraph, as well as of the instruments of ratification, shall be immediately sent by the Netherlands Government, through the diplomatic channel, to the Powers invited to the Second Peace Conference, as well as to the other Powers which have adhered to the Convention. In the cases contemplated in the preceding paragraph the said Government shall at the same time inform them of the date on which it received the notification.

. . .

Annex to the Convention: Regulations Respecting the Laws and Customs of War on Land

SECTION I: ON BELLIGERENTS
CHAPTER I: The Qualifications of Belligerents
Article 1.

The laws, rights, and duties of war apply not only to armies, but also to militia and volunteer corps fulfilling the following conditions:

To be commanded by a person responsible for his subordinates;

To have a fixed distinctive emblem recognizable at a distance;

To carry arms openly; and

To conduct their operations in accordance with the laws and customs of war.

In countries where militia or volunteer corps constitute the army, or form part of it, they are included under the denomination "army."

Art. 2.

The inhabitants of a territory which has not been occupied, who, on the approach of the enemy, spontaneously take up arms to resist the invading troops without having had time to organize themselves in accordance with Article 1, shall be regarded as belligerents if they carry arms openly and if they respect the laws and customs of war.

Art. 3.

The armed forces of the belligerent parties may consist of combatants and non-combatants. In the case of capture by the enemy, both have a right to be treated as prisoners of war.

CHAPTER II: Prisoners of War

Art. 4.

Prisoners of war are in the power of the hostile Government, but not of the individuals or corps who capture them.

They must be humanely treated.

All their personal belongings, except arms, horses, and military papers, remain their property.

. . .

SECTION II: HOSTILITIES

CHAPTER I: Means of Injuring the Enemy, Sieges, and bombardments

Art. 22.

The right of belligerents to adopt means of injuring the enemy is not unlimited.

Art. 23.

In addition to the prohibitions provided by special Conventions, it is especially forbidden—

To employ poison or poisoned weapons;

To kill or wound treacherously individuals belonging to the hostile nation or army;

To kill or wound an enemy who, having laid down his arms, or having no longer means of defence, has surrendered at discretion;

To declare that no quarter will be given;

To employ arms, projectiles, or material calculated to cause unnecessary suffering;

To make improper use of a flag of truce, of the national flag or of the military insignia and uniform of the enemy, as well as the distinctive badges of the Geneva Convention;

To destroy or seize the enemy's property, unless such destruction or seizure be imperatively demanded by the necessities of war;

To declare abolished, suspended, or inadmissible in a court of law the rights and actions of the nationals of the hostile party. A belligerent is likewise forbidden to compel the nationals of the hostile party to take part in the operations of war directed against their own country, even if they were in the belligerent's service before the commencement of the war.

Art. 24.

Ruses of war and the employment of measures necessary for obtaining information about the enemy and the country are considered permissible.

Art. 25.

The attack or bombardment, by whatever means, of towns, villages, dwellings, or buildings which are undefended is prohibited.

Art. 26.

The officer in command of an attacking force must, before commencing a bombardment, except in cases of assault, do all in his power to warn the authorities.

Art. 27.

In sieges and bombardments all necessary steps must be taken to spare, as far as possible, buildings dedicated to religion, art, science, or charitable purposes, historic monuments, hospitals, and places where the sick and wounded are collected, provided they are not being used at the time for military purposes.

It is the duty of the besieged to indicate the presence of such buildings or places by distinctive and visible signs, which shall be notified to the enemy beforehand.

Art. 28.

The pillage of a town or place, even when taken by assault, is prohibited.

. . .

SECTION III: MILITARY AUTHORITY OVER THE TERRITORY OF THE HOSTILE STATE

Art. 42.

Territory is considered occupied when it is actually placed under the authority of the hostile army

The occupation extends only to the territory where such authority has been established and can be exercised.

Art. 43.

The authority of the legitimate power having in fact passed into the hands of the occupant, the latter shall take all the measures in his power to restore, and ensure, as far as possible, public order and safety, while respecting, unless absolutely prevented, the laws in force in the country.

Art. 44.

A belligerent is forbidden to force the inhabitants of territory occupied by it to furnish information about the army of the other belligerent, or about its means of defense.

Art. 45.

It is forbidden to compel the inhabitants of occupied territory to swear allegiance to the hostile Power.

Art. 46.

Family honour and rights, the lives of persons, and private property, as well as religious convictions and practice, must be respected.

Private property cannot be confiscated.

Art. 47.

Pillage is formally forbidden.

Art. 48.

If, in the territory occupied, the occupant collects the taxes, dues, and tolls imposed for the benefit of the State, he shall do so, as far as is possible, in accordance with the rules of assessment and incidence in force, and shall in consequence be bound to defray the expenses of the administration of the occupied territory to the same extent as the legitimate Government was so bound.

Art. 49.

If, in addition to the taxes mentioned in the above article, the occupant levies other money contributions in the occupied territory, this shall only be for the needs of the army or of the administration of the territory in question.

Art. 50.

No general penalty, pecuniary or otherwise, shall be inflicted upon the population on account of the acts of individuals for which they cannot be regarded as jointly and severally responsible.

Art. 51.

No contribution shall be collected except under a written order, and on the responsibility of a commander-in-chief.

The collection of the said contribution shall only be effected as far as possible in accordance with the rules of assessment and incidence of the taxes in force.

For every contribution a receipt shall be given to the contributors.

Art. 52.

Requisitions in kind and services shall not be demanded from municipalities or inhabitants except for the needs of the army of occupation. They shall be in proportion to the resources of the country, and of such a nature as not to involve the inhabitants in the obligation of taking part in military operations against their own country.

Such requisitions and services shall only be demanded on the authority of the commander in the locality occupied.

Contributions in kind shall as far as possible be paid for in cash; if not, a receipt shall be given and the payment of the amount due shall be made as soon as possible.

Art. 53.

An army of occupation can only take possession of cash, funds, and realizable securities which are strictly the property of the State, depots of arms, means of transport, stores and supplies, and, generally, all movable property belonging to the State which may be used for military operations.

All appliances, whether on land, at sea, or in the air, adapted for the transmission of news, or for the transport of persons or things, exclusive of cases governed by naval law, depots of arms, and, generally, all kinds of munitions of war, may be seized, even if they belong to private individuals, but must be restored and compensation fixed when peace is made.

Art. 54.

Submarine cables connecting an occupied territory with a neutral territory shall not be seized or destroyed except in the case of absolute necessity. They must likewise be restored and compensation fixed when peace is made.

Art. 55. The occupying State shall be regarded only as administrator and usufructuary of public buildings, real estate, forests, and agricultural estates belonging to the hostile State, and situated in the occupied country. It must safeguard the capital of these properties, and administer them in accordance with the rules of usufruct.

Art. 56.

The property of municipalities, that of institutions dedicated to religion, charity and education, the arts and sciences, even when State property, shall be treated as private property.

All seizure of, destruction or wilful damage done to institutions of this character, historic monuments, works of art and science, is forbidden, and should be made the subject of legal proceedings.

Geneva Protocol for the Prohibition of the Use in War of Asphyxiating, Poisonous or Other Gases, and of Bacteriological Methods of Warfare, 1925

After the horrors of gas warfare during World War I, the international community got together to address the use of this type of weaponry. The upshot was the 1925 protocol that prohibited a nation-state from "first use" of poison gas.

Protocol for the Prohibition of the Use in War of Asphyxiating, Poisonous or Other Gases, and of Bacteriological Methods of Warfare (June 17, 1925)

The undersigned Plenipotentiaries, in the name of their respective governments:

Whereas the use in war of asphyxiating, poisonous or other gases, and of all analogous liquids, materials or devices, has been justly condemned by the general opinion of the civilised world; and

Whereas the prohibition of such use has been declared in Treaties to which the majority of Powers of the world are Parties; and

To the end that this prohibition shall be universally accepted as a part of International Law, binding alike the conscience and the practice of nations;

Declare:

That the High Contracting Parties, so far as they are not already Parties to Treaties prohibiting such use, accept this prohibition, agree to extend this prohibition to the use of bacteriological methods of warfare and agree to be bound as between themselves according to the terms of this declaration.

The High Contracting Parties will exert every effort to induce other States to accede to the present Protocol. Such accession will be notified to the Government of the French Republic, and by the latter to all signatories and acceding Powers, and will take effect on the date of the notification by the Government of the French Republic.

The ratifications of the present Protocol shall be addressed to the Government of the French Republic, which will at once notify the deposit of such ratification to each of the signatory and acceding Powers.

The instruments of ratification of and accession to the present Protocol will remain deposited in the archives of the Government of the French Republic.

The present Protocol will come into force for each signatory Power as from the date of deposit of its ratification, and, from that moment, each Power will be bound as regards other Powers which have already deposited their ratifications.

Treaty of Paris (Kellogg-Briand Pact for the Renunciation of War as an Instrument of National Policy), 1928

This treaty, reflecting the world's revulsion of total war, was an effort by the international community to resort to peaceful means to remove or ameliorate conflicts between two nation-states. The pact was the first international agreement renunciating the use of war as an instrument of national policy. It was conceived by French diplomat A. Briand, who hoped to engage the United States in a system of protective alliances to guard against aggression from a resurgent Germany. The U.S. secretary of state, F. Kellogg, proposed a general multilateral treaty, and the French agreed. Most states signed the treaty, but its lack of enforceability and exceptions to its pacifist pledges rendered it useless.

Kellogg-Briand Pact, August 27, 1928

By the President of the United States of America: A proclamation

THE PRESIDENT OF THE GERMAN REICH, THE PRESIDENT OF THE UNITED STATES OF AMERICA, HIS MAJESTY THE KING OF THE BELGIANS, THE PRESIDENT OF THE FRENCH REPUBLIC, HIS MAJESTY THE KING OF GREAT BRITAIN, IRELAND AND THE BRITISH DOMINIONS BEYOND THE SEAS, EMPEROR OF INDIA, HIS MAJESTY THE KING OF ITALY, HIS MAJESTY THE EMPEROR OF JAPAN, THE PRESIDENT OF THE REPUBLIC OF POLAND THE PRESIDENT OF THE CZECHOSLOVAK REPUBLIC,

Deeply sensible of their solemn duty to promote the welfare of mankind;

Persuaded that the time has come when a frank renunciation of war as an instrument of national policy should be made to the end that the peaceful and friendly relations now existing between their peoples may be perpetuated;

Convinced that all changes in their relations with one another should be sought only by pacific means and be the result of a peaceful and orderly process, and that any signatory Power which shall hereafter seek to promote its national interests by resort to war a should be denied the benefits furnished by this Treaty;

Hopeful that, encouraged by their example, all the other nations of the world will join in this humane endeavor and by adhering to the present Treaty as soon as it comes into force bring their peoples within the scope of its beneficent provisions, thus uniting the civilized nations of the world in a common renunciation of war as an instrument of their national policy;

Have decided to conclude a Treaty and for that purpose . . . having communicated to one another their full powers found in good and due form have agreed upon the following articles:

ARTICLE I

The High Contracting Parties solemnly declare in the names of their respective peoples that they condemn recourse to war for the solution of international controversies, and renounce it, as an instrument of national policy in their relations with one another.

ARTICLE II

The High Contracting Parties agree that the settlement or solution of all disputes or conflicts of whatever nature or of whatever origin they may be, which may arise among them, shall never be sought except by pacific means.

ARTICLE III

The present Treaty shall be ratified by the High Contracting Parties named in the Preamble in accordance with their respective constitutional requirements, and shall take effect as between them as soon as all their several instruments of ratification shall have been deposited at Washington.

This Treaty shall, when it has come into effect as prescribed in the preceding paragraph, remain open as long as may be necessary for adherence by all the other Powers of the world. Every instrument evidencing the adherence of a Power shall be deposited at Washington and the Treaty shall immediately upon such deposit become effective as; between the Power thus adhering and the other Powers parties hereto.

It shall be the duty of the Government of the United States to furnish each Government named in the Preamble and every Government subsequently adhering to this Treaty with a certified copy of the Treaty and of every instrument of ratification or adherence. It shall also be the duty of the Government of the United States telegraphically to notify such Governments immediately upon the deposit with it of each instrument of ratification or adherence.

IN FAITH WHEREOF the respective Plenipotentiaries have signed this Treaty in the French and English languages both texts having equal force, and hereunto affix their seals.

DONE at Paris, the twenty seventh day of August in the year one thousand nine hundred and twenty-eight.

AND WHEREAS it is stipulated in the said Treaty that it shall take effect as between the High Contracting Parties as soon as all the several instruments of ratification shall have been deposited at Washington;

AND WHEREAS the said Treaty has been duly ratified on the parts of all the High Contracting Parties and their several instruments of ratification have been deposited with the Government of the United States of America, the last on July 24, 1929;

NOW THEREFORE, be it known that I, Herbert Hoover, President of the United States of America, have caused the said Treaty to be made public, to the end that the same and every article and clause thereof may be observed and fulfilled with good faith by the United States and the citizens thereof.

IN TESTIMONY WHEREOF, I have hereunto set my hand and caused the seal of the United States to be affixed.

HERBERT HOOVER
By the President:
HENRY L STIMSON
Secretary of State

Red Cross Convention Regarding the Amelioration of the Condition of Wounded and Sick of Armies in the Field (1929)

The International Committee of the Red Cross (ICRC), in the continuing effort to improve the condition of the sick and wounded on the field of battle, convened an international conference to enhance the protections afforded these injured combatants in the 1864 and 1907 treaties. Given the terrible loss of lives during World War I, it was inevitable that revisions would be created in the earlier treaties. Indeed, this 1929 treaty was revised and modified in 1949, after the end of World War II.

Convention for the Amelioration of the Condition of the Wounded and Sick in Armies in the Field, entered into force June 19, 1931

[The Contracting Parties] being equally animated by the desire to lessen, so far as lies in their power, the evils inseparable from war and desiring, for this purpose, to perfect and complete the provisions agreed to at Geneva on 22 August 1864, and 6 July 1906, for the amelioration of the condition of the wounded and sick in armies in the field,

Have resolved to conclude a new Convention for that purpose and have appointed as their Plenipotentiaries who, after having communicated to each other their full powers, found in good and due form, have agreed as follows.

CHAPTER I: WOUNDED AND SICK

Article 1. Officers and soldiers and other persons officially attached to the armed forces who are wounded or sick shall be respected and protected in all circumstances; they shall be treated with humanity and cared for medically, without distinction of nationality, by the belligerent in whose power they may be. Nevertheless, the belligerent who is compelled to abandon wounded or sick to the enemy, shall, as far as military exigencies permit, leave with them a portion of his medical personnel and material to help with their treatment.

Art. 2. Except as regards the treatment to be provided for them in virtue of the preceding Article, the wounded and sick of an army who fall into the hands of the enemy shall be prisoners of war, and the general provisions of international law concerning prisoners of war shall be applicable to them.

Belligerents shall, however, be free to prescribe, for the benefit of wounded or sick prisoners such arrangements as they may think fit beyond the limits of the existing obligations.

Art. 3. After each engagement the occupant of the field of battle shall take measures to search for the wounded and dead, and to protect them against pillage and maltreatment.

Whenever circumstances permit, a local armistice or a suspension of fire shall be arranged to permit the removal of the wounded remaining between the lines.

Art. 4. Belligerents shall communicate to each other reciprocally, as soon as possible, the names of the wounded, sick and dead, collected or discovered, together with any indications which may assist in their identification.

They shall establish and transmit to each other the certificates of death.

They shall likewise collect and transmit to each other all articles of a personal nature found on the field of battle or on the dead, especially one half of their identity discs, the other hall to remain attached to the body.

They shall ensure that the burial or cremation of the dead is preceded by a careful, and if possible medical, examination of the bodies, with a view to confirming death, establishing identity and enabling a report to be made.

They shall further ensure that the dead are honourably interred, that their graves are respected and marked so that they may always be found.

To this end, at the commencement of hostilities, they shall organize officially a graves registration service, to render eventual exhumations possible, and to ensure the identification of bodies whatever may be the subsequent site of the grave.

After the cessation of hostilities they shall exchange the list of graves and of dead interred in their cemeteries and elsewhere.

Art. 5. The military authorities may appeal to the charitable zeal of the inhabitants to collect and afford medical assistance under their direction to the wounded or sick of armies, and may accord to persons who have responded to this appeal special protection and certain facilities.

CHAPTER II: MEDICAL FORMATIONS AND ESTABLISHMENTS

Art. 6. Mobile medical formations, that is to say, those which are intended to accompany armies in the field, and the fixed establishments of the medical service shall be respected and protected by the belligerents.

. . .

CHAPTER III: PERSONNEL

Art. 9. The personnel engaged exclusively in the collection, transport and treatment of the wounded and sick, and in the administration of medical formations and establishments, and chaplains attached to armies, shall be respected and protected under all circumstances. If they fall into the hands of the enemy they shall not be treated as prisoners of war.

Soldiers specially trained to be employed, in case of necessity, as auxiliary nurses or stretcher-bearers for the collection, transport and treatment of the wounded and sick, and furnished with a proof of identity, shall enjoy the same treatment as the permanent medical personnel if they are taken prisoners while carrying out these functions.

Art. 10. The personnel of Voluntary Aid Societies, duly recognized and authorized by their Government, who may be employed on the same duties as those of the personnel mentioned in the rust paragraph of Article 9, are placed on the same footing as the personnel contemplated in that paragraph, provided that the personnel of such societies are subject to military law and regulations. . . .

Geneva Convention Relative to the Treatment of Prisoners of War (1929)

In 1929, the Geneva Convention on prisoners of war (POWs) was signed by 47 governments. Chief among the nations that did not adhere to this Geneva Convention were Japan and the Soviet Union. Japan, however, gave a qualified promise (1942) to abide by the Geneva rules, and the Soviet Union announced (1941) that it would observe the terms of the Hague Convention of 1907, which did not provide (as does the 1929 Geneva Convention) for neutral inspection of prison camps, for the exchange of prisoners' names, and for correspondence with prisoners.

According to the 1929 Geneva Convention, no POW could be forced to disclose to his captor any information other than his identity (i.e., his name and rank, but not his military unit, hometown, or address of relatives). Every POW was entitled to adequate food and medical care and had the right to exchange correspondence and receive parcels. He was required to observe ordinary military discipline and courtesy, but he could attempt to escape at his own risk.

Once recaptured, he was not to be punished for his attempt. Officers were to receive pay either according to the pay scale of their own country or to that of their captor, whichever was less; they could not be required to work. Enlisted men might be required to work for pay, but the nature and location of their work were not to expose them to danger, and in no case could they be required to perform work directly related to military operations.

Camps were to be open to inspection by authorized representatives of a neutral power.

In World War II, Switzerland and Sweden acted as protecting powers. The Red Cross in Geneva acted as a clearinghouse for the exchange of all information regarding POWs and had charge of transmitting correspondence and parcels. With minor and inevitable exceptions on the lower levels, the United States and Great Britain generally honored the Geneva Convention throughout the conflict. Japan at first committed such atrocities as the death march at Bataan but began to abide by the rules after a sufficient number of Japanese prisoners had fallen into Allied hands to make reprisals possible. Germany did not treat all its prisoners alike. Americans and British subjects received the best treatment, Polish prisoners the worst.

Convention of July 27, 1929, Relative to the Treatment of Prisoners of War

The President of the German Reich, the President of the United States of America, the Federal President of the Republic of Austria, His Majesty the King of the Belgians, the President of the Republic of Bolivia, the President of the Republic of the United States of Brazil, His Majesty the King of Great Britain, Ireland, and the British Dominions beyond the Seas, Emperor of India, His Majesty the King of the Bulgarians, the President of the Republic of Chile, the President of the Republic of China, the President of the Republic of Colombia, the President of the Republic of Cuba, His Majesty the King of Denmark and Iceland, the President of the Dominican Republic, His Majesty the King of Egypt, His Majesty the King of Spain, the President of the Republic of Estonia, the President of the Republic of Finland, the President of the French Republic, the President of the Hellenic Republic, His Serene Highness the Regent of Hungary, His Majesty the King of Italy, His Majesty the Emperor of Japan, the President of the Republic of Latvia, Her Royal Highness the Grand Duchess of Luxembourg, the President of the United States of Mexico, the President of the Republic of Nicaragua, His Majesty the King of Norway, Her Majesty the Queen of the Netherlands, His Imperial Majesty the Shah of Persia the President of the Republic of Poland, the President of the Portuguese Republic, His Majesty the King of Rumania, His Majesty the

King of the Serbs, Croats and Slovenes, His Majesty the King of Siam, His Majesty the King of Sweden, the Swiss Federal Council, the President of the Czechoslovak Republic, the President of the Turkish Republic, the President of the Oriental Republic of Uruguay, [and] the President of the Republic of the United States of Venezuela,

-recognizing that, in the extreme case of a war, it will be the duty of every Power to diminish, so far as possible the unavoidable rigors thereof an to mitigate the fate of prisoners of war;

-desirous of developing the principles which inspired the international conventions of The Hague, in particular the Convention relative to the laws and customs of war and the Regulations annexed thereto;

-have decided to conclude a Convention to that end.

TITLE I: GENERAL PROVISIONS

ARTICLE 1.

The present Convention shall apply, without prejudice to the stipulations of Title VII:

To all persons mentioned in Articles 1, 2 and 3 of the Regulations annexed to the Hague Convention respecting the laws and customs of war on land, of October 18, 1907, and captured by the enemy.

To all persons belonging to the armed forces of belligerent parties, captured by the enemy in the course of military operations at sea or in the air, except for such derogations as might be rendered inevitable by the conditions of capture. However, such derogations shall not infringe upon the fundamental principles of the present Convention; they shall cease from the moment when the persons captured have rejoined a prisoners-of-war camp.

ARTICLE 2.

Prisoners of war are in the power of the hostile Power, but not of the individuals or corps who have captured them.

They must at all times be humanely treated and protected, particularly against acts of violence, insults and public curiosity.

Measures of reprisal against them are prohibited.

ARTICLE 3

Prisoners of war have the right to have their person and their honor respected. Women shall be treated with all the regard due to their sex.

Prisoners retain their full civil status.

ARTICLE 4.

The Power detaining prisoners of war is bound to provide for their maintenance.

Difference in treatment among prisoners is lawful only when it is based on the military rank, state of physical or mental health, professional qualifications or sex of those who profit thereby.

TITLE II: CAPTURE

ARTICLE 5.

Every prisoner of war is bound to give, if he is questioned on the subject, his true name and rank, or else his regimental number.

If he infringes this rule, he is liable to have the advantages given to prisoners of his class curtailed.

No coercion may be used on prisoners to secure information as to the condition of their army or country. Prisoners who refuse to answer may not be threatened, insulted, or exposed to unpleasant or disadvantageous treatment of any kind whatever.

If, because of his physical or mental condition, a prisoner is unable to identify himself, he shall be turned over to the medical corps.

ARTICLE 6.

All effects and objects of personal use except arms, horses, military equipment and military papers shall remain in the possession of prisoners of war, as well as metal helmets and gas masks.

Money in the possession of prisoners may not be taken away from them except by order of an officer and after the amount is determined.

A receipt shall be given. Money thus taken away shall be entered to the amount of each prisoner.

Identification documents, insignia of rank, decorations and objects of value may not be taken from prisoners.

TITLE III: CAPTIVITY

SECTION I: EVACUATION OF PRISONERS OF WAR

ARTICLE 7.

Prisoners of war shall be evacuated within the shortest possible period after their capture, to spots located in a region far enough from the zone of combat for them to be out of danger.

Only prisoners who, because of wounds or sickness would run greater risks by being evacuated than by remaining where they are may be temporarily kept in a dangerous zone.

Prisoners shall not be needlessly exposed to danger while awaiting their evacuation from the combat zone.

Evacuation of prisoners on foot may normally be effected only by stages of 20 kilometers a day, unless the necessity of reaching water and food depots requires longer stages.

ARTICLE 8.

Belligerents are bound mutually to notify each other of their capture of prisoners within the shortest period possible, through the intermediary of the information bureaus, such as are organized according to Article 77. They are likewise bound to inform each other of the official addresses to which the correspondence of their families may be sent to prisoners of war.

As soon as possible, every prisoner must be enabled to correspond with his family himself, under the conditions provided in Articles 36 et seq.

As regards prisoners captured at sea, the provisions of the present article shall be observed as soon as possible after arrival at port.

SECTION II: PRISONERS-OF-WAR CAMPS

ARTICLE 9.

Prisoners of war may be interned in a town, fortress, or other place, and bound not to go beyond certain fixed limits. They may also be interned in enclosed camps; they may not be confined or imprisoned except as an indispensable measure of safety or sanitation, and only while the circumstances which necessitate the measure continue to exist.

Prisoners captured in unhealthful regions or where the climate is injurious for persons coming from temperate regions, shall be transported, as soon as possible, to a more favorable climate.

Belligerents shall, so far as possible, avoid assembling in a single camp prisoners of different races or nationalities.

No prisoner may, at any time, be sent into a region where he might be exposed to the fire of the combat zone, nor used to give protection from bombardment to certain points or certain regions by his presence.

CHAPTER 1: Installation of Camps

ARTICLE 10.

Prisoners of war shall be lodged in buildings or in barracks affording all possible guarantees of hygiene and healthfulness.

The quarters must be fully protected from. dampness, sufficiently heated and lighted. All precautions must be taken against danger of fire.

With regard to dormitories the total surface, minimum cubic amount of air, arrangement and material of bedding-the conditions shall be the same as for the troops at base camps of the detaining Power.

CHAPTER 2: Food and Clothing of Prisoners of War

ARTICLE 11.

The food ration of prisoners of war shall be equal in quantity and quality to that of troops at base camps.

Furthermore, prisoners shall receive facilities for preparing, themselves, additional food which they might have.

Sufficiency of potable water shall be furnished them. The use of tobacco shall be permitted. Prisoners may be employed in the kitchens.

All collective disciplinary measures affecting the food are prohibited.

ARTICLE 12.

Clothing, linen and footwear shall be furnished prisoners of war by the detaining Power. Replacement and repairing of these effects must be assured regularly. In addition, laborers must receive work clothes wherever the nature of the work requires it.

Canteens shall be installed in all camps where prisoners may obtain, at the local market price, food products and ordinary objects.

Profits made by the canteens for camp administrations shall be used for the benefit of prisoners.

CHAPTER 3: Sanitary Service in Camps

ARTICLE 13.

Belligerents shall. be bound to take all sanitary measures necessary to assure the cleanliness and healthfulness of camps and to prevent epidemics.

Prisoners of war shall have at their disposal, day and night, installations conforming to sanitary rules and constantly maintained in a state of cleanliness.

Furthermore, and without Prejudice to baths and showers of which the camp shall be as well provided as possible, prisoners shall be furnished a sufficient quantity of water for the care of their own bodily cleanliness.

It shall be possible for them to take physical exercise and enjoy the open air.

ARTICLE 14.

Every camp shall have an infirmary, where prisoners of war shall receive every kind of attention they need. If necessary, isolated quarters shall be reserved for the sick affected with contagious diseases.

Expenses of treatment, including therein those of temporary prosthetic equipment, shall become by the detaining Power.

Upon request, belligerents shall be bound to deliver to every prisoner treated an official statement showing the nature and duration of his illness as well as the attention received.

It shall be lawful for belligerents reciprocally to authorize, by means of private arrangements the retention in the camps of physicians and attendants to care for prisoners of their own country.

Prisoners affected with a serious illness or whose condition necessitates an important surgical operation, must be admitted, at the expense of the detaining Power, to any military or civil medical unit qualified to treat them.

ARTICLE 15.

Medical inspections of prisoners of war shall be arranged at least once a month. Their purpose shall be the supervision of the general state of health and cleanliness, and the detection of contagious diseases, particularly tuberculosis and venereal diseases.

CHAPTER 4: Intellectual and Moral Needs of Prisoners of War

ARTICLE 16

Prisoners of war shall enjoy complete liberty in the exercise of their religion, including attendance at the services of their faith, on the sole condition that they comply with the measures of order and police issued by the military authorities.

Ministers of a religion, prisoners of war, whatever their denomination, shall be allowed to minister fully to members of the same religion.

ARTICLE 17.

So far as possible belligerents shall encourage intellectual diversions and sports organized by prisoners of war. . . .

Nuremberg Principles, 1946, 1950

The United Nations (UN) General Assembly in 1945 directed one of its agencies, the International Law Commission, to "formulate the principles of international law recognized in the Charter of the Nuremberg Tribunal and in the judgment of the Tribunal." In the course of the consideration of this subject, the question arose as to whether or not the commission should ascertain to what extent the principles contained in the UN Charter and judgment constituted principles of international law. The conclusion was that since the Nuremberg Principles had been affirmed by the General Assembly in 1946, the task entrusted to the commission was not to express any appreciation of these principles as principles of international law but merely to formulate them.

Principles of International Law Recognized in the Charter of the Nuremberg Tribunal and in the Judgment of the Tribunal, Adopted by the International Law Commission of the United Nations (1950)

Principle I

Any person who commits an act which constitutes a crime under international law is responsible therefor and liable to punishment.

Principle II

The fact that internal law does not impose a penalty for an act which constitutes a crime under international law does not relieve the person who committed the act from responsibility under international law.

Principle III

The fact that a person who committed an act which constitutes a crime under international law acted as Head of State or responsible Government official does not relieve him from responsibility under international law.

Principle IV

The fact that a person acted pursuant to order of his Government or of a superior does not relieve him from responsibility under international law, provided a moral choice was in fact possible to him.

Principle V

Any person charged with a crime under international law has the right to a fair trial on the facts and law.

Principle VI

The crimes hereinafter set out are punishable as crimes under international law:

a. Crimes against peace:

i. Planning, preparation, initiation or waging of a war of aggression or a war in violation of international treaties, agreements or assurances;

ii. Participation in a common plan or conspiracy for the accomplishment of any of the acts mentioned under (i).

b. War crimes:

Violations of the laws or customs of war which include, but are not limited to, murder, ill-treatment or deportation to slave-labor or for any other purpose of civilian population of or in occupied territory, murder or ill-treatment of prisoners of war, of persons on the seas, killing of hostages, plunder of public or private property, wanton destruction of cities, towns, or villages, or devastation not justified by military necessity.

c. Crimes against humanity:

Murder, extermination, enslavement, deportation and other inhuman acts done against any civilian population, or persecutions on political, racial or religious grounds, when such acts are done or such persecutions are carried on in execution of or in connection with any crime against peace or any war crime.

Principle VII

Complicity in the commission of a crime against peace, a war crime, or a crime against humanity as set forth in Principles VI is a crime under international law.

UN Convention on the Prevention and Punishment of the Crime of Genocide (1948)

The atrocities directed toward civilians and the implementation of the final solution (the extermination of Jews) by the Nazi dictatorship led to the deaths of many millions of Jews, Gypsies, and other groups thought to be inferior to the Aryan race. In 1946, at the instigation of a number of member states of the United Nations, the world community began to examine the question of genocide and quickly fashioned an international convention to try to prevent and then punish those who perpetrated genocide. It is important to note that a state's policy of genocide became a crime in international law whether committed during peace or during war. In the 1990s, the crime of genocide fell under the jurisdiction of both the International Criminal Tribunal for the Former Yugoslavia (ICTY) and the International Criminal Tribunal for Rwanda (ICTR). It is also within the jurisdiction of the recently ratified International Criminal Court.

Convention on the Prevention and Punishment of the Crime of Genocide; December 9, 1948

The Contracting Parties,

Having considered the declaration made by the General Assembly of the United Nations in its resolution 96 (I) dated 11 December 1946 that genocide is a crime under international law, contrary to the spirit and aims of the United Nations and condemned by the civilized world;

Recognizing that at all periods of history genocide has inflicted great losses on humanity; and

Being convinced that, in order to liberate mankind from such an odious scourge, international co-operation is required;

Hereby agree as hereinafter provided.

Article 1.

The Contracting Parties confirm that genocide, whether committed in time of peace or in time of war, is a crime under international law which they undertake to prevent and to punish.

Art. 2.

In the present Convention, genocide means any of the following acts committed with intent to destroy, in whole or in part, a national, ethnical, racial or religious group, as such:

(a) Killing members of the group; (b) Causing serious bodily or mental harm to members of the group; (c) Deliberately inflicting on the group conditions of life calculated to bring about its physical destruction in whole or in part; (d) Imposing measures intended to prevent births within the group; (e) Forcibly transferring children of the group to another group.

Art. 3.

The following acts shall be punishable:

(a) Genocide; (b) Conspiracy to commit genocide; (c) Direct and public incitement to commit genocide; (d) Attempt to commit genocide; (e) Complicity in genocide.

Art. 4.

Persons committing genocide or any of the other acts enumerated in Article 3 shall be punished, whether they are constitutionally responsible rulers, public officials or private individuals.

Art. 5.

The Contracting Parties undertake to enact, in accordance with their respective Constitutions, the necessary legislation to give effect to the provisions of the present Convention and, in particular, to provide effective penalties for persons guilty of genocide or any of the other acts enumerated in Article 3.

Art. 6.

Persons charged with genocide or any of the other acts enumerated in Article 3 shall be tried by a competent tribunal of the State in the territory of which the act was committed, or by such international penal tribunal as may have jurisdiction with respect to those

Contracting Parties which shall have accepted its jurisdiction.

Art. 7.

Genocide and the other acts enumerated in Article 3 shall not be considered as political crimes for the purpose of extradition.

The Contracting Parties pledge themselves in such cases to grant extradition in accordance with their laws and treaties in force.

Art. 8.

Any Contracting Party may call upon the competent organs of the United Nations to take such action under the Charter of the United Nations as they consider appropriate for the prevention and suppression of acts of genocide or any of the other acts enumerated in Article 3.

Art. 9.

Disputes between the Contracting Parties relating to the interpretation, application or fulfilment of the present Convention, including those relating to the responsibility of a State for genocide or any of the other acts enumerated in Article 3, shall be submitted to the International Court of Justice at the request of any of the parties to the dispute. . . .

The Four Geneva Conventions, 1949

I. For the Amelioration of the Condition of Wounded and Sick in Armed Forces in the Field;
II. For the Amelioration of the Condition of Wounded, Sick, and Shipwrecked Members of the Armed Forces at Sea;
III. Relative to the Treatment of Prisoners of War,
IV. Relative to the Protection of Civilian Persons in Time of War

The four Geneva Conventions of 1949, although directed at different cohorts, focused centrally on protecting the victims of war: wounded and sick combatants, POWs, and civilian populations. The horrors of World War II in the Pacific and European theaters, death marches, extermination of civilians, civilian reprisal murders, medical experiments on POWs and on civilians, and other crimes against humanity led to the convening of a conference in Geneva in the spring and summer of 1949, attended by more than sixty nation-states.

Some of the conventions (e.g., Convention I) updated earlier conventions signed in Geneva in 1864, 1907, and 1929. Convention III, on POWs, updated and revised earlier treaties on the same subject ratified in 1899, 1907, and 1929. Convention IV, however, was unique: For the first time, the international community addressed the plight of civilians during war, whether under the authority and control of the occupying power or who were interned by a belligerent during war.

Geneva Convention III Relative to the Treatment of Prisoners of War; August 12, 1949

. . .

PART I: GENERAL PROVISIONS

ARTICLE 1

The High Contracting Parties undertake to respect and to ensure respect for the present Convention in all circumstances.

ARTICLE 2

In addition to the provisions which shall be implemented in peace time, the present Convention shall apply to all cases of declared war or of any other armed conflict which may arise between two or more of the High Contracting Parties, even if the state of war is not recognized by one of them.

The Convention shall also apply to all cases of partial or total occupation of the territory of a High Contracting Party, even if the said occupation meets with no armed resistance.

Although one of the Powers in conflict may not be a party to the present Convention, the Powers who are parties thereto shall remain bound by it in their mutual relations. They shall furthermore be bound by the Convention in relation to the said Power, if the latter accepts and applies the provisions thereof.

ARTICLE 3

In the case of armed conflict not of an international character occurring in the territory of one of the High Contracting Parties, each Party to the conflict shall be bound to apply, as a minimum, the following provisions:

(1) Persons taking no active part in the hostilities, including members of armed forces who have laid down their arms and those placed hors de combat by sickness, wounds, detention, or any other cause, shall in all circumstances be treated humanely, without any adverse distinction founded on race, colour, religion or faith, sex, birth or wealth, or any other similar criteria. To this end the following acts are and shall remain prohibited at any time and in any place whatsoever with respect to the above-mentioned persons:

(a) violence to life and person, in particular murder of all kinds, mutilation, cruel treatment and torture; (b) taking of hostages; (c) outrages upon personal dignity, in particular, humiliating and degrading treatment; (d) the passing of sentences and the carrying out of executions without previous judgment pronounced by a regularly constituted court affording all the judicial guarantees which are recognized as indispensable by civilized peoples.

(2) The wounded and sick shall be collected and cared for.

An impartial humanitarian body, such as the International Committee of the Red Cross, may offer its services to the Parties to the conflict.

The Parties to the conflict should further endeavour to bring into force, by means of special agreements, all or part of the other provisions of the present Convention.

The application of the preceding provisions shall not affect the legal status of the Parties to the conflict.

ARTICLE 4

A. Prisoners of war, in the sense of the present Convention, are persons belonging to one of the following categories, who have fallen into the power of the enemy:

(1) Members of the armed forces of a Party to the conflict, as well as members of militias or volunteer corps forming part of such armed forces.

(2) Members of other militias and members of other volunteer corps, including those of organized resistance movements, belonging to a Party to the conflict and operating in or outside their own territory, even if this territory is occupied, provided that such militias or volunteer corps, including such organized resistance movements, fulfil the following conditions: (a) that of being commanded by a person responsible for his subordinates; (b) that of having a fixed distinctive sign recognizable at a distance; (c) that of carrying arms openly; (d) that of conducting their operations in accordance with the laws and customs of war.

(3) Members of regular armed forces who profess allegiance to a government or an authority not recognized by the Detaining Power.

(4) Persons who accompany the armed forces without actually being members thereof, such as civilian members of military aircraft crews, war correspondents, supply contractors, members of labour units or of services responsible for the welfare of the armed forces, provided that they have received authorization, from the armed forces which they accompany, who shall provide them for that purpose with an identity card similar to the annexed model.

(5) Members of crews, including masters, pilots and apprentices, of the merchant marine and the crews of civil aircraft of the Parties to the conflict, who do not benefit by more favourable treatment under any other provisions of international law.

(6) Inhabitants of a non-occupied territory, who on the approach of the enemy spontaneously take up arms to resist the invading forces, without having had time to form themselves into regular armed units, provided they carry arms openly and respect the laws and customs of war.

B. The following shall likewise be treated as prisoners of war under the present Convention:

(1) Persons belonging, or having belonged, to the armed forces of the occupied country, if the occupying Power consid-

ers it necessary by reason of such allegiance to intern them, even though it has originally liberated them while hostilities were going on outside the territory it occupies, in particular where such persons have made an unsuccessful attempt to rejoin the armed forces to which they belong and which are engaged in combat, or where they fail to comply with a summons made to them with a view to internment.

(2) The persons belonging to one of the categories enumerated in the present Article, who have been received by neutral or non-belligerent Powers on their territory and whom these Powers are required to intern under international law, without prejudice to any more favourable treatment which these Powers may choose to give and with the exception of Articles 8, 10, 15, 30, fifth paragraph, 58–67, 92, 126 and, where diplomatic relations exist between the Parties to the conflict and the neutral or non-belligerent Power concerned, those Articles concerning the Protecting Power. Where such diplomatic relations exist, the Parties to a conflict on whom these persons depend shall be allowed to perform towards them the functions of a Protecting Power as provided in the present Convention, without prejudice to the functions which these Parties normally exercise in conformity with diplomatic and consular usage and treaties.

C. This Article shall in no way affect the status of medical personnel and chaplains as provided for in Article 33 of the present Convention.

ARTICLE 5

The present Convention shall apply to the persons referred to in Article 4 from the time they fall into the power of the enemy and until their final release and repatriation.

Should any doubt arise as to whether persons, having committed a belligerent act and having fallen into the hands of the enemy, belong to any of the categories enumerated in Article 4, such persons shall enjoy the protection of the present Convention until such time as their status has been determined by a competent tribunal.

ARTICLE 6

In addition to the agreements expressly provided for in Articles 10, 23, 28, 33, 60, 65, 66, 67, 72, 73, 75, 109, 110, 118, 119, 122 and 132, the High Contracting Parties may conclude other special agreements for all matters concerning which they may deem it suitable to make separate provision. No special agreement shall adversely affect the situation of prisoners of war, as defined by the present Convention, nor restrict the rights which it confers upon them.

Prisoners of war shall continue to have the benefit of such agreements as long as the Convention is applicable to them, except where express provisions to the contrary are contained in the aforesaid or in subsequent agreements, or where more favourable measures have been taken with regard to them by one or other of the Parties to the conflict.

ARTICLE 7

Prisoners of war may in no circumstances renounce in part or in entirety the rights secured to them by the present Convention, and by the special agreements referred to in the foregoing Article, if such there be.

ARTICLE 8

The present Convention shall be applied with the cooperation and under the scrutiny of the Protecting Powers whose duty it is to safeguard the interests of the Parties to the conflict. For this purpose, the Protecting Powers may appoint, apart from their diplomatic or consular staff, delegates from amongst their own nationals or the nationals of other neutral Powers. The said delegates shall be subject to the approval of the Power with which they are to carry out their duties.

The Parties to the conflict shall facilitate to the greatest extent possible the task of the representatives or delegates of the Protecting Powers.

The representatives or delegates of the Protecting Powers shall not in any case exceed their mission under the present Convention. They shall, in particular, take account of the imperative necessities of security of the State wherein they carry out their duties.

ARTICLE 9

The provisions of the present Convention constitute no obstacle to the humanitarian activities which the International Committee of the Red Cross or any other impartial humanitarian organization may, subject to the consent of the Parties to the conflict concerned, undertake for the protection of prisoners of war and for their relief.

ARTICLE 10

The High Contracting Parties may at any time agree to entrust to an organization which offers all guarantees of impartiality and efficacy the duties incumbent on the Protecting Powers by virtue of the present Convention.

When prisoners of war do not benefit or cease to benefit, no matter for what reason, by the activities of a Protecting Power or of an organization provided for in the first paragraph above, the Detaining Power shall request a neutral State, or such an organization, to undertake the functions performed under the present Convention by a Protecting Power designated by the Parties to a conflict.

If protection cannot be arranged accordingly, the Detaining Power shall request or shall accept, subject to the provisions of this Article, the offer of the services of a humanitarian organization, such as the International Committee of the Red Cross to assume the humanitarian functions performed by Protecting Powers under the present Convention.

Any neutral Power or any organization invited by the Power concerned or offering itself for these purposes, shall be required to act with a sense of responsibility towards the Party to the conflict on which persons protected by the present Convention depend, and shall be required to furnish sufficient assurances that it is in a position to undertake the appropriate functions and to discharge them impartially.

No derogation from the preceding provisions shall be made by special agreements between Powers one of which is restricted, even temporarily, in its freedom to negotiate with the other Power or its allies by reason of military events, more particularly where the whole, or a substantial part, of the territory of the said Power is occupied.

Whenever in the present Convention mention is made of a Protecting Power, such mention applies to substitute organizations in the sense of the present Article.

Geneva Convention [IV] relative to the Protection of Civilian Persons in Time of War; Geneva, August 12, 1949

Preamble

The undersigned Plenipotentiaries of the Governments represented at the Diplomatic Conference held at Geneva from April 21 to August 12, 1949, for the purpose of establishing a Convention for the Protection of Civilian Persons in Time of War, have agreed as follows:

Part I: General Provisions

Article 1. The High Contracting Parties undertake to respect and to ensure respect for the present Convention in all circumstances.

Art. 2. In addition to the provisions which shall be implemented in peace-time, the present Convention shall apply to all cases of declared war or of any other armed conflict which may arise between two or more of the High Contracting Parties, even if the state of war is not recognized by one of them.

The Convention shall also apply to all cases of partial or total occupation of the territory of a High Contracting Party, even if the said occupation meets with no armed resistance.

Although one of the Powers in conflict may not be a party to the present Convention, the Powers who are parties thereto shall remain bound by it in their mutual relations. They shall furthermore be bound by the Convention in relation to the said Power, if the latter accepts and applies the provisions thereof.

Art. 3. In the case of armed conflict not of an international character occurring in the territory of one of the High Contracting Parties, each Party to the conflict shall be bound to apply, as a minimum, the following provisions:

(1) Persons taking no active part in the hostilities, including members of armed forces who have laid down their arms and those placed hors de combat by sickness, wounds, detention, or any other cause, shall in all circumstances be treated humanely, without any adverse distinction founded on race, colour, religion or faith, sex, birth or wealth, or any other similar criteria.

To this end the following acts are and shall remain prohibited at any time and in any place whatsoever with respect to the above-mentioned persons:

(a) violence to life and person, in particular murder of all kinds, mutilation, cruel treatment and torture;

(b) taking of hostages;

(c) outrages upon personal dignity, in particular humiliating and degrading treatment;

(d) the passing of sentences and the carrying out of executions without previous judgment pronounced by a regularly constituted court, affording all the judicial guarantees which are recognized as indispensable by civilized peoples.

(2) The wounded and sick shall be collected and cared for.

An impartial humanitarian body, such as the International Committee of the Red Cross, may offer its services to the Parties to the conflict.

The Parties to the conflict should further endeavour to bring into force, by means of special agreements, all or part of the other provisions of the present Convention.

The application of the preceding provisions shall not affect the legal status of the Parties to the conflict.

Art. 4. Persons protected by the Convention are those who, at a given moment and in any manner whatsoever, find themselves, in case of a conflict or occupation, in the hands of a Party to the conflict or Occupying Power of which they are not nationals.

Nationals of a State which is not bound by the Convention are not protected by it. Nationals of a neutral State who find themselves in the territory of a belligerent State, and nationals of a co-belligerent State, shall not be regarded as protected persons while the State of which they are nationals has normal diplomatic representation in the State in whose hands they are.

The provisions of Part II are, however, wider in application, as defined in Article 13.

Persons protected by the Geneva Convention for the Amelioration of the Condition of the Wounded and Sick in Armed Forces in the Field of 12 August 1949, or by the Geneva Convention for the Amelioration of the Condition of Wounded, Sick and Shipwrecked Members of Armed Forces at Sea of 12 August 1949, or by the Geneva Convention relative to the Treatment of Prisoners of War of 12 August 1949, shall not be considered as protected persons within the meaning of the present Convention.

Art. 5 Where in the territory of a Party to the conflict, the latter is satisfied that an individual protected person is definitely suspected of or engaged in activities hostile to the security of the State, such individual person shall not be entitled to claim such rights and privileges under the present Convention as would, if exercised in the favour of such individual person, be prejudicial to the security of such State.

Where in occupied territory an individual protected person is detained as a spy or saboteur, or as a person under definite suspicion of activity hostile to the security of the Occupying Power, such person shall, in those cases where absolute military security so requires, be regarded as having forfeited rights of communication under the present Convention.

In each case, such persons shall nevertheless be treated with humanity and, in case of trial, shall not be deprived of the rights of fair and regular trial prescribed by the present Convention. They shall also be granted the full rights and privileges of a protected person under the present Convention at the earliest date consistent with the security of the State or Occupying Power, as the case may be.

Art. 6. The present Convention shall apply from the outset of any conflict or occupation mentioned in Article 2.

In the territory of Parties to the conflict, the application of the present Convention shall cease on the general close of military operations.

In the case of occupied territory, the application of the present Convention shall cease one year after the general close of military operations; however, the Occupying Power shall be bound, for the duration of the occupation, to the extent that such Power exercises the functions of government in such territory, by the provisions of the following Articles of the present Convention: 1 to 12, 27, 29 to 34, 47, 49, 51, 52, 53, 59, 61 to 77, 143.

Protected persons whose release, repatriation or re-establishment may take place after such dates shall meanwhile continue to benefit by the present Convention.

Art. 7. In addition to the agreements expressly provided for in Articles 11, 14, 15, 17, 36, 108, 109, 132, 133 and 149, the High Contracting Parties may conclude other special agreements for all matters concerning which they may deem it suitable to make separate provision. No special agreement shall adversely affect the situation of protected persons, as defined by the present Convention, not restrict the rights which it confers upon them.

Protected persons shall continue to have the benefit of such agreements as long as the Convention is applicable to them, except where express provisions to the contrary are contained in the aforesaid or in subsequent agreements, or where more favourable measures have been taken with regard to them by one or other of the Parties to the conflict.

Art. 8. Protected persons may in no circumstances renounce in part or in entirety the rights secured to them by the present Convention, and by the special agreements referred to in the foregoing Article, if such there be.

Art. 9. The present Convention shall be applied with the co-operation and under the scrutiny of the Protecting Powers whose duty it is to safeguard the interests of the Parties to the conflict. For this purpose, the Protecting Powers may appoint, apart from their diplomatic or consular staff, delegates from amongst their own nationals or the nationals of other neutral

Powers. The said delegates shall be subject to the approval of the Power with which they are to carry out their duties.

The Parties to the conflict shall facilitate to the greatest extent possible the task of the representatives or delegates of the Protecting Powers.

The representatives or delegates of the Protecting Powers shall not in any case exceed their mission under the present Convention.

They shall, in particular, take account of the imperative necessities of security of the State wherein they carry out their duties.

Art. 10. The provisions of the present Convention constitute no obstacle to the humanitarian activities which the International Committee of the Red Cross or any other impartial humanitarian organization may, subject to the consent of the Parties to the conflict concerned, undertake for the protection of civilian persons and for their relief.

Art. 11. The High Contracting Parties may at any time agree to entrust to an international organization which offers all guarantees of impartiality and efficacy the duties incumbent on the Protecting Powers by virtue of the present Convention.

When persons protected by the present Convention do not benefit or cease to benefit, no matter for what reason, by the activities of a Protecting Power or of an organization provided for in the first paragraph above, the Detaining Power shall request a neutral State, or such an organization, to undertake the functions performed under the present Convention by a Protecting Power designated by the Parties to a conflict.

If protection cannot be arranged accordingly, the Detaining Power shall request or shall accept, subject to the provisions of this Article, the offer of the services of a humanitarian organization, such as the International Committee of the Red Cross, to assume the humanitarian functions performed by Protecting Powers under the present Convention.

Any neutral Power or any organization invited by the Power concerned or offering itself for these purposes, shall be required to act with a sense of responsibility towards the Party to the conflict on which persons protected by the present Convention depend, and shall be required to furnish sufficient assurances that it is in a position to undertake the appropriate functions and to discharge them impartially.

Geneva Protocol I Additional to the Geneva Conventions of 12 August 1949 and Relating to the Protection of Victims of International Armed Conflicts, 1977; Geneva Protocol II Additional to the Geneva Conventions of 12 August 1949 Relating to the Protection of Victims of Non-International Armed Conflicts, 1977

After 1949, the increase in armed conflicts across the globe and the use of new methods of warfare and new technologies of killing led to the 1977 Geneva Protocols that attempted to modify and revise the four 1949 Geneva Conventions. Many of these armed conflicts were not covered by the earlier conventions because the armed clashes were manifestations of an internal conflict (i.e., a civil war fought between rival claimants for power). As was the case in 1949, the focus of these revisions was on protection of the victims of war, including civil wars. The two protocols supplemented the 1949 Geneva Conventions; they did not set the earlier treaties aside.

Protocol 1 Additional to the Geneva Conventions (1977)

. . .

PART IV: CIVILIAN POPULATION

Section 1: General Protection Against Effects of Hostilities
Chapter I: Basic Rule and Field of Application
Article 48: Basic Rule In order to ensure respect for and protection of the civilian population and civilian objects, the Parties to the conflict shall at all times distinguish between the civilian population and combatants and between civilian objects and military objectives and accordingly shall direct their operations only against military objectives.

Article 49: Definition of Attacks and Scope of Application 1. "Attacks" means acts of violence against the adversary, whether in offense or in defense.

2. The provisions of this Protocol with respect to attacks apply to all attacks in whatever territory conducted, including the national territory belonging to a Party to the conflict but under the control of an adverse Party.

3. The provisions of this Section apply to any land, air or sea warfare which may affect the civilian population, individual civilians or civilian objects on land. They further apply to all attacks from the sea or from the air against objectives on land but do not otherwise affect the rules of international law applicable in armed conflict at sea or in the air.

4. The provisions of this Section are additional to the rules concerning humanitarian protection contained in the Fourth Convention, particularly in Part II thereof, and in other international agreements binding upon the High Contracting Parties, as well as to other rules of international law relating to the protection of civilians and civilian objects on land, at sea or in the air against the effects of hostilities.

Chapter II: Civilians and Civilian Population

Article 50: Definition of Civilians and Civilian Population 1. A civilian is any person who does not belong to one of the categories of persons referred to in Article 4 A 111, (Articles 31 and 161 of the Third Convention and in Article 43 of this Protocol). In case of doubt whether a person is a civilian, that person shall be considered to be a civilian.

2. The civilian population comprises all persons who are civilians.

3. The presence within the civilian population of individuals who do not come within the definition of civilians does not deprive the population of its civilian character.

Article 51: Protection of the Civilian Population 1. The civilian population and individual civilians shall enjoy general protection against dangers arising from military operations. To give effect to this protection, the following rules, which are additional to other applicable rules of international law, shall be observed in all circumstances.

2. The civilian population as such, as well as individual civilians, shall not be the object of attack. Acts or threats of violence the primary purpose of which is to spread terror among the civilian population are prohibited.

3. Civilians shall enjoy the protection afforded by this Section, unless and for such time as they take a direct part in hostilities.

4. Indiscriminate attacks are prohibited. Indiscriminate attacks are:

a. those which are not directed at a specific military objective;

b. those which employ a method or means of combat which cannot be directed at a specific military objective; or

c. those which employ a method or means of combat the effects of which cannot be limited as required by this Protocol; and consequently, in each such case, are of a nature to strike military objectives and civilians or civilian objects without distinction.

5. Among others, the following types of attacks are to be considered as indiscriminate:

a. an attack by bombardment by any methods or means which treats as a single military objective a number of clearly separated and distinct military objectives located in a city, town, village or other area containing a similar concentration of civilians or civilian objects; and

b. an attack which may be expected to cause incidental loss of civilian life, injury to civilians, damage to civilian objects, or a combination thereof, which would be excessive in relation to the concrete and direct military advantage anticipated.

6. Attacks against the civilian population or civilians by way of reprisals are prohibited.

7. The presence or movements of the civilian population or individual civilians shall not be used to render certain points or areas immune from military operations, in particular in attempts to shield military objectives from attacks or to shield, favor or impede military operations. The Parties to the conflict shall not direct the movement of the civilian population or individual civilians in order to attempt to shield military objectives from attacks or to shield military operations.

8. Any violation of these prohibitions shall not release the Parties to the conflict from their legal obligations with respect to the civilian population and civilians, including the obligation to take the precautionary measures provided for in Article 57.

Chapter III: Civilian Objects

Article 52: General Protection of Civilian Objects 1. Civilian objects shall not be the object of attack or of reprisals. Civilian objects are all objects which are not military objectives as defined in paragraph 2.

2. Attacks shall be limited strictly to military objectives. In so far as objects are concerned, military objectives are limited to those objects which by their nature, location, purpose or use make an effective contribution to military action and whose total or partial destruction, capture or neutralization, in the circumstances ruling at the time, offers a definite military advantage.

3. In case of doubt whether an object which is normally dedicated to civilian purposes, such as a place of worship, a house or other dwelling or a school, is being used to make an effective contribution to military action, it shall be presumed not to be so used.

Article 53 Protection of cultural objects and of places of worship without prejudice to the provisions of the Hague Convention for the Protection of Cultural Property in the Event of Armed Conflict of 14 May 1954, and of other relevant international instruments, it is prohibited:

a. to commit any acts of hostility directed against the historic monuments, works of art or places

of worship which constitute the cultural or spiritual heritage of peoples;

b. to use such objects in support of the military effort;

c. to make such objects the object of reprisals.

Article 54: Protection of Objects Indispensable to the Survival of the Civilian Population 1. Starvation of civilians as a method of warfare is prohibited

2. It is prohibited to attack, destroy, remove or render useless objects indispensable to the survival of the civilian population, such as foodstuffs, agricultural areas for the production of foodstuffs, crops, livestock, drinking water installations and supplies and irrigation works, for the specific purpose of denying them for their sustenance value to the civilian population or to the adverse Party, whatever the motive, whether in order to starve out civilians, to cause them to move away, or for any other motive.

3. The prohibitions in paragraph 2 shall not apply to such of the objects covered by it as are used by an adverse Party:

a. as sustenance solely for the members of its armed forces; or

b. if not as sustenance, then in direct support of military action, provided, however, that in no event shall actions against these objects be taken which may be expected to leave the starvation or force its movement.

4. These objects shall not be made the object of reprisals.

5. In recognition of the vital requirements of any Party to the conflict in the defense of its national territory against invasion, derogation from the prohibitions contained in paragraph 2 may be made by a Party to the conflict within such territory under its own control where required by imperative military necessity.

Article 55: Protection of the Natural Environment 1. Care shall be taken in warfare to protect the natural environment against widespread, long-term and severe damage. This protection includes a prohibition of the use of methods or means of warfare which are intended or may be expected to cause such damage to the natural environment and thereby to prejudice the health or survival of the population.

2. Attacks against the natural environment by way of reprisals are prohibited.

Article 56: Protection of Works and Installations Containing Dangerous Forces 1. Works or installations containing dangerous forces, namely dams, dikes and nuclear electrical generating stations, shall not be made the object of attack, even where these objects are military objectives, if such attack may cause the release of dangerous forces and consequent severe losses among the civilian population. Other military objectives located at or in the vicinity of these works or installations shall not be made the object of attack if such attack may cause the release of dangerous forces from the works or installations and consequent severe losses among the civilian population.

2. The special protection against attack provided by paragraph I shall cease:

a. for a dam or a dike only if it is used for other than its normal function and in regular, significant and direct support of military operations and if such attack is the only feasible way to terminate such support;

b. for a nuclear electrical generating station only if it provides electric power in regular, significant and direct support of military operations and if such attack is the only feasible way to terminate such support;

c. for other military objectives located at or in the vicinity of these works or installations only if they are used in regular, significant and direct support of military operations and if such attack is the only feasible way to terminate such support.

3. In all cases, the civilian population and individual civilians shall remain entitled to all the protection accorded them by international law, including the protection of the precautionary measures provided for in Article 57. If the protection ceases and any of the works, installations or military objectives mentioned in paragraph 1 is attacked, all practical precautions shall be taken to avoid the release of the dangerous forces.

4. It is prohibited to make any of the works, installations or military objectives mentioned in paragraph 1 the object of reprisals.

5. The Parties to the conflict shall endeavor to avoid locating any military objectives in the vicinity of the works or installations mentioned in paragraph 1. Nevertheless, installations erected for the sole purpose of defending the protected works or installations from attack are permissible and shall not themselves be made the object of attack, provided that they are not used in hostilities except for defensive actions necessary to respond to attacks against the protected works or installations and that their armament is limited to weapons capable only of repelling hostile

6. The High Contracting Parties and the Parties to the conflict are urged to conclude further agreements among themselves to provide additional protection for objects containing dangerous forces.

7. In order to facilitate the identification of the objects protected by this Article, the Parties to the conflict may mark them with a special sign consisting of a group of three bright orange circles placed on the same axis, as specified in Article 16 of Annex I to this Protocol. The absence of such marking in no way relieves any Party to the conflict of its obligations under this Article.

Chapter IV: Precautionary Measures

Article 57: Precautions in Attack 1. In the conduct of military operations, constant care shall be taken to spare the civilian population, civilians and civilian objects.

2. With respect to attacks, the following precautions shall be taken:

a. those who plan or decide upon an attack shall:

i. do everything feasible to verify that the objectives to be attacked are neither civilians nor civilian objects and are not subject to special protection but are military objectives within the meaning of paragraph 2 of Article 52 and that it is not prohibited by the provisions of this Protocol to attack them;

ii. take all feasible precautions in the choice of means and methods of attack with a view to avoiding, and in any event to minimizing, incidental loss of civilian life, injury to civilians and damage to civilian objects;

iii. refrain from deciding to launch any attack which may be expected to cause incidental loss of civilian life, injury to civilians, damage to civilian objects, or a combination thereof, which would be excessive in relation to the concrete and direct military advantage anticipated;

b. an attack shall be canceled or suspended if it becomes apparent that the objective is not a military one or is subject to special protection or that the attack may be expected to cause incidental loss of civilian life, injury to civilians, damage to civilian objects, or a combination thereof, which would be excessive in relation to the concrete and direct military advantage anticipated;

c. effective advance warning shall be given of attacks which may affect the civilian population, unless circumstances do not permit.

3. When a choice is possible between several military objectives for obtaining a similar military advantage, the objective to be selected shall be that the attack on which may be expected to cause the least danger to civilian lives and to civilian objects.

4. In the conduct of military operations at sea or in the air, each Party to the conflict shall, in conformity with its rights and duties under the rules of international law applicable in armed conflict, take all reasonable precautions to avoid losses of civilian lives and damage to civilian objects

5. No provision of this article may be construed as authorizing any attacks against the civilian population, civilians or civilian objects.

UN Statute of the International Criminal Tribunal for the Former Yugoslavia, 1993

For only the third time in world history, the international community established an ad hoc international criminal tribunal to try to deal with the perpetrators of war crimes, crimes against humanity, and genocide, this time in the former Yugoslavia between 1991 and 1995. In that period of time, more than 400,000 persons, mostly civilians, were killed, primarily by Serbs and Bosnian Serbs. More than 4 million persons became refugees or displaced persons in the former Yugoslavia. Laws of war were continually violated by the Serbs and the Bosnian Serbs in their efforts to create an "ethnically pure" Greater Serbia at the expense of Bosnian Croats and Bosnian Muslims. After more than two years of violence, the United Nations created the ICTY in 1993. It did not begin to function until a prosecutor was appointed in 1995. Since then, almost one hundred persons have been indicted, with more than fifty actually held in jail at The Hague. More than thirty indicted men are still at large, living in Serbia and other places in Europe.

STATUTE OF THE INTERNATIONAL TRIBUNAL (ADOPTED 25 MAY 1993 by Resolution 827) (AS AMENDED 13 MAY 1998 by Resolution 1166) (AS AMENDED 30 NOVEMBER 2000 by Resolution 1329)

Article 1: Competence of the International Tribunal

The International Tribunal shall have the power to prosecute persons responsible for serious violations of international humanitarian law committed in the territory of the former Yugoslavia since 1991 in accordance with the provisions of the present Statute.

Article 2: Grave breaches of the Geneva Conventions of 1949

The International Tribunal shall have the power to prosecute persons committing or ordering to be committed grave breaches of the Geneva Conventions of 12 August 1949, namely the following acts against persons or property protected under the provisions of the relevant Geneva Convention:

(a) wilful killing;

(b) torture or inhuman treatment, including biological experiments;

(c) wilfully causing great suffering or serious injury to body or health;

(d) extensive destruction and appropriation of property, not justified by military necessity and carried out unlawfully and wantonly;

(e) compelling a prisoner of war or a civilian to serve in the forces of a hostile power;

(f) wilfully depriving a prisoner of war or a civilian of the rights of fair and regular trial;

(g) unlawful deportation or transfer or unlawful confinement of a civilian;

(h) taking civilians as hostages.

Article 3: Violations of the laws or customs of war

The International Tribunal shall have the power to prosecute persons violating the laws or customs of war. Such violations shall include, but not be limited to:

(a) employment of poisonous weapons or other weapons calculated to cause unnecessary suffering;

(b) wanton destruction of cities, towns or villages, or devastation not justified by military necessity;

(c) attack, or bombardment, by whatever means, of undefended towns, villages, dwellings, or buildings;

(d) seizure of, destruction or wilful damage done to institutions dedicated to religion, charity and education, the arts and sciences, historic monuments and works of art and science;

(e) plunder of public or private property.

Article 4: Genocide

1. The International Tribunal shall have the power to prosecute persons committing genocide as defined in paragraph 2 of this article or of committing any of the other acts enumerated in paragraph 3 of this article.

2. Genocide means any of the following acts committed with intent to destroy, in whole or in part, a national, ethnical, racial or religious group, as such:

(a) killing members of the group;

(b) causing serious bodily or mental harm to members of the group;

(c) deliberately inflicting on the group conditions of life calculated to bring about its physical destruction in whole or in part;

(d) imposing measures intended to prevent births within the group;

(e) forcibly transferring children of the group to another group.

3. The following acts shall be punishable:

(a) genocide;

(b) conspiracy to commit genocide;

(c) direct and public incitement to commit genocide;

(d) attempt to commit genocide;

(e) complicity in genocide.

Article 5: Crimes against humanity

The International Tribunal shall have the power to prosecute persons responsible for the following crimes when committed in armed conflict, whether international or internal in character, and directed against any civilian population:

(a) murder;

(b) extermination;

(c) enslavement;
(d) deportation;
(e) imprisonment;
(f) torture;
(g) rape;
(h) persecutions on political, racial and religious grounds;
(i) other inhumane acts.

Article 6: Personal jurisdiction

The International Tribunal shall have jurisdiction over natural persons pursuant to the provisions of the present Statute.

Article 7: Individual criminal responsibility

1. A person who planned, instigated, ordered, committed or otherwise aided and abetted in the planning, preparation or execution of a crime referred to in articles 2 to 5 of the present Statute, shall be individually responsible for the crime.

2. The official position of any accused person, whether as Head of State or Government or as a responsible Government official, shall not relieve such person of criminal responsibility nor mitigate punishment.

3. The fact that any of the acts referred to in articles 2 to 5 of the present Statute was committed by a subordinate does not relieve his superior of criminal responsibility if he knew or had reason to know that the subordinate was about to commit such acts or had done so and the superior failed to take the necessary and reasonable measures to prevent such acts or to punish the perpetrators thereof.

4. The fact that an accused person acted pursuant to an order of a Government or of a superior shall not relieve him of criminal responsibility, but may be considered in mitigation of punishment if the International Tribunal determines that justice so requires.

Article 8: Territorial and temporal jurisdiction

The territorial jurisdiction of the International Tribunal shall extend to the territory of the former Socialist Federal Republic of Yugoslavia, including its land surface, airspace and territorial waters. The temporal jurisdiction of the International Tribunal shall extend to a period beginning on 1 January 1991.

Article 9: Concurrent jurisdiction

1. The International Tribunal and national courts shall have concurrent jurisdiction to prosecute persons for serious violations of international humanitarian law committed in the territory of the former Yugoslavia since 1 January 1991.

2. The International Tribunal shall have primacy over national courts. At any stage of the procedure, the International Tribunal may formally request national courts to defer to the competence of the International Tribunal in accordance with the present Statute and the Rules of Procedure and Evidence of the International Tribunal.

Article 10: Non-bis-in-idem

1. No person shall be tried before a national court for acts constituting serious violations of international humanitarian law under the present Statute, for which he or she has already been tried by the International Tribunal.

2. A person who has been tried by a national court for acts constituting serious violations of international humanitarian law may be subsequently tried by the International Tribunal only if:

(a) the act for which he or she was tried was characterized as an ordinary crime; or

(b) the national court proceedings were not impartial or independent, were designed to shield the accused from international criminal responsibility, or the case was not diligently prosecuted.

3. In considering the penalty to be imposed on a person convicted of a crime under the present Statute, the International Tribunal shall take into account the extent to which any penalty imposed by a national court on the same person for the same act has already been served.

Article 11: Organization of the International Tribunal

The International Tribunal shall consist of the following organs:

(a) the Chambers, comprising three Trial Chambers and an Appeals Chamber;

(b) the Prosecutor; and

(c) a Registry, servicing both the Chambers and the Prosecutor.

Article 12: Composition of the Chambers

1. The Chambers shall be composed of sixteen permanent independent judges, no two of whom may be nationals of the same State, and a maximum at any one time of nine ad litem independent judges appointed in accordance with article 13 ter, paragraph 2, of the Statute, no two of whom may be nationals of the same State.

2. Three permanent judges and a maximum at any one time of six ad litem judges shall be members of each Trial Chamber. Each Trial Chamber to which ad litem judges are assigned may be divided into sections of three judges each, composed of both permanent and ad litem judges. A section of a Trial Chamber shall have the same powers and responsibilities as a Trial Chamber under the Statute and shall render judgement in accordance with the same rules.

3. Seven of the permanent judges shall be members of the Appeals Chamber. The Appeals Chamber shall, for each appeal, be composed of five of its members.

Article 13: Qualifications of judges

The permanent and ad litem judges shall be persons of high moral character, impartiality and integrity who possess the qualifications required in their respective countries for appointment to the highest judicial offices.

In the overall composition of the Chambers and sections of the Trial Chambers, due account shall be taken of the experience of the judges in criminal law, international law, including international humanitarian law and human rights law.

Article 13 bis: Election of permanent judges

1. Fourteen of the permanent judges of the International Tribunal shall be elected by the General Assembly from a list submitted by the Security Council, in the following manner:

(a) The Secretary-General shall invite nominations for judges of the International Tribunal from States Members of the United Nations and non-member States maintaining permanent observer missions at United Nations Headquarters.

(b) Within sixty days of the date of the invitation of the Secretary-General, each State may nominate up to two candidates meeting the qualifications set out in article 13 of the Statute, no two of whom shall be of the same nationality and neither of whom shall be of the same nationality as any judge who is a member of the Appeals Chamber and who was elected or appointed a judge of the International Criminal Tribunal for the Prosecution of Persons Responsible for Genocide and Other Serious Violations of International Humanitarian Law Committed in the Territory of Rwanda and Rwandan Citizens Responsible for Genocide and Other Such Violations Committed in the Territory of Neighbouring States, between 1 January 1994 and 31 December 1994 (hereinafter referred to as "The International Tribunal for Rwanda") in accordance with article 12 of the Statute of that Tribunal.

(c) The Secretary-General shall forward the nominations received to the Security Council. From the nominations received the Security Council shall establish a list of not less than twenty-eight and not more than forty-two candidates, taking due account of the adequate representation of the principal legal systems of the world.

(d) The President of the Security Council shall transmit the list of candidates to the President of the General Assembly. From that list the General Assembly shall elect fourteen permanent judges of the International Tribunal. The candidates who receive an absolute majority of the votes of the States Members of the United Nations and of the non-member States maintaining permanent observer missions at United Nations Headquarters, shall be declared elected. Should two candidates of the same nationality obtain the required majority vote, the one who received the higher number of votes shall be considered elected.

2. In the event of a vacancy in the Chambers amongst the permanent judges elected or appointed in accordance with this article, after consultation with the Presidents of the Security Council and of the General Assembly, the Secretary-General shall appoint a person meeting the qualifications of article 13 of the Statute, for the remainder of the term of office concerned.

3. The permanent judges elected in accordance with this article shall be elected for a term of four years. The terms and conditions of service shall be those of the judges of the International Court of Justice. They shall be eligible for re-election.

Article 13 ter: Election and appointment of ad litem judges

1. The ad litem judges of the International Tribunal shall be

elected by the General Assembly from a list submitted by the Security Council, in the following manner:

(a) The Secretary-General shall invite nominations for ad litem judges of the International Tribunal from States Members of the United Nations and non-member States maintaining permanent observer missions at United Nations Headquarters.

(b) Within sixty days of the date of the invitation of the Secretary-General, each State may nominate up to four candidates meeting the qualifications set out in article 13 of the Statute, taking into account the importance of a fair representation of female and male candidates.

(c) The Secretary-General shall forward the nominations received to the Security Council. From the nominations received the Security Council shall establish a list of not less than fifty-four candidates, taking due account of the adequate representation of the principal legal systems of the world and bearing in mind the importance of equitable geographical distribution.

(d) The President of the Security Council shall transmit the list of candidates to the President of the General Assembly. From that list the General Assembly shall elect the twenty-seven ad litem judges of the International Tribunal. The candidates who receive an absolute majority of the votes of the States Members of the United Nations and of the non-member States maintaining permanent observer missions at United Nations Headquarters shall be declared elected.

(e) The ad litem judges shall be elected for a term of four years. They shall not be eligible for re-election.

2. During their term, ad litem judges will be appointed by the Secretary-General, upon request of the President of the International Tribunal, to serve in the Trial Chambers for one or more trials, for a cumulative period of up to, but not including, three years. When requesting the appointment of any particular ad litem judge, the President of the International Tribunal shall bear in mind the criteria set out in article 13 of the Statute regarding the composition of the Chambers and sections of the Trial Chambers, the considerations set out in paragraphs 1 (b) and (c) above and the number of votes the ad litem judge received in the General Assembly.

Article 13 quater: Status of ad litem judges

1. During the period in which they are appointed to serve in the International Tribunal, ad litem judges shall:

(a) benefit from the same terms and conditions of service mutatis mutandis as the permanent judges of the International Tribunal;

(b) enjoy, subject to paragraph 2 below, the same powers as the permanent judges of the International Tribunal;

(c) enjoy the privileges and immunities, exemptions and facilities of a judge of the International Tribunal.

2. During the period in which they are appointed to serve in the International Tribunal, ad litem judges shall not:

(a) be eligible for election as, or to vote in the election of, the President of the Tribunal or the Presiding Judge of a Trial Chamber pursuant to article 14 of the Statute;

(b) have power:

(i) to adopt rules of procedure and evidence pursuant to article 15 of the Statute. They shall, however, be consulted before the adoption of those rules;

(ii) to review an indictment pursuant to article 19 of the Statute;

(iii) to consult with the President in relation to the assignment of judges pursuant to article 14 of the Statute or in relation to a pardon or commutation of sentence pursuant to article 28 of the Statute;

(iv) to adjudicate in pre-trial proceedings.

Article 14: Officers and members of the Chambers

1. The permanent judges of the International Tribunal shall elect a President from amongst their number.

2. The President of the International Tribunal shall be a member of the Appeals Chamber and shall preside over its proceedings.

3. After consultation with the permanent judges of the International Tribunal, the President shall assign four of the permanent judges elected or appointed in accordance with Article 13 bis of the Statute to the Appeals Chamber and nine to the Trial Chambers.

4. Two of the judges elected or appointed in accordance with article 12 of the Statute of the International Tribunal for Rwanda shall be assigned by the President of that Tribunal, in consultation with the President of the International Tribunal, to be members of the Appeals Chamber and permanent judges of the International Tribunal.

5. After consultation with the permanent judges of the In-

ternational Tribunal, the President shall assign such ad litem judges as may from time to time be appointed to serve in the International Tribunal to the Trial Chambers.

6. A judge shall serve only in the Chamber to which he or she was assigned.

7. The permanent judges of each Trial Chamber shall elect a Presiding Judge from amongst their number, who shall oversee the work of the Trial Chamber as a whole.

Article 15: Rules of procedure and evidence

The judges of the International Tribunal shall adopt rules of procedure and evidence for the conduct of the pre-trial phase of the proceedings, trials and appeals, the admission of evidence, the protection of victims and witnesses and other appropriate matters.

Article 16: The Prosecutor

1. The Prosecutor shall be responsible for the investigation and prosecution of persons responsible for serious violations of international humanitarian law committed in the territory of the former Yugoslavia since 1 January 1991.

2. The Prosecutor shall act independently as a separate organ of the International Tribunal. He or she shall not seek or receive instructions from any Government or from any other source.

3. The Office of the Prosecutor shall be composed of a Prosecutor and such other qualified staff as may be required.

4. The Prosecutor shall be appointed by the Security Council on nomination by the Secretary-General. He or she shall be of high moral character and possess the highest level of competence and experience in the conduct of investigations and prosecutions of criminal cases. The Prosecutor shall serve for a four-year term and be eligible for reappointment. The terms and conditions of service of the Prosecutor shall be those of an Under-Secretary-General of the United Nations.

5. The staff of the Office of the Prosecutor shall be appointed by the Secretary-General on the recommendation of the Prosecutor.

Article 17: The Registry

1. The Registry shall be responsible for the administration and servicing of the International Tribunal.

2. The Registry shall consist of a Registrar and such other staff as may be required.

3. The Registrar shall be appointed by the Secretary-General after consultation with the President of the International Tribunal. He or she shall serve for a four-year term and be eligible for reappointment. The terms and conditions of service of the Registrar shall be those of an Assistant Secretary-General of the United Nations.

4. The staff of the Registry shall be appointed by the Secretary-General on the recommendation of the Registrar.

Article 18: Investigation and preparation of indictment

1. The Prosecutor shall initiate investigations ex-officio or on the basis of information obtained from any source, particularly from Governments, United Nations organs, intergovernmental and non-governmental organisations. The Prosecutor shall assess the information received or obtained and decide whether there is sufficient basis to proceed.

2. The Prosecutor shall have the power to question suspects, victims and witnesses, to collect evidence and to conduct on-site investigations. In carrying out these tasks, the Prosecutor may, as appropriate, seek the assistance of the State authorities concerned.

3. If questioned, the suspect shall be entitled to be assisted by counsel of his own choice, including the right to have legal assistance assigned to him without payment by him in any such case if he does not have sufficient means to pay for it, as well as to necessary translation into and from a language he speaks and understands.

4. Upon a determination that a prima facie case exists, the Prosecutor shall prepare an indictment containing a concise statement of the facts and the crime or crimes with which the accused is charged under the Statute.

The indictment shall be transmitted to a judge of the Trial Chamber.

Article 19: Review of the indictment

1. The judge of the Trial Chamber to whom the indictment has been transmitted shall review it. If satisfied that a prima facie case has been established by the Prosecutor, he shall confirm the indictment. If not so satisfied, the indictment shall be dismissed.

2. Upon confirmation of an indictment, the judge may, at the request of the Prosecutor, issue such orders and warrants for the arrest, detention, surrender or transfer of persons, and any other orders as may be required for the conduct of the trial.

Article 20: Commencement and conduct of trial proceedings

1. The Trial Chambers shall ensure that a trial is fair and expeditious and that proceedings are conducted in accordance with the rules of procedure and evidence, with full respect for the rights of the accused and due regard for the protection of victims and witnesses.

2. A person against whom an indictment has been confirmed shall, pursuant to an order or an arrest warrant of the International Tribunal, be taken into custody, immediately informed of the charges against him and transferred to the International Tribunal.

3. The Trial Chamber shall read the indictment, satisfy itself that the rights of the accused are respected, confirm that the accused understands the indictment, and instruct the accused to enter a plea. The Trial Chamber shall then set the date for trial.

4. The hearings shall be public unless the Trial Chamber decides to close the proceedings in accordance with its rules of procedure and evidence.

Article 21: Rights of the accused

1. All persons shall be equal before the International Tribunal.

2. In the determination of charges against him, the accused shall be entitled to a fair and public hearing, subject to article 22 of the Statute.

3. The accused shall be presumed innocent until proved guilty according to the provisions of the present Statute.

4. In the determination of any charge against the accused pursuant to the present Statute, the accused shall be entitled to the following minimum guarantees, in full equality:

(a) to be informed promptly and in detail in a language

which he understands of the nature and cause of the charge against him;

(b) to have adequate time and facilities for the preparation of his defence and to communicate with counsel of his own choosing;

(c) to be tried without undue delay;

(d) to be tried in his presence, and to defend himself in person or through legal assistance of his own choosing; to be informed, if he does not have legal assistance, of this right; and to have legal assistance assigned to him, in any case where the interests of justice so require, and without payment by him in any such case if he does not have sufficient means to pay for it;

(e) to examine, or have examined, the witnesses against him and to obtain the attendance and examination of witnesses on his behalf under the same conditions as witnesses against him;

(f) to have the free assistance of an interpreter if he cannot understand or speak the language used in the International Tribunal;

(g) not to be compelled to testify against himself or to confess guilt.

Article 22: Protection of victims and witnesses

The International Tribunal shall provide in its rules of procedure and evidence for the protection of victims and witnesses. Such protection measures shall include, but shall not be limited to, the conduct of in camera proceedings and the protection of the victim's identity.

Article 23: Judgment

1. The Trial Chambers shall pronounce judgments and impose sentences and penalties on persons convicted of serious violations of international humanitarian law.

2. The judgment shall be rendered by a majority of the judges of the Trial Chamber, and shall be delivered by the Trial Chamber in public. It shall be accompanied by a reasoned opinion in writing, to which separate or dissenting opinions may be appended.

Article 24: Penalties

1. The penalty imposed by the Trial Chamber shall be limited to

imprisonment. In determining the terms of imprisonment, the Trial Chambers shall have recourse to the general practice regarding prison sentences in the courts of the former Yugoslavia.

2. In imposing the sentences, the Trial Chambers should take into account such factors as the gravity of the offence and the individual circumstances of the convicted person.

3. In addition to imprisonment, the Trial Chambers may order the return of any property and proceeds acquired by criminal conduct, including by means of duress, to their rightful owners.

Article 25: Appellate proceedings

1. The Appeals Chamber shall hear appeals from persons convicted by the Trial Chambers or from the Prosecutor on the following grounds:

(a) an error on a question of law invalidating the decision; or

(b) an error of fact which has occasioned a miscarriage of justice.

2. The Appeals Chamber may affirm, reverse or revise the decisions taken by the Trial Chambers.

Article 26: Review proceedings

Where a new fact has been discovered which was not known at the time of the proceedings before the Trial Chambers or the Appeals Chamber and which could have been a decisive factor in reaching the decision, the convicted person or the Prosecutor may submit to the International Tribunal an application for review of the judgement.

Article 27: Enforcement of sentences

Imprisonment shall be served in a State designated by the International Tribunal from a list of States which have indicated to the Security Council their willingness to accept convicted persons. Such imprisonment shall be in accordance with the applicable law of the State concerned, subject to the supervision of the International Tribunal.

Article 28: Pardon or commutation of sentences

If, pursuant to the applicable law of the State in which the convicted person is imprisoned, he or she is eligible for pardon or commutation of sentence, the State concerned shall notify the International Tribunal accordingly. The President of the International Tribunal, in consultation with the judges, shall decide the matter on the basis of the interests of justice and the general principles of law.

Article 29: Co-operation and judicial assistance

1. States shall co-operate with the International Tribunal in the investigation and prosecution of persons accused of committing serious violations of international humanitarian law.

2. States shall comply without undue delay with any request for assistance or an order issued by a Trial Chamber, including, but not limited to:

(a) the identification and location of persons;

(b) the taking of testimony and the production of evidence;

(c) the service of documents;

(d) the arrest or detention of persons;

(e) the surrender or the transfer of the accused to the International Tribunal.

Article 30: The status, privileges and immunities of the International Tribunal

1. The Convention on the Privileges and Immunities of the United Nations of 13 February 1946 shall apply to the International Tribunal, the judges, the Prosecutor and his staff, and the Registrar and his staff.

2. The judges, the Prosecutor and the Registrar shall enjoy the privileges and immunities, exemptions and facilities accorded to diplomatic envoys, in accordance with international law.

3. The staff of the Prosecutor and of the Registrar shall enjoy the privileges and immunities accorded to officials of the United Nations under articles V and VII of the Convention referred to in paragraph 1 of this article.

4. Other persons, including the accused, required at the seat of the International Tribunal shall be accorded such treatment as is necessary for the proper functioning of the International Tribunal.

Article 31: Seat of the International Tribunal

The International Tribunal shall have its seat at The Hague.

Article 32: Expenses of the International Tribunal

The expenses of the International Tribunal shall be borne by the regular budget of the United Nations in accordance with Article 17 of the Charter of the United Nations.

Article 33: Working languages

The working languages of the International Tribunal shall be English and French.

Article 34: Annual report

The President of the International Tribunal shall submit an annual report of the International Tribunal to the Security Council and to the General Assembly.

UN Statute of the International Criminal Tribunal for Rwanda, 1994

Between April and July 1994, almost 1 million civilians, mostly members of the Tutsi tribe, were exterminated by Hutus in Rwanda. During that period, almost 1 million persons (mostly Tutsi civilians) were massacred by Hutu paramilitaries and civilians, one of the clearest examples of genocidal actions condemned and prohibited in the 1948 Geneva Genocide Convention. The world did nothing to prevent the slaughter of the innocents, which ended after Tutsi military took decisive action and defeated their Hutu enemy. Neither Belgium, the former colonial master of Rwanda (then a part of the Belgium Congo), the European Community, the United States, nor the United Nations took any action to halt the genocide.

The tragedy was the culmination of ethnic hatred and violent clashes that surfaced while Rwanda was still a part of the Belgian Congo. The most recent civil war between the Hutu and the Tutsi began in 1990 when Hutu rebels crossed the Uganda border into Rwanda. In 1993, a peace agreement was reached in Arusha, Tanzania. The United Nations committed a small number of peacekeeping military forces—the UN Assistance Mission for

Rwanda—to help implement the movement toward a transitional government. In early April 1994, the presidents of Rwanda and Burundi were killed when the plane they were on was shot down as it was landing at the Kigali airport. Within days the 1994 machete genocide began.

In July 1994, a few days before the genocide ended, the United Nations sent the Commission of Experts to determine what happened in Rwanda. In October 1994, they gave their recommendations to the Security Council: A terrible genocide had occurred, and the principle leaders and implementers of the genocide must face justice before an international criminal tribunal modeled after the ICTY.

In November 1994, the UN Security Council created the International Criminal Tribunal for Rwanda to try to bring to justice those who ordered and who implemented the machete genocide. It was also a unique tribunal, for it was the first such entity created to deal with war crimes and genocide that occurred in a civil war.

Statute of the International Tribunal for Rwanda

The Security Council,

Reaffirming all its previous resolutions on the situation in Rwanda, . . .

Expressing once again its grave concern at the reports indicating that genocide and other systematic, widespread and flagrant violations of international humanitarian law have been committed in Rwanda,

Determining that this situation continues to constitute a threat to international peace and security,

Determined to put an end to such crimes and to take effective measures to bring to justice the persons who are responsible for them,

Convinced that in the particular circumstances of Rwanda, the prosecution of persons responsible for serious violations of international humanitarian law would enable this aim to be achieved and would contribute to the process of national reconciliation and to the restoration and maintenance of peace,

Believing that the establishment of an international tribunal for the prosecution of persons responsible for genocide and the other above-mentioned violations of international humanitarian law will contribute to ensuring that such violations are halted and effectively redressed,

Stressing also the need for international cooperation to strengthen the courts and judicial system of Rwanda, having regard in particular to the necessity for those courts to deal with large numbers of suspects,

Considering that the Commission of Experts established pursuant to resolution 935 (1994) should continue on an urgent basis the collection of information relating to evidence of grave violations of international humanitarian law committed in the territory of Rwanda and should submit its final report to the Secretary-General by 30 November 1994,

Acting under Chapter VII of the Charter of the United Nations,

1. Decides hereby, having received the request of the Government of Rwanda (S/1994/1115), to establish an international tribunal for the sole purpose of prosecuting persons responsible for genocide and other serious violations of international humanitarian law committed in the territory of Rwanda and Rwandan citizens responsible for genocide and other such violations committed in the territory of neighbouring states, between 1 January 1994 and 31 December 1994 and to this end to adopt the Statute of the International Criminal Tribunal for Rwanda annexed hereto;

2. Decides that all States shall cooperate fully with the International Tribunal and its organs in accordance with the present resolution and the Statute of the International Tribunal and that consequently all States shall take any measures necessary under their domestic law to implement the provisions of the present resolution and the Statute, including the obligation of States to comply with requests for assistance or orders issued by a Trial Chamber under Article 28 of the Statute, and requests States to keep the Secretary-General informed of such measures;

3. Considers that the Government of Rwanda should be notified prior to the taking of decisions under articles 26 and 27 of the Statute;

4. Urges States and intergovernmental and non-governmental organisations to contribute funds, equipment and services to the International Tribunal, including the offer of expert personnel;

5. Requests the Secretary-General to implement this resolution urgently and in particular to make practical arrangements for the effective functioning of the International Tribunal, in-

cluding recommendations to the Council as to possible locations for the seat of the International Tribunal at the earliest time to report periodically to the Council;

6. Decides that the seat of the International Tribunal shall be determined by the Council having regard to considerations of justice and fairness as well as administrative efficiency, including access to witnesses, and economy, and subject to the conclusion of appropriate arrangements between the United Nations and the State of the seat, acceptable to the Council, having regard to the fact that the International Tribunal may meet away from its seat when it considers necessary for the efficient exercise of its functions; and decides that an office will be established and proceedings will be conducted in Rwanda, where feasible and appropriate, subject to the conclusion of similar appropriate arrangements;

7. Decides to consider increasing the number of judges and Trial Chambers of the International Tribunal if it becomes necessary;

8. Decides to remain actively seized of the matter.

Annex: Statute of the International Tribunal for Rwanda

Having been established by the Security Council acting under Chapter VII of the Charter of the United Nations, the International Criminal Tribunal for the Prosecution of Persons Responsible for Genocide and Other Serious Violations of International Humanitarian Law Committed in the Territory of Rwanda and Rwandan Citizens responsible for genocide and other such violations committed in the territory of neighbouring States, between 1 January 1994 and 31 December 1994 (hereinafter referred to as "The International Tribunal for Rwanda") shall function in accordance with the provisions of the present Statute.

Article 1: Competence of the International Tribunal for Rwanda

The International Tribunal for Rwanda shall have the power to prosecute persons responsible for serious violations of international humanitarian law committed in the territory of Rwanda and Rwandan citizens responsible for such violations committed in the territory of neighbouring States between 1 January 1994 and 31 December 1994, in accordance with the provisions of the present Statute.

. . .

Article 7: Territorial and temporal jurisdiction

The territorial jurisdiction of the International Tribunal for Rwanda shall extend to the territory of Rwanda including its land surface and airspace as well as to the territory of neighbouring States in respect of serious violations of international humanitarian law committed by Rwandan citizens. The temporal jurisdiction of the International Tribunal for Rwanda shall extend to a period beginning on 1 January 1994 and ending on 31 December 1994. . . .

Dayton Peace Accord, 1995

In November 1995, after more than three years of war in Bosnia and the death of more than 400,000 persons, mostly civilians, the leaders of Bosnia, Croatia, and Serbia signed a peace accord ending the armed conflict. It was negotiated at a former Air Force base in Dayton, Ohio, and signed under intense pressure from the U.S. President, Bill Clinton. Six days later, in OPERATION JOINT ENDEAVOR, more than 60,000 North Atlantic Treaty Organization (NATO) and U.S. forces arrived in Bosnia to implement the accord. This force was replaced one year later, in December 1996, by a stabilization force (SFOR) of 30,000 armed troops from 16 NATO nations and 13 other partner nations, including 1,200 troops from Russia. SFOR troops still remain in Bosnia, albeit in smaller numbers.

The Dayton Peace Accord divided Bosnia into two separate republics: the federation of Bosnia-Herzegovina, and the Republika Srpska. They were to be joined under a central Bosnian government in Sarajevo, where political power was to be shared in a Parliament.

General Framework Agreement for Peace in Bosnia and Herzegovina (Dayton Peace Accord, November 21, 1995)

The Republic of Bosnia and Herzegovina, the Republic of Croatia and the Federal Republic of Yugoslavia (the "Parties"),

Recognizing the need for a comprehensive settlement to bring an end to the tragic conflict in the region,

Desiring to contribute toward that end and to promote an enduring peace and stability,

Affirming their commitment to the Agreed Basic Principles issued on September 8, 1995, the Further Agreed Basic Principles issued on September 26, 1995, and the cease-fire agreements of September 14 and October 5, 1995,

Noting the agreement of August 29, 1995, which authorized the delegation of the Federal Republic of Yugoslavia to sign, on behalf of the Republika Srpska, the parts of the peace plan concerning it, with the obligation to implement the agreement that is reached strictly and consequently,

Have agreed as follows:

Article I

The Parties shall conduct their relations in accordance with the principles set forth in the United Nations Charter, as well as the Helsinki Final Act and other documents of the Organization for Security and Cooperation in Europe. In particular, the Parties shall fully respect the sovereign equality of one another, shall settle disputes by peaceful means, and shall refrain from any action, by threat or use of force or otherwise, against the territorial integrity or political independence of Bosnia and Herzegovina or any other State.

Article II

The Parties welcome and endorse the arrangements that have been made concerning the military aspects of the peace settlement and aspects of regional stabilization, as set forth in the Agreements at Annex 1-A and Annex 1-B. The Parties shall fully respect and promote fulfillment of the commitments made in Annex 1-A, and shall comply fully with their commitments as set forth in Annex 1-B.

Article III

The Parties welcome and endorse the arrangements that have been made concerning the boundary demarcation between the two Entities, the Federation of Bosnia and Herzegovina and Republika Srpska, as set forth in the Agreement at Annex 2. The Parties shall fully respect and promote fulfillment of the commitments made therein.

Article IV

The Parties welcome and endorse the elections program for Bosnia and Herzegovina as set forth in Annex 3. The Parties shall fully respect and promote fulfillment of that program.

Article V

The Parties welcome and endorse the arrangements that have been made concerning the Constitution of Bosnia and Herzegovina, as set forth in Annex 4. The Parties shall fully respect and promote fulfillment of the commitments made therein.

Article VI

The Parties welcome and endorse the arrangements that have been made concerning the establishment of an arbitration tribunal, a Commission on Human Rights, a Commission on Refugees and Displaced Persons, a Commission to Preserve National Monuments, and Bosnia and Herzegovina Public Corporations, as set forth in the Agreements at Annexes 5–9. The Parties shall fully respect and promote fulfillment of the commitments made therein.

Article VII

Recognizing that the observance of human rights and the protection of refugees and displaced persons are of vital importance in achieving a lasting peace, the Parties agree to and shall comply fully with the provisions concerning human rights set forth in Chapter One of the Agreement at Annex 6, as well as the provisions concerning refugees and displaced persons set forth in Chapter One of the Agreement at Annex 7.

Article VIII

The Parties welcome and endorse the arrangements that have been made concerning the implementation of this peace settlement, including in particular those pertaining to the civilian (non-military) implementation, as set forth in the Agreement at Annex 10, and the international police task force, as set forth in the Agreement at Annex 11. The Parties shall fully respect and promote fulfillment of the commitments made therein.

Article IX

The Parties shall cooperate fully with all entities involved in implementation of this peace settlement, as described in the Annexes to this Agreement, or which are otherwise authorized by the United Nations Security Council, pursuant to the obligation of all Parties to cooperate in the investigation and prosecution of war crimes and other violations of international humanitarian law.

Article X

The Federal Republic of Yugoslavia and the Republic of Bosnia and Herzegovina recognize each other as sovereign independent States within their international borders. Further aspects of their mutual recognition will be subject to subsequent discussions.

Article XI

This Agreement shall enter into force upon signature.

DONE at Paris, this [21st] day of [November], 1995, in the Bosnian, Croatian, English and Serbian languages, each text being equally authentic.

For the Republic of Bosnia and Herzegovina

For the Republic of Croatia

For the Federal Republic of Yugoslavia

Witnessed by:

European Union Special Negotiator

For the French Republic

For the Federal Republic of Germany

For the Russian Federation

For the United Kingdom of Great Britain and Northern Ireland

For the United States of America

Rome Statute of the International Criminal Court (ICC; 1998)

More than fifty years after it was proposed after World War II, and after a decade of intense work by NGOs such as Human Rights Watch, the Lawyers Committee for Human Rights, and the International Committee of the Red Cross, nation-states, and the United Nations, the 1998 Rome Statute of the International Criminal Court was signed in August 1998 by 139 nations. In mid-April 2002, the requisite number of nation-states, sixty, ratified the ICC, and it was in force in July 2002.

The ICC is a major milestone. For the first time in history, a permanent international criminal court came into being—despite the fierce opposition of the United States. The ICC, as seen below, is dedicated to trying individuals responsible for war crimes, including crimes against humanity, genocide, and torture. UN Secretary-General Kofi Annan said after the sixtieth nation (actually, ten nations became the "sixtieth" to ratify on April 11, 2002) ratified the treaty: "The long-held dream of a permanent international criminal court will now be realized. Impunity has been dealt a decisive blow."

Located in The Hague, Netherlands, it will begin to function after the United Nations selects the independent prosecutor and the judges who will sit in judgment of alleged war criminals. Richard Dicker, an official with Human Rights Watch, stated, "It will be the court where Saddam Husseins, Pol Pots, and Augusto

Pinochets of the future are held to account." Two major international actors, the United States and Russia, signed the ICC treaty. However, neither one has ratified it. Another major power, China, neither signed the treaty nor ratified it.

Rome Statute of the International Criminal Court; July 12, 1999

PREAMBLE

The States Parties to this Statute,

Conscious that all peoples are united by common bonds, their cultures pieced together in a shared heritage, and concerned that this delicate mosaic may be shattered at any time,

Mindful that during this century millions of children, women and men have been victims of unimaginable atrocities that deeply shock the conscience of humanity,

Recognizing that such grave crimes threaten the peace, security and well-being of the world,

Affirming that the most serious crimes of concern to the international community as a whole must not go unpunished and that their effective prosecution must be ensured by taking measures at the national level and by enhancing international cooperation,

Determined to put an end to impunity for the perpetrators of these crimes and thus to contribute to the prevention of such crimes,

Recalling that it is the duty of every State to exercise its criminal jurisdiction over those responsible for international crimes,

Reaffirming the Purposes and Principles of the Charter of the United Nations, and in particular that all States shall refrain from the threat or use of force against the territorial integrity or political independence of any State, or in any other manner inconsistent with the Purposes of the United Nations,

Emphasizing in this connection that nothing in this Statute shall be taken as authorizing any State Party to intervene in an armed conflict or in the internal affairs of any State,

Determined to these ends and for the sake of present and future generations, to establish an independent permanent International Criminal Court in relationship with the United Nations system, with jurisdiction over the most serious crimes of concern to the international community as a whole,

Emphasizing that the International Criminal Court established under this Statute shall be complementary to national criminal jurisdictions,

Resolved to guarantee lasting respect for and the enforcement of international justice,

Have agreed as follows . . .

PART 2. JURISDICTION, ADMISSIBILITY AND APPLICABLE LAW

Article 5: Crimes within the jurisdiction of the Court

1. The jurisdiction of the Court shall be limited to the most serious crimes of concern to the international community as a whole. The Court has jurisdiction in accordance with this Statute with respect to the following crimes:

(a) The crime of genocide;

(b) Crimes against humanity;

(c) War crimes;

(d) The crime of aggression.

2. The Court shall exercise jurisdiction over the crime of aggression once a provision is adopted in accordance with articles 121 and 123 defining the crime and setting out the conditions under which the Court shall exercise jurisdiction with respect to this crime. Such a provision shall be consistent with the relevant provisions of the Charter of the United Nations.

Article 6: Genocide

For the purpose of this Statute, "genocide" means any of the following acts committed with intent to destroy, in whole or in part, a national, ethnical, racial or religious group, as such:

(a) Killing members of the group;

(b) Causing serious bodily or mental harm to members of the group;

(c) Deliberately inflicting on the group conditions of life calculated to bring about its physical destruction in whole or in part;

(d) Imposing measures intended to prevent births within the group;

(e) Forcibly transferring children of the group to another group.

Article 7: Crimes against humanity

1. For the purpose of this Statute, "crime against humanity" means any of the following acts when committed as part of a

widespread or systematic attack directed against any civilian population, with knowledge of the attack:

(a) Murder;

(b) Extermination;

(c) Enslavement;

(d) Deportation or forcible transfer of population;

(e) Imprisonment or other severe deprivation of physical liberty in violation of fundamental rules of international law;

(f) Torture;

(g) Rape, sexual slavery, enforced prostitution, forced pregnancy, enforced sterilization, or any other form of sexual violence of comparable gravity;

(h) Persecution against any identifiable group or collectivity on political, racial, national, ethnic, cultural, religious, gender as defined in paragraph 3, or other grounds that are universally recognized as impermissible under international law, in connection with any act referred to in this paragraph or any crime within the jurisdiction of the Court;

(i) Enforced disappearance of persons;

(j) The crime of apartheid;

(k) Other inhumane acts of a similar character intentionally causing great suffering, or serious injury to body or to mental or physical health.

2. For the purpose of paragraph 1:

(a) "Attack directed against any civilian population" means a course of conduct involving the multiple commission of acts referred to in paragraph 1 against any civilian population, pursuant to or in furtherance of a State or organizational policy to commit such attack;

(b) "Extermination" includes the intentional infliction of conditions of life, inter alia the deprivation of access to food and medicine, calculated to bring about the destruction of part of a population;

(c) "Enslavement" means the exercise of any or all of the powers attaching to the right of ownership over a person and includes the exercise of such power in the course of trafficking in persons, in particular women and children;

(d) "Deportation or forcible transfer of population" means forced displacement of the persons concerned by expulsion or other coercive acts from the area in which they are lawfully present, without grounds permitted under international law;

(e) "Torture" means the intentional infliction of severe pain or suffering, whether physical or mental, upon a person in the custody or under the control of the accused; except that torture shall not include pain or suffering arising only from, inherent in or incidental to, lawful sanctions;

(f) "Forced pregnancy" means the unlawful confinement of a woman forcibly made pregnant, with the intent of affecting the ethnic composition of any population or carrying out other grave violations of international law. This definition shall not in any way be interpreted as affecting national laws relating to pregnancy;

(g) "Persecution" means the intentional and severe deprivation of fundamental rights contrary to international law by reason of the identity of the group or collectivity;

(h) "The crime of apartheid" means inhumane acts of a character similar to those referred to in paragraph 1, committed in the context of an institutionalized regime of systematic oppression and domination by one racial group over any other racial group or groups and committed with the intention of maintaining that regime;

(i) "Enforced disappearance of persons" means the arrest, detention or abduction of persons by, or with the authorization, support or acquiescence of, a State or a political organization, followed by a refusal to acknowledge that deprivation of freedom or to give information on the fate or whereabouts of those persons, with the intention of removing them from the protection of the law for a prolonged period of time.

3. For the purpose of this Statute, it is understood that the term "gender" refers to the two sexes, male and female, within the context of society. The term "gender" does not indicate any meaning different from the above.

Article 13: Exercise of jurisdiction

The Court may exercise its jurisdiction with respect to a crime referred to in article 5 in accordance with the provisions of this Statute if:

(a) A situation in which one or more of such crimes appears to have been committed is referred to the Prosecutor by a State Party in accordance with article 14;

(viii) A situation in which one or more of such crimes appears to have been committed is referred to the Prosecutor by the Security Council acting under Chapter VII of the Charter of the United Nations; or

(c) The Prosecutor has initiated an investigation in respect of such a crime in accordance with article 15.

Major Reports/Rules/Speeches

Justice Robert H. Jackson, Allied Chief Prosecutor for the International Military Tribunal in Nuremberg, Opening Remarks, 1945

For almost one year, prosecutors from the four victorious Allied powers—the United States, Great Britain, France, and Russia—presented their case against twenty-two Nazi leaders. In trying to fix German guilt, the prosecutors had charged the defendants with conspiring and launching aggressive war and committing war crimes and crimes against humanity. In the end, three of the defendants were acquitted. Eight received long prison sentences, and the rest were sentenced to death. At 10:45 P.M. on October 15, 1946, Hermann Goering cheated the hangman with a cyanide capsule. Two hours later, the executions began.

The trial of Goering, Rudolf Hess, Albert Speer, and the others was part show-trial and part noble effort to create new international law in the face of crimes that negated civilization's progress. To some extent, it reflected the optimistic sentiments for world cooperation (which were rapidly eclipsed by the Cold War) that led to the creation of the United Nations. It was a political effort to find human-sized justice for crimes that were so hideous. U.S. Supreme Court Associate Justice Robert H. Jackson, on leave to serve as the Allies' chief prosecutor, opened up the proceedings with the following remarks.

Prosecutor's Opening Statement, November 21, 1945 (part 4, pp. 98–102)

The privilege of opening the first trial in history for crimes against the peace of the world imposes a grave responsibility. The wrongs which we seek to condemn and punish have been so calculated, so malignant, and so devastating, that civilization cannot tolerate their being ignored, because it cannot survive their being repeated. That four great nations, flushed with victory and stung with injury stay the hand of vengeance and voluntarily submit their captive enemies to the judgment of the law is one of the most significant tributes that Power has ever paid to Reason.

. . .

Unfortunately the nature of these crimes is such that both prosecution and judgment must be by victor nations over vanquished foes. The worldwide scope of the aggressions carried out by these men has left but few real neutrals. Either the victors must judge the vanquished or we must leave the defeated to judge themselves. After World War I, we learned the futility of the latter course. The former high station of these defendants, the notoriety of their acts, and the adaptability of their conduct to provoke retaliation make it hard to distinguish between the demand for a just and measured retribution, and the unthinking cry for vengeance which arises from the anguish of war. It is our task, so far as humanly possible, to draw the line between the two. We must never forget that the record on which we judge these defendants today is the record on which history will judge us tomorrow. To pass these defendants a poisoned chalice is to put it to our own lips as well. We must summon such detachment and intellectual integrity to our task that this Trial will commend itself to posterity as fulfilling humanity's aspirations to do justice. . . .

Red Cross Fundamental Rules of International Humanitarian Law Applicable in Armed Conflicts, 1983

In 1975, the ICRC called for the creation of a document that concisely summarized the essential principles of the laws of war codified in the major treaties applicable to armed conflicts ratified since 1945. The texts of these treaties are complex and not always easily grasped by readers. The four 1949 Geneva Conventions and the two 1977 Additional Protocols, for example, contain almost 600 articles, many very complex and difficult to understand.

In 1979, the task was completed, and the 63-page book (*Basic Rules of the Geneva Conventions and Their Additional Protocols*) was published by the ICRC in 1983. The summary, reprinted below, is entitled "Basic Rules of International Humanitarian Law in Armed Conflicts." It succeeded in summarizing the essence of these hundreds of articles in the laws of war relating to protecting the victims of war in less than two pages. Neither the book nor the summary is an international legal treaty; rather, they offer the reader the core themes contained in post-1945 treaties and conventions.

Basic Rules of the Geneva Conventions and Their Additional Protocols, September 1, 1983

. . .

Foreword

The aim of this document, "The Geneva Conventions and the Additional Protocols-Basic Rules," is to provide a condensed synthesis of the rules of international humanitarian law in armed conflicts as contained in these legal instruments. This presentation itself is preceded by a summary which sets out, as simply and briefly as possible, the fundamental rules which are the basis of these treaties and the law of armed conflicts as a whole. Prepared for dissemination purposes, this work cannot in any circumstances serve as a substitute for the complete provisions of the international agreements to which the marginal notes refer.

Summary: Basic rules of international humanitarian law in Armed Conflicts

1. Persons hors de combat and those who do not take a direct part in hostilities are entitled to respect for their lives and their moral and physical integrity. They shall in all circumstances be protected and treated humanely without any adverse distinction.

2. It is forbidden to kill or injure an enemy who surrenders or who is hors de combat.

3. The wounded and sick shall be collected and cared for by the party to the conflict which has them in its power. Protection also covers medical personnel, establishments, transports and equipment. The emblem of the red cross or the red crescent is the sign of such protection and must be respected.

4. Captured combatants and civilians under the authority of an adverse party are entitled to respect for their lives, dignity, personal rights and convictions. They shall be protected against all acts of violence and reprisals. They shall have the right to correspond with their families and to receive relief.

5. Everyone shall be entitled to benefit from fundamental judicial guarantees. No one shall be held responsible for an act he has not committed. No one shall be subjected to physical or

mental torture, corporal punishment or cruel or degrading treatment.

6. Parties to a conflict and members of their armed forces do not have an unlimited choice of methods and means of warfare. It is prohibited to employ weapons or methods of warfare of a nature to cause unnecessary losses or excessive suffering.

7. Parties to a conflict shall at all times distinguish between the civilian population and combatants in order to spare civilian population and property. Neither the civilian population as such nor civilian persons shall be the object of attack. Attacks shall be directed solely against military objectives.

Note

This text constitutes the quintessence of the provisions of international humanitarian law summarized in the following pages. It does not have the force of an international legal instrument and is in no way intended to replace the treaties in force. It is designed, as is this whole work, to facilitate dissemination of international humanitarian law.

"One Sad Night" (a poem by Hajrie Lajqi, Kosovo, May 1999)

In a small village a short distance from Pec, in western Kosovo, the town's population of about 200 villagers came out to mourn the deaths of a dozen of their own, Albanian Muslims slaughtered by Serb paramilitary forces. Hajrie Lajqi, a 23-year-old woman, was there to mourn the deaths of her grandfather, her father, and his two brothers. They had been killed and then decapitated by the Serbs in part because they were wearing their chalms, a fezlike white hat worn by Kosovar Albanian Muslim men. She read a poem she had written.

"One Sad Night"

Tragedy struck on May 2nd
Four people were taken away from our homes
It happened at midnight to all of us,
Soldiers filling our gardens with fear.
They took all our men,

Divided young from old.
They took all our money,
And promised us death.
They robbed our last penny
Still it wasn't enough.
They beat us at home
And promised us death.
They took my grandfather in his 103rd year,
Simply because he wore a white chalm.
That showed he was proud to be Albanian,
Who would never betray his fair land.
And then they came for his three sons, too.
Took them from their families and homes,
And in front of their children,
They promised to cut off their heads.
Like grandpa they wore white chalms
On their heads,
Like many Albanians do.
And the last word they told us as they
Left us that night,
Was 'Keep these white chalms safe for us.' . . .

Text of Kosovo Peace Plan, June 1999

In the winter of 1999, Yugoslav President Slobodan Milosevic sent Yugoslav armed forces and Serbian paramilitary groups into Kosovo, a once semiautonomous province of Serbia. (In 1989, it lost its autonomy when threatened with force by then Serbian President Milosevic, who began his effort to create an ethnically pure Greater Serbia.) The task of the military and paramilitary forces was to protect the Serbian minority residing in Kosovo from attacks by the Kosovar Muslim majority. The intervention led to war crimes, crimes against humanity, and genocide in Kosovo.

However, this time NATO and the United States acted decisively to force Milosevic to withdraw his military from Kosovo. After more than three months of NATO bombing of military sites in both Kosovo and Serbia, including targets in the Serb capital city, Belgrade, an international peace plan, crafted jointly by Russia and the European Union, won the backing of the Serbian parliament and then, very reluctantly, President Milosevic. The plan (reproduced below) called for the cessation of hostilities in Kosovo and the complete withdrawal of all Serb and Yugoslavian military forces within seven days. The NATO bombing stopped after Milosevic ordered and the military and paramilitary leaders implemented a total troop withdrawal. As was the case in Bosnia after the Dayton Peace Accord, an international military force, including Russian troops and with a "substantial" NATO component, entered Kosovo—under a unified military command. In addition, the Kosovo Liberation Army (a paramilitary organization made up of Kosovar Albanian Muslims) was required to disarm.

On June 10, 1999, the UN Security Council authorized the Secretary-General to establish in Kosovo an interim international civilian administration under which the people of the war-ravaged province could enjoy substantial autonomy. The Security Council has vested in the UN mission authority over the territory and people of Kosovo, including all legislative and executive powers, as well as the administration of the judiciary. Never before has the United Nations assumed such broad, far-reaching, and important executive tasks. Among its key tasks, the mission will: promote the establishment of substantial autonomy and self-government in Kosovo; perform basic civilian administrative functions; facilitate a political process to determine Kosovo's future status; support the reconstruction of key infrastructure and humanitarian and disaster relief; maintain civil law and order; promote human rights; and assure the safe and unimpeded return of all refugees and displaced persons to their homes in Kosovo.

Kosovo Peace Accord (presented April 2, 1999; accepted June 3, 1999)

In order to move forward toward solving the Kosovo crisis, an agreement should be reached on the following principles.

1. Imminent and verifiable end to violence and repression of Kosovo.

2. Verifiable withdrawal from Kosovo of military, police and paramilitary forces according to a quick timetable.

3. Deployment in Kosovo, under UN auspices, of efficient international civilian and security presences which would act as can be decided according to Chapter 7 of the UN Charter and be capable of guaranteeing fulfillment of joint goals.

4. International security presence, with an essential NATO

participation, must be deployed under a unified control and command and authorized to secure safe environment for all the residents in Kosovo and enable the safe return of the displaced persons and refugees to their homes.

5. Establishment of an interim administration for Kosovo . . . which the UN Security Council will decide and under which the people of Kosovo will enjoy substantial autonomy within the Federal Republic of Yugoslavia. The interim administration [will] secure transitional authority during the time [for the] interim democratic and self-governing institutions, [establish] conditions for peaceful and normal life of all citizens of Kosovo.

6. After the withdrawal, an agreed number of Serb personnel will be allowed to return to perform the following duties: liaison with the international civilian mission and international security presence, marking mine fields, maintaining a presence at places of Serb heritage, maintaining a presence at key border crossings,

7. Safe and free return of all refugees and the displaced under the supervision of [UN High Commissioner for Refugees] and undisturbed access for humanitarian organizations to Kosovo.

8. Political process directed at reaching interim political agreement which would secure essential autonomy for Kosovo, with full taking into consideration of the Rambouillet agreement, the principles of sovereignty and territorial integrity of the Federal Republic of Yugoslavia and other states in the region as well as demilitarization of the Kosovo Liberation Army. The talks between the sides about the solution should not delay or disrupt establishment of the democratic self-governing institutions.

9. General approach to the economic development of the crisis region. That would include carrying out a pact of stability for southeastern Europe, wide international participation in order to advance democracy and economic prosperity, and stability and regional cooperation.

10. The end of military activities will depend on acceptance of the listed principles and simultaneous agreement with other previously identified elements which are identified in the footnote below. Then a military-technical agreement will be agreed which will among other things specify additional modalities, including the role and function of the Yugoslav, i.e., Serb, personnel in Kosovo.

11. The process of withdrawal includes a phased, detailed timetable and the marking of a buffer zone in Serbia behind which the troops will withdraw.

12. The returning personnel: The equipment of the returning personnel, the range of their functional responsibilities, the timetable for their return, determination of the geographic zones of their activity, the rules guiding their relations with the international security presence and the international civilian mission.

Newsweek Article, 2000

One problem facing an international criminal tribunal, as seen so clearly in recent armed conflicts involving genocidal actions in Bosnia, Rwanda, and Kosovo, is the task of finding the victims of war crimes and genocide, determining who they were and how they died, and then trying to find the perpetrators of the crime. Building the case against the perpetrators in these kinds of war zones, where there is no documentation (as was the case with Nazi German executioners), is a grisly process. As seen in the activities of the ICTY forensic experts depicted in the *Newsweek* story, there are seven steps in the process. The forensic team must:

1. Exhume human remains from marked and unmarked gravesites;

2. collect evidence at the crime scene;

3. bag the body and transport it to a mortuary, where it is refrigerated awaiting the autopsy by ICTY forensic experts;

4. bring body bag to radiology lab, where it is x-rayed for bullet or shrapnel fragments and identifying objects such as keys, rings, etc.;

5. remove the body from the bag, take off clothing, which is hosed down and available for family members to possibly identify;

6. place stripped body on a "wet" table for autopsy, including taking of DNA samples; and then

7. turn over identification findings to Victim Recovery and Identification Commission at The Hague. The Commission assists relatives in identifying victims and helps arrange proper burial of the body.

"On the Trail of the Hard Truth" (an article by Joshua Hammer, *Newsweek,* July 17, 2000)

The four skulls lie in a clearing in the forest, just off the main road through the village of Meja. A Kosovar shepherd spotted them three months ago, and they have remained there, untouched, until the arrival of the United Nations homicide squad on this steamy July afternoon. Italian troops from NATO's explosives unit move in first, sweeping the earth for mines and cluster bombs. Then the forensics experts creep down a cleared path through bramble and scrub oak and kneel beside the remains, carefully recording the evidence: the small round hole in the back of each skull, the used 9mm cartridges with Cyrillic markings, the grooves in the bullets probably made by a Skorpio automatic pistol, a favorite of Serb paramilitary and police units. "They caught them here, made them kneel, then shot each in the back of the head," says Paolo Pastore Stocchi, the lead investigator, as he drops two bullet fragments into a plastic container. Stocchi gestures to a pile of charred clothing and touches a woman's blackened shoe, with the bones of a foot still inside. "See this?" he says, chomping on an Antico Toscano cigar. "The Serbs burned the bodies after executing them."

Stocchi has witnessed plenty of similar scenes during his nine months in Kosovo. The 40-year-old Italian detective belongs to an international team of policemen and forensic scientists engaged in one of the world's most ambitious murder investigations, attempting to identify both the victims and the perpetrators of last year's slaughter in Kosovo. Investigators estimate that Serb forces murdered between 5,000 and 10,000 Albanian civilians during the three months of NATO bombing, including 500 massacred around Meja in April 1999, the worst atrocity of the conflict. But while the slaughter was relentlessly documented by the media, the investigators' work has been carried out far from the spotlight of publicity. Last week NEWSWEEK was permitted to spend four days in the field with Stocchi's team as it scoured the countryside for bodies and evidence—a search through the past that shed new light on the horrors of the war and on the difficulty of bringing the murderers to justice.

Prosecutors at the International Criminal Tribunal for the Former Yugoslavia (ICTY) in The Hague hope that nailing down the details of the crimes and interviewing eyewitnesses will help build cases against Serb officers and ordinary triggermen involved in the killing campaign. They also expect it to bolster last year's murder indictment of Yugoslav President Slobodan Milosevic and four other high-ranking Serb officials. So far, Milosevic and most of his top henchmen are beyond the tribunal's reach. Last week the Yugoslav Parliament even amended the country's Constitution so that Milosevic can seek reelection when his term expires next year.

Stocchi, the tribunal's man in the town of Gjakova, ignores politics and keeps digging for evidence. The boyishly handsome plainclothesman spent years chasing drug traffickers and international car thieves across Europe from his base in Rome. But by 1997, newly divorced and restless, he accepted an offer to work on loan for the tribunal. He documented ethnic killings in Bosnia for two years, then was asked by The Hague prosecutors to become one of five field investigators in Kosovo. "Even Bosnia didn't prepare me for this," he says.

Much of Gjakova, a former Kosovo Liberation Army stronghold of 60,000 near the Albanian border, had been burned down during a rampage by Serb troops the first night of the NATO bombing. Hundreds of people had been killed by Serb police and paramilitary units. Because of all the destruction, the investigators had no electricity or heat last winter. Stocchi set up shop in the back office of an abandoned bank building and spent the frigid Balkan nights "shivering in my sleeping bag, wearing every piece of clothing that I had." The work helped keep his mind off the hardships. Stocchi's goal was to document exactly what had happened in Gjakova between March and June 1999.

Cruising the icy streets with his Albanian interpreter in his United Nations-issue Toyota Land Cruiser, he visited 400 separate murder scenes, including two homes in which a total of 28 people had been massacred, and tracked down hundreds of eyewitnesses. During the war, he learned, Serb police had dispatched Gypsies in trucks to collect bodies each morning. The body collectors then buried the victims without identification in the town's graveyard.

When the ground began to thaw in April, Stocchi and his teams exhumed the corpses from the Gjakova cemetery, and tried to identify them and determine how they'd died. The forensics work could be hazardous: one exhumation team pried opened a coffin and noticed three packages lying beside the corpse.

The team called in the bomb squad, which detonated a

booby trap planted there by Serbs. The exhumations of more than 200 bodies ended earlier this summer. Stocchi then set out to solve what remains one of the deepest mysteries of the war: the fate of the missing. The International Committee of the Red Cross has estimated that 3,300 people disappeared in Kosovo last year, more than half of them in and around Gjakova. Serb killers almost certainly burned or otherwise disposed of many victims—including 90 bodies removed one May night from Gjakova's cemetery. But the Kosovo countryside, Stocchi soon learned, was littered with remains. Acting on tips from local human-rights workers and Albanian informants who served with the Serb police, Stocchi has spent weeks driving down Kosovo's back roads looking for corpses. The hunt has often been frustrating. Suspected graves routinely turn out to contain nothing but cattle bones.

False leads are abundant. "Everybody in Kosovo," Stocchi says, "thinks he has a body buried in his backyard."

Sometimes they do. With the temperature soaring on a July morning, Stocchi and his team of forensic scientists—a Peruvian, an Argentine, an Irish woman, two Americans and a Canadian—receive a tip from the U.N. police.

The owner of a farmhouse in Zhabeli, deep in rural Kosovo, recently returned home from a year abroad to find a decomposed corpse dumped in the mechanics' pit in his garage.

After a quick cup of coffee at the Italian soldiers' PX in Gjakova, they're off. The two white U.N. Land Cruisers and a pickup truck kick up clouds of dust as they bounce over unpaved roads past cornfields and ruined farmhouses. Two armored personnel carriers filled with Italian NATO troops follow them for protection. Investigators have begun to feel more vulnerable in Kosovo since ICTY chief prosecutor Carla del Ponte announced last spring that she would consider indicting Albanian Kosovars for crimes against Serbs. A couple of weeks ago a three-car U.N. convoy was attacked and burned by ethnic Albanians in Mitrovica. "It's tense," says Stocchi. "These people are not so tolerant."

The body lies in a pool of black oil and sludge, four feet down in the concrete pit. A blanket has entwined itself about the corpse, but the skull and left leg are clearly visible. Three members of the team don white plastic suits and green rubber boots. Aldo Bolanos, a Peruvian forensic anthropologist who spent years identifying Shining Path victims in his own country, climbs in wearing only shorts and sandals. Stocchi watches, swigging mineral water in the 100-degree heat. "It's been lying in liquid so long, it's going to be heavy," he says. "The body is well kept because of the oil, but it's filthy work." Cautiously, the team members lift the disintegrating blanket and heave the rotting corpse into a body bag. The stench is terrible. The soldiers grimace; Stocchi wraps a bandanna around his face as his workers carry the body to the truck and its next stop on the road to justice: the ICTY mortuary, where it will lie with 200 other sets of human remains awaiting autopsies.

Stocchi is under no illusions that he can provide a complete accounting of Kosovo's dead. So far his team has recovered the remains of just a handful of the 500 men and boys pulled out of a convoy and massacred on April 27, 1999, by Serb police and paramilitaries near Meja. Identifying the decomposed bodies is often next to impossible in a country without decent dental records. He has tried to be frank with local Albanians who are impatient with the investigation.

"It might be possible that you will never get an answer about the people you've lost, but I hope that doesn't happen," he tells a group of Albanian men in Meja. Justice, too, may be hard to come by. Using Serb informants and police contacts, Stocchi has made some progress identifying triggermen in Kosovo, but he admits that "until there's a change of leadership in Serbia, we won't be able to touch them." Stocchi refuses to be discouraged, and he plans to stay in Kosovo for at least another year. "We've got to be thorough," he says. "If we don't try to bring them justice, who will?" And so the hunt goes on.

U.S. President Bill Clinton's Speech Ratifying the ICC, December 31, 2000

President Clinton announced on December 31, 2000, that the United States was going to sign the 1998 Rome Treaty on the International Criminal Court but said he would recommend that President-elect George W. Bush not submit the treaty to the Senate until "fundamental concerns are satisfied."

Statement by the President: Signature of the International Criminal Court Treaty

THE WHITE HOUSE Office of the Press Secretary (Camp David, Maryland)

December 31, 2000

The United States is today signing the 1998 Rome Treaty on the International Criminal Court. In taking this action, we join more than 130 other countries that have signed by the December 31, 2000 deadline established in the Treaty. We do so to reaffirm our strong support for international accountability and for bringing to justice perpetrators of genocide, war crimes, and crimes against humanity. We do so as well because we wish to remain engaged in making the ICC an instrument of impartial and effective justice in the years to come.

The United States has a long history of commitment to the principle of accountability, from our involvement in the Nuremberg tribunals that brought Nazi war criminals to justice, to our leadership in the effort to establish the International Criminal Tribunals for the Former Yugoslavia and Rwanda. Our action today sustains that tradition of moral leadership.

Under the Rome Treaty, the International Criminal Court (ICC) will come into being with the ratification of 60 governments, and will have jurisdiction over the most heinous abuses that result from international conflict, such as war crimes, crimes against humanity, and genocide. The Treaty requires that the ICC not supercede or interfere with functioning national judicial systems; that is, the ICC Prosecutor is authorized to take action against a suspect only if the country of nationality is unwilling or unable to investigate allegations of egregious crimes by their national. The U.S. delegation to the Rome Conference worked hard to achieve these limitations, which we believe are essential to the international credibility and success of the ICC.

In signing, however, we are not abandoning our concerns about significant flaws in the Treaty. In particular, we are concerned that when the Court comes into existence, it will not only exercise authority over personnel of states that have ratified the Treaty, but also claim jurisdiction over personnel of states that have not. With signature, however, we will be in a position to influence the evolution of the Court. Without signature, we will not. Signature will enhance our ability to further protect U.S. officials from unfounded charges and to achieve the human rights and accountability objectives of the ICC.

In fact, in negotiations following the Rome Conference, we have worked effectively to develop procedures that limit the likelihood of politicized prosecutions. For example, U.S. civilian and military negotiators helped to ensure greater precision in the definitions of crimes within the Court's jurisdiction.

But more must be done. Court jurisdiction over U.S. personnel should come only with U.S. ratification of the Treaty. The United States should have the chance to observe and assess the functioning of the Court, over time, before choosing to become subject to its jurisdiction. Given these concerns, I will not, and do not recommend that my successor submit the Treaty to the Senate for advice and consent until our fundamental concerns are satisfied.

Nonetheless, signature is the right action to take at this point. I believe that a properly constituted and structured International Criminal Court would make a profound contribution in deterring egregious human rights abuses worldwide, and that signature increases the chances for productive discussions with other governments to advance these goals in the months and years ahead.

Press Release of the International Criminal Tribunal for Rwanda (non official—for media information only) (ICTR/INFO-9-2-314.EN, Arusha, April 10, 2002)

The International Criminal Tribunal for Rwanda issued its first indictment against eight accused persons on 28 November 1995. Since that date the Tribunal has made steady progress towards the fulfillment of its mandate and has made a notable contribution to the development of international criminal justice. To date over seventy suspects have been indicted of whom more than fifty have been arrested and transferred to the Tribunal's custody. Of those so far apprehended the trials of nine have been completed resulting in eight convictions and one acquittal. The Appeals Chamber has confirmed six of the convictions and two appeals are still pending. Seven trials are currently in progress involving seventeen defendants. As a result, the total of completed cases and trials in progress involve over half of the total number of persons arrested.

Those convicted include Jean Kambanda, the Prime Minister of the Rwandan Government during the genocide, who was the first head of Government to be indicted and subsequently convicted for genocide. His conviction made it clear that international criminal law applied to the highest authorities and helped to create the conditions in which prosecutions could be undertaken against former Heads of State General Augusto Pinochet of Chile, President Hissène Habeé of Chad and Slobodan Milosevic of Serbia.

A further eleven Ministers of the 1994 interim government of Rwanda are also in the Tribunal's custody as well as senior military commanders, high ranking central and regional government officials, prominent businessmen, church leaders, journalists, intellectuals and other influential figures. Arrests are effected with the assistance of judicial and police authorities in the States where suspects are located.

Nineteen countries, including twelve African countries, have cooperated with the Tribunal in this way. Other countries have assisted the Tribunal by facilitating the movement of witnesses, by offering their own prison facilities for the execution of sentences of persons convicted by the Tribunal and by making contributions to the Tribunal's Trust Fund. Based upon international confidence in its organization and management, the Tribunal has thus enjoyed a high degree of support and assistance from the international community, in particular from Rwanda and Tanzania, its host states.

Priest Nsengimana Transferred to Arusha

Hormidas Nsengimana, a former priest who was Rector of Christ-Roi College in Nyanza, Nyabisindu Commune in Butare Prefecture (Rwanda) was today transferred from Yaoundé, Cameroon to the United Nations Detention Facility in Arusha. Cameroonian authorities arrested the accused on 21 March 2002 in Yaoundé on the basis of an arrest warrant submitted by the Tribunal. Nsengimana is the fifth clergyman to be arrested at the request of the Tribunal on charges connected with the genocide in Rwanda in 1994. Nsengimana, 48, faces four counts charging him with genocide, conspiracy to commit genocide and crimes against humanity for murder and extermination.

The accused is alleged to have played a leading role in a group of killers called Les Dragons (The Dragons) or Escadron de la mort (Death Squad). This group is alleged to have played a crucial role in the killing of Tutsis in and around the Christ-Roi College and in other parts of Butare Prefecture.

Nsengimana will shortly make his initial appearance before

a Judge of the Tribunal to answer the charges preferred against him. Duty Counsel will be assigned by the Registrar to represent him until he engages Counsel of his own or is assigned Counsel under the rules of the Tribunal.

Official U.S. Letter Renunciating the ICC, May 6, 2002

For the first time in history, a U.S. president formally renounced previous U.S. support of an international treaty. President Bill Clinton signed the treaty on the very last possible day (December 31, 2000) for signing the Rome Statute creating the ICC. Less than two years later, the George W. Bush administration, declaring that the permanent ICC would be an unchecked power able to prosecute U.S. soldiers and their superiors, notified UN Secretary-General Kofi Annan that the United States considers itself free of any obligation to comply with its terms. U.S. Undersecretary of State Marc Grossman said: "We believe the ICC is built on a flawed foundation. These flaws leave it open for exploitation and politically motivated prosecutions. Pierce-Richard Prosper, the U.S. ambassador for war crimes, bluntly stated that "we have washed our hands. It's over."

U.S. President George W. Bush's Renunciation of U.S. Support for the ICC [Letter], May 6, 2002

May 6, 2002

UN Secretary General Kofi Annan

New York, New York

This is to inform you in connection with the Rome Statute of the ICC, adopted on July 17, 1998, that the United States does not intend to become a party to the treaty. Accordingly, the United States has no legal obligations arising from its signature on December 31, 2000. The United States requests that its intention not to become a party, as expressed in this letter, be reflected in the depository's status list relating to this treaty.

[Signed]

John R. Bolton

U.S. Undersecretary for Arms Control and International Security

. . .

[Followed by Secretary of State Colin Powell's authorization and the official seal of the U.S. State Department]

6

Directory of Nongovernmental and Governmental Organizations

Protecting and seeking justice for the innocent victims of armed conflict has been the task of nongovernmental organizations (NGOs) since the International Committee of the Red Cross (ICRC) was created in 1863. Since the end of World War II, NGOs have proliferated across the globe and have been instrumental in addressing serious issues associated with the laws of war, including the creation of the International Criminal Court (ICC), the Ottawa Convention (banning the production, sale, and use of landmines), and so on. The essay by Rachel Brett (reproduced below) addresses the growth and the place of the NGO in the international community.

"Non-Governmental Human Rights Organizations and International Humanitarian Law" (an essay by Rachel Brett, New England School of Law Library, Research Guide, April 1999, www.nesl.edu/research/RSGUIDES/warpath.html)

At the heart of human rights work is the attempt to protect individuals from the abuse of power or neglect on the part of their own governments. At the international level, this translates into State responsibility for the way in which the government treats its own people, supplementing the older international law regarding the treatment of aliens and the law of war which also (originally) addressed only the treatment of non-nationals.

It is therefore not surprising that non-governmental organizations (NGOs) involved in safeguarding human rights have always focused on the implementation (or violation) of universal or regional human rights standards by governments. This reflects the traditional view of governments as the centres of power and responsibility as well as the general principle that States are bound by international law (either by virtue of becoming party to a treaty or because the rule is recognized as a norm of customary international law) and the classic human rights view that governments and only governments can violate human rights. Killings committed by individuals or groups are crimes. Such acts become violations of human rights if the perpetrator is the agent of a State or if the State fails in its duty to protect the individual or to prosecute the alleged perpetrator.

However, the world has changed and the law along with it. The growing number of internal (non-international) armed conflicts and the attention they receive internationally has produced a number of developments.

International humanitarian law has moved from its exclusive concern for international armed conflict to active interest in internal armed conflicts as well. The first of this was Article 3 common to the 1949 Geneva Conventions. The second came in 1977 with Additional Protocol II, which is applicable to non-international armed conflict. Humanitarian law has thus moved into the human rights arena, as it were, in the sense that it now addresses the relationship between those in authority and the people they govern. This raises the question of the relationship between international humanitarian law and human rights law, since human rights law continues to apply (though with limitations) in time of armed conflict. This same development raises questions about some of the fundamental tenets of international humanitarian law: the equal standing of the parties to an armed conflict and the reciprocal nature of their obligations. Finally, the regulation of internal armed conflicts raises the whole question of accountability on the part of non-State entities under international law.

Traditionally, human rights NGOs have tended to feel that international humanitarian law was the province of the International Committee of the Red Cross and that it was complicated, containing as it does all sorts of strange and ambiguous (at least to human rights people) concepts such as "collateral damage" and "military necessity," so that even something as apparently straightforward as the killing of civilians might, though regrettable, not constitute a violation of international humanitarian law.

For human rights NGOs, there have been questions about how to interpret the law and whether there is a danger of lowering standards by applying international humanitarian law rather than human rights law.

However, the proliferation of armed conflicts—in particular internal armed conflicts—and the apparent convergence of human rights law and international humanitarian law has led certain human rights NGOs to reconsider their position. A basic principle for human rights NGOs is that it is unacceptable to ignore violations on the grounds that they occur during armed conflicts. How then can these organizations respond effectively to such violations? Does international humanitarian law provide a useful framework? These questions will be examined with respect to two issues: applicable standards and the accountability of non-State forces.

. . .

As knowledge of international humanitarian law has grown among human rights NGOs, there has been an increasing recognition that at least some of the standards provide a degree of specialization and specificity that human rights standards lack, even in relation to internal armed conflicts. A notable example of this is the rules governing displacement of the civilian population. Such displacement is a common phenomenon in internal armed conflicts but one on which human rights law provides little assistance. By contrast, Article 17, paragraph 1 of Additional Protocol II provides that people may be relocated only for their own security or for "imperative military reasons," and specifies that "all possible measures" must be taken to ensure "satisfactory conditions of shelter, hygiene, health, safety and nutrition" for those displaced. This provision was used by Human Rights Watch in its recent report on Burundi as the yardstick for judging the camps set up by the government. The reality of today's world is that there are countries with no government or with titular governments only partially in control of the territory. Can (or should?) human rights NGOs either ignore such situations or go on considering only governments accountable under human rights law. The legal and conceptual ambivalence about non-State forces is not exclusive to NGOs. It is also nicely reflected in the proposed optional protocol to the Convention on the Rights of the Child on involvement of children in armed conflict (another example of convergence of human rights and international humanitarian law) in the latest draft of that text's provision on military recruitment by non-States forces.

The preambular paragraph recalls "the obligation of each

party to an armed conflict to abide by the provisions of international humanitarian law," while draft Article 3, paragraph 1 balances the moral (not legal) obligation not to recruit children under 18 with a legal obligation on States to prevent such recruitment: "Persons under the age of 18 years should not be recruited into armed groups, distinct from the armed forces of a State, which are parties to an armed conflict. States Parties shall take all feasible measures to prevent such recruitment." For human rights NGOs, therefore, it might seem that the obvious solution to the problem of non-State entities is to use international humanitarian law.

However, it is not as simple as that. Firstly, humanitarian law applies only if there is an armed conflict, and there are situations in which non-State entities are involved without there being an armed conflict. Still other situations are simply difficult to define. Secondly, even where there unequivocally is an armed conflict, human rights law continues to be binding on governments, although in certain circumstances they are permitted to derogate from some of its provisions. Human rights NGOs could, therefore, find themselves invoking both human rights law and international humanitarian law vis-à-vis the government while referring only to international humanitarian law vis-à-vis armed opposition group. Does it matter whether the government is held to higher or different standards than the opposition? Furthermore, Protocol II only applies if the State concerned is party to it. Should the non-adherence of a government prevent human rights NGOs from insisting that its provisions be complied with by non-State entities to whom those provisions would otherwise apply? The increasing interest in international humanitarian law on the part of human rights NGOs highlights the problems with which they are wrestling: in particular, how to maintain or improve protection of human rights in armed conflicts and internal disturbances. It is in the nature of NGOs that there will be no unified response to these problems though a number of key points on which they agree emerge from their work and from their discussions. They are as follows.

1. International humanitarian law provides agreed standards specifically designed to address issues arising in armed conflict. On the basis of these, NGOs can hold governments and armed opposition groups alike accountable for their actions.

2. In the event of non-international armed conflict, NGOs can remind the warring parties of the provisions of Protocol II

even where the State is not bound by that treaty or where it is not applicable (because a condition for its applicability is not met, e.g., control of territory), since the Protocol provides authoritative guidance regarding humane treatment. Moreover, at least part of its provisions belong to international customary law.

3. In addition to including violations committed by non-State entities in their reports on government violations, human rights NGOs need to engage non-State entities and to be able frankly to condemn violations committed by them. There are at least four possible bases for such action by human rights NGOs. Their use would depend on various factors, including the sensitive problem of possibly giving "recognition" to such groups, and the body of law which the individual NGO considers most appropriate or with which it feels most comfortable.- the principles of human rights law (though that law itself binds only States). Human rights NGOs are unlikely ever to feel completely at ease with international humanitarian law. Its concepts, language and approach are different from those of human rights. However, the strength of the human rights movement is its ability to learn and to adapt on order to meet the changing challenges of the world while guarding the integrity of the human rights concept in the face of pressure from governments and the public. International humanitarian law provides valuable tools for human rights NGOs in their struggle to safeguard human rights.

Directory

Amnesty International
International Secretariat
1 Easton Street
London WC1X 8DJ, United Kingdom
website: http://www.amnesty.org/;
email: amnestyis@amnesty.org

Amnesty International is an international human rights organization, a worldwide movement of people who are united by their desire to protect and promote human rights. It was founded in 1961 by Peter Benenson, a London lawyer who organized a letter-writing campaign calling for amnesty for "prisoners of conscience." Amnesty International seeks to inform the public about violations of human rights, especially abridgments of freedom of speech and religion and the imprisonment and torture of political dissidents. It actively seeks the release of political prisoners and support for their families when necessary. Its members and supporters are said to number 1 million in 162 countries. Its first director, S. MacBride, won the 1974 Nobel Prize; Amnesty International itself won the award in 1977.

Campaign to End Genocide
c/o The World Federalist Association
418-420 7th Street SE
Washington, DC 20003
Phone: (202) 546-3950; fax: (202) 546-3749;
email: info@endgenocide.org

Genocide and mass murder took more lives during the twentieth century than all wars combined. In the twenty-first century, we have the ability to end genocide forever and build a more just and peaceful world. Through strong and effective international institutions, coupled with the necessary political will, the world can end this egregious human rights crime.

Center for Economic and Social Rights
105 E. 22nd St. #909
New York, NY 10010 USA
Phone: (212) 982-1950; fax: (212) 982-2163;
email: rights@cesr.org; website: http://www.cesr.org

The Center for Economic and Social Rights was established in 1993 to address issues of poverty (access to health, food, housing, education, and other basic needs) as human rights under international and domestic laws.

Coalition for an International Criminal Court
American Non-Governmental Organizations
Coalition for the ICC
Address: United Nations Association-USA
801 Second Ave., 2nd Fl
New York, NY 10017
Phone: (212) 907-1317/1358; fax: (212) 682-9185;
email: jwashburn@unausa.org/aheindel@unausa.org;
Contacts: John Washburn, Convenor; Anne Heindel, Deputy Convenor

The main purpose of the NGO-sponsored Coalition for an International Criminal Court is to advocate for the creation of an effective, just, and independent International Criminal Court. The coalition brings together a broad-based network of more than

1,000 NGOs, international law experts, and other civil society groups. The multitrack approach of the coalition involves: promoting education and awareness of the ICC and the Rome Statute at the national, regional, and global levels; supporting the successful completion of the mandate of the Preparatory Commission and facilitating NGO involvement in the process; promoting the universal acceptance and ratification of the Rome Statute, including the adoption of comprehensive national implementing legislation following ratification; and expanding and strengthening the coalition's global network.

Coalition for International Justice (CIJ)
2001 S Street NW, 7th Floor
Washington, DC 20009
Phone: (202) 483-9234; fax: (202) 483-9263;
email: coalition@cij.org; website: http://www.cij.org

The Hague
Javastraat 119
2585 AH
The Hague, Netherlands
Telephone/Fax: 011-31-70-352-1171

The Coalition for International Justice is an international non-profit organization that supports the international war crimes tribunals for Rwanda and the former Yugoslavia, as well as justice initiatives in East Timor, Sierra Leone, and Cambodia. CIJ initiates and conducts advocacy and public education campaigns, targeting decisionmakers in Washington and other capitals, the media, and the public. Working with other NGOs in Washington and elsewhere, CIJ helps focus and maximize the impact of individual and collective advocacy. In the field, CIJ provides practical assistance on legal, technical, and outreach matters to the tribunals and other justice initiatives. CIJ has offices in Washington and The Hague, as well as contracted employees in East Timor.

Derechos Human Rights
46 Estabrook St.
San Leandro, CA 94577
Phone: (510) 483-4005; fax: (208) 275-3406;
email: rights@derechos.org;
website: http://www.derechos.org

Derechos Human Rights is the first Internet-based human rights organization. Its purpose is to work for the promotion and respect of human rights all over the world, for the right to privacy, and against impunity for human rights violators. It uses the Internet as its primary information and communication tool. Derechos works with human rights organizations in Latin America and the world to bring accurate and timely information on human rights situations, as well as opportunities to help. It also coordinates several human rights mailing lists, publishes an internet human rights journal, and works on the preservation of memory and for justice for the disappeared. (Derechos website)

Dr. Homa Darabi Foundation
P.O. Box 11049
Truckee, CA 96162
Phone: (916) 582 4197; fax: (916) 582 0156;
website: http://www.homa.org

Its mission is to raise public awareness about the violence afflicted upon women and children all over the world in the name of God, religion, culture, family values, and the preservation of the society and to promote activism for change.

Doctors Without Borders (Medecins Sans Frontieres)
Doctors Without Borders USA
Eastern Office:
P.O. Box 2247
New York, NY 10116-2247
Phone: (212) 679-6800; fax: (212) 679-7016
Western Office:
2040 Ave. of the Stars, C-216
Los Angeles, CA 90067
Phone: (310) 277-2793; fax: (310) 277-166

Doctors Without Borders/Medecins Sans Frontieres, the 1999 Nobel Prize laureate, is the world's largest independent international medical relief agency aiding victims of armed conflict, epidemics, and natural and man-made disasters and others who lack health care due to geographic remoteness or ethnic marginalization. Annually, more than 2,000 volunteers representing 45 nationalities work in more than 80 countries in front-line hospitals, refugee camps, disaster sites, towns, and villages. Doctors Without Borders teams provide primary health care, perform surgery, vaccinate children, rehabilitate hospitals, operate emergency nutrition and sanitation programs, and train local medical staff.

Human Rights Watch
350 Fifth Avenue, 34th floor
New York, NY 10118-3299 USA
Phone: (212) 290-4700; fax: (212) 736-1300;
email: hrwnyc@hrw.org

1630 Connecticut Avenue, N.W., Suite 500
Washington, DC 20009 USA
Phone: (202) 612-4321; fax: (202) 612-4333;
email: hrwdc@hrw.org

11500 W. Olympic Blvd., Suite 441
Los Angeles, CA 90064
Phone: (310) 477-5540; fax: (310) 477-4622;
email: hrwla@hrw.org

312 Sutter Street, Suite 407
San Francisco CA 94108
Phone: (415) 362-3250; fax: (415) 362-3255;
email: hrwsf@hrw.org

33 Islington High Street
N1 9LH London, UK
Phone: (20) 7713 1995; fax: (20) 7713 1800;
email: hrwuk@hrw.org

Rue Van Campenhout 15
1000 Brussels, Belgium
Phone: 32 (2) 732-2009; fax: 32 (2) 732-0471

An NGO "dedicated to protecting the human rights of people around the world. We stand with victims and activists to prevent discrimination, to uphold political freedom, to protect people from inhumane conduct in wartime, and to bring offenders to justice. We investigate and expose human rights violations and hold abusers accountable. We challenge governments and those who hold power to end abusive practices and respect international human rights law. We enlist the public and the international community to support the cause of human rights for all. Human Rights Watch is an independent, non-governmental organization, supported by contributions from private individuals and foundations worldwide. It accepts no government funds, directly or indirectly."

Institute of War and Peace Reporting (IWPR)
Lancaster House, 33 Islington High Street
London N1 9LH, UK
Phone: +44 (0)20 7713 7130; fax: +44 (0)20 7713 7140

Founded in 1991, the Institute of War and Peace Reporting is an independent educational charity based in the United Kingdom. The board of trustees includes prominent journalists, peace researchers, and regional specialists. Staff are mostly journalists with international or regional backgrounds. IWPR supports democratization and development in crisis zones by providing an international platform, professional training, and financial assistance to independent media, human rights activists, and other democratic voices.

International Campaign to Ban Landmines (ICBL)
110 Maryland Ave NE
Box 6, Suite 509
Washington DC 20002
Phone: (202) 547-2667; fax: (202) 547-2687
email: icbl@icbl.org; website: www.icbl.org

Works toward an international ban on the use, production, stockpiling, and sale, transfer, or export of antipersonnel landmines; the signing, ratification, implementation, and monitoring of the mine-ban treaty; increasing resources for humanitarian demining and mine awareness programs; and increasing resources for landmine victim rehabilitation and assistance.

International Commission of Jurists (ICJ)
Centre for the Independence of Judges and lawyers
P.O. Box 216, 81A avenue de Châtelaine,
1219 Geneva, Switzerland.
Phone: +41(0)22 979-38-00; fax: +41(0)22 979-38-01;
email: info@icj.org

The International Commission of Jurists was founded in Berlin in 1952. It is dedicated to the primacy, coherence, and implementation of international law and principles that advance human rights. What distinguishes the ICJ is its impartial, objective, and authoritative legal approach to the protection and promotion of human rights through the rule of law. The ICJ provides legal expertise at both the international and national levels to ensure that developments in international law adhere to human rights principles and that international standards are implemented at the national level.

International Committee of the Red Cross (ICRC)
19 avenue de la Paix

CH 1202 Genève
Phone: ++ 41 (22) 734 60 01; fax: ++ 41 (22) 733 20 57 (Public Information Division, Web Server);
email : dc_com_pmd.gva@icrc.org;
website: http://www.icrc.org/

The International Committee of the Red Cross is an impartial, neutral, and independent organization whose exclusively humanitarian mission is to protect the lives and dignity of victims of war and internal violence and to provide them with assistance. Established in 1863, the ICRC is at the origin of the International Red Cross and Red Crescent Movement. It directs and coordinates the international relief activities conducted by the movement in situations of conflict. It also endeavors to prevent suffering by promoting and strengthening humanitarian law and universal humanitarian principles.

International Rescue Committee (IRC)
122 East 42nd Street
New York, NY 10165
Phone: (212) 551-3000; fax: (212) 551-3180;
email: bode@intrescom.org;
website: http://www.theIRC.org

Founded in 1933, the International Rescue Committee is the leading nonprofit, nonsectarian voluntary organization providing relief, protection, and resettlement services for refugees and victims of oppression or violent conflict. IRC is committed to freedom, human dignity, and self reliance. This commitment is reflected in well planned resettlement assistance, global emergency relief, rehabilitation, and advocacy for refugees.

Lawyers Committee for Human Rights
New York Headquarters
Lawyers Committee for Human Rights
333 Seventh Avenue
New York, NY 10001-5004
Phone: (212) 845 5200; fax: (212) 845-5299;
email: nyc@lchr.org

Washington, DC, Office:
Lawyers Committee for Human Rights
100 Maryland Avenue NE, Suite 500
Washington, DC 20002-5625
Phone: (202) 547 5692; fax: (202) 543-5999

San Francisco Office
Lawyers Committee for Human Rights
275 Battery St., 23rd Floor
San Francisco, CA 94111
Phone: (415) 365 7400; fax: (415) 986 9014

Since 1978, the Lawyers Committee for Human Rights has worked to protect and promote fundamental human rights. Its work is impartial, holding all governments accountable to the standards affirmed in the International Bill of Human Rights. Its programs focus on building the legal institutions and structures that will guarantee human rights in the long term. Strengthening independent human rights advocacy at the local level is a key feature of its work.

Organization of American States
OAS/Public Information
17th St. and Constitution Ave. NW
Washington, DC 20006
Phone: (202) 458-3754; Fax: (202) 458-6421;
website: http://www.oas.org

The Organization of American States is the world's oldest regional organization. It is the principal forum in the hemisphere for dialogue on political, economic, and social issues. Every country in the Americas is a member of the organization.

Peace Brigades International
International Secretariat
5 Caledonian Road
London N1 9DX
United Kingdom
Phone: +44-171-713-0392; fax: +44-171-837-2290;
website: http://www.peacebrigades.org/index.html

Peace Brigades International is a unique grassroots organization exploring and implementing nonviolent approaches to peacekeeping and support for basic human rights.

Physicians for Human Rights (PHR)
100 Boylston Street, Suite 702
Boston, MA 02116
Phone: (617) 695-0041; fax: (617) 695-0307

Physicians for Human Rights is an organization of health professionals, scientists, and concerned citizens that uses the knowledge and skills of the medical and forensic sciences to investigate and prevent violations of international human rights and humanitarian law. Since 1986, PHR members have worked to stop torture, disappearances, and political killings by governments and opposition groups; to improve health and sanitary conditions in prisons and detention centers; to investigate the physical and psychological consequences of violations of humanitarian law in internal and international conflicts; to defend medical neutrality and the right of civilians and combatants to receive medical care during times of war; to protect health professionals who are victims of violations of human rights; and to prevent medical complicity in torture and other abuses.

United Nations High Commissioner/
Commission on Human Rights
Commission on Human Rights
Geneva, Switzerland
Phone: (41-22) 917-9000; website: http://193.135.156.15

The mission of the United Nations High Commissioner for Human Rights is to ensure the universal enjoyment of all human rights by giving practical effect to the will and resolve of the world community as expressed by the United Nations.

Witness Program
330 Seventh Avenue, 10th Floor
New York, NY 10001
Phone: (212) 274-1664; fax: (212) 274-1262
email: witbin@lchr.org; website: http://www.witness.org

The Witness program, conceived in 1992 in partnership with the Lawyers Committee for Human Rights, Peter Gabriel, and the Reebok Foundation, gives human rights advocates the tools to document human rights abuses. Witness provides video cameras and training to human rights groups around the world.

World Organisation Against Torture
World Organization Against Torture USA
1725 K St. NW, Suite 610
Washington, DC 20006
Phone: (202) 296-5702; fax (202) 296-5704;
email: woatusa@woatusa.org;
website: http://www.woatusa.org

The World Organisation Against Torture is today the largest international coalition of NGOs fighting against torture, summary executions, forced disappearances, and all other forms of cruel, inhuman, and degrading treatment in order to preserve Human Rights. It has at its disposal a network—SOS Torture—consisting of some 240 NGOs that act as sources of information. Its urgent interventions reach daily more than 90,000 governmental and intergovernmental institutions, nongovernmental associations, and pressure and interest groups.

7

Selected Print and Nonprint Resources

War Crimes and Justice: "Resources and Research Steps"

(New England School of Law, Sandra J. Lamar, Reference Librarian, April 1999.)

Professor Lamar's essay serves as an introduction to doing research on war crimes and justice.

Print Resources: Check for treatises, articles on topic.
Why? War crimes and other human rights issues often require either finding controlling treaties and conventions, or finding authoritative sources which interpret them. Secondary sources can provide background; leads to primary sources by supplying needed numbers, dates, and exact titles; and English translations of primary material.

How? Use Portia, linked from http://www.nesl.edu/library/ For articles, search in the paper indexes or the links from http://www.nesl.edu/research/indices.cfm. Index to Legal Periodicals, Wilsondisc, and Index to Foreign Legal Periodicals are all linked from this page; Legaltrac is also a networked CD-ROM. Suggestions for subject searches in Portia, and a listing of major treatises in the NESL collection, are attached.

Tip: Do not rely on the full text databases of Westlaw and Lexis for law reviews. Some of the articles, and ILM documents, are very long. It will be more efficient to identify the cite, then find the source in paper and copy the sections needed.

. . .

Use Lexis to find resources which analyze and translate (http://lawschool.lexis.com).
Why? Lexis is a logical starting place because of its large international database and sophisticated search capability. Many times

the first English translations of key documents are available here, in the news databases: look in the Lexis "World" and "Intlaw" libraries. Specific country's materials may or may not be available. Likewise, Lexis has not collected the war crimes materials you are apt to need. Westlaw has some materials, but should not be the first research stop as it does not have as many world-wide sources as Lexis.

How? Use the enhanced search features, especially segment searching, to identify the resources which discuss, identify and analyze. Ask for help to identify available databases.

Tip: Search HLEAD (boolean search terms). HLEAD requires the terms to be in the headline or the lead sentence, helping your retrieval of more analytical news.

Utilize the power of the Internet

Why? The Internet has become essential for this kind of research. Many documents will only be available to you on the web. Recent treaties, constitutions, and United Nations [UN] materials are all appearing on the World Wide Web at a staggering rate. They are often posted by authoritative sources, and may well be the only practical source for some resources. Trial and Tribunal materials, and evidentiary procedures for example, are often only available on the web.

How? Start with War Crimes, at http://www.nesl.edu/research/warcrim.cfm. Human rights links are at http://www.nesl.edu/research/hrights.cfm and the United Nations materials are at http://www.un.org.

Tip: Evaluate your source: Who produced this material? If the author is a government agency, an advocacy group, or a scholar, does the resource have an ideological bent? Is the document current? Is the translation accurate?

Use the networked CD-ROM's

Why? The Internet may have key treaties or conventions, and may have recent documents, but is unlikely to have everything you need.

How? Access Hein's Treaty Index, on all library workstations, for treaties to which the U.S. is a party. The United Nations material is also networked: UNBIS PLUS databases provide bibliographic access to the documentary output of the United Nations. This CD-ROM also includes the full text of UN resolutions since the early 70's; voting records; and citations to speeches.

Finding Primary Resources: Treaties, Conventions, and other Agreements between Nations

Find the citation:

Is the United States a party?

Use Hein's United States Treaty Index, on CD-ROM or the TIARA index, http://www.oceanalaw.com.

Hein's Treaty Index (on CD-ROM) is quite current, and cited by "KAV number."

Finding Treaties, Conventions, and other Agreements which do not involve the United States

Through 1980, check The World Treaty Index. After that, search the news databases on Westlaw & Lexis, and the Internet to get a number and date.

Find the Document

Treaties to which the United States is a party are published by the United States Department of State: TIAS ("Treaties and Other International Acts"), and from 1950 on, the United States Treaties and Other International Agreements (UST). The lag time may be as much as 7 to 10 years before the first official publication in slip form. Other books to check: Treaties In Force, published annually. Subject-oriented treatises may also collect treaties and resolutions.

International Legal Materials (ILM)

Published by the American Society of International Law, ILM reproduces select U.S. draft treaties, treaties entered into force, and the Treaty Section of the Department of State Bulletin. Provides selective translations of important international treaties and conventions, UN documents, and court decisions. Not comprehensive but a highly valuable source. The annual index is in the November issue. The most efficient way is to find the cite online, and then go to the paper.

Online Treaty databases

Lexis: INTLAW library; DSTATE file from 1984 (use "treaty actions" as search term); INTLAW library; ILM file.

Westlaw databases: USTREATIES and ILM.

Internet: Links on the Web

Start with the links from [http://www.nesl.edu/research].

The Fletcher School Multilateral Treaty Project, http://www.fletcher.tufts.edu/multilaterals.html, is an especially good resource, and with full text of selected current and historical treaties in both "rules of warfare" and "human rights" categories. The site is keyword searchable.

Human rights treaties are collected at http://www1.umn.edu/humanrts/treaties.htm.

Various United Nations Conventions provide the substantive law of war. These include, inter alia, the Geneva conventions, see http://www.un.org, the Hague Conventions, see http://www.hcch.net/e/conventions, and the Genocide Convention, http://www.yale.edu/cgp/dccam/genocide.htm.

Primary Resources: Legislative, Executive, Judicial

Legislative: To the extent the code of the nation is needed to determine process or criminal procedure, you may need not only the most recent version of a code but also the official gazette. These may not be available in English, and may not be indexed. Use other sources to find a number and a date to increase your chances of locating.

Tip: The Reynolds & Flores treatise on CD-ROM can tell you the titles of applicable codes, and the language, but other resources may be able to give you more specific sections.

Executive: Many civil law countries include the executive orders, decrees, and the equivalent of regulations in their gazette. Decisions of administrative tribunals will be difficult.

Judicial: Be aware that many civil law jurisdictions do not place much value on caselaw. Statutes, treaties, and academic interpretations of those laws may be considered more authoritative than case law.

Where a formal tribunal of some sort is set up to handle war crimes, the Internet is the most likely resource for these decisions. Westlaw and Cornell's web site provide access to the International Court of Justice decisions, but those issues generally will not be applicable to individual war crimes cases.

Accessing Print Resources:

Search online catalog: Url: http://38.232.116.10/ ; or, telnet to portia.nesl.edu (telnet://portia.nesl.edu)

Key words to search

"war crimes" "human rights" "atrocities" "genocide" "war crime trials" "Crimes against humanity"

Applicable Subject Searches (using Library of Congress subject headings):

"International Offenses"; "Crimes against Humanity" ; "War victims —Kuwait [or whatever country]" ; "United Nations. General Assembly— Resolutions"; "International law—Sources";

"United Nations—Armed Forces"; "International police"; "International offenses"; "War crimes"

Selected treatises

M. Cherif Bassiouni, The Law of the International Criminal Tribunal for the former Yugoslavia (Transnational Publishers, 1996).

M. Cherif Bassiouni, Crimes Against Humanity in International Criminal Law (Kluwer 1992).

Global war crimes tribunal collection. Vol. 1, The Rwanda Tribunal (Global Law Association, 1997);

John R. W. D. Jones, the Practice of the International Criminal Tribunals for the former Yugoslavia and Rwanda (Transnational Publishers, 1997). Virginia Morris and Michael Scharf, An Insider's Guide to the International Criminal Tribunal for the Former Yugoslavia (Transnational Publishers, 1995).

Virginia Morris and Michael Scharf, The International Criminal Tribunal for Rwanda (Transnational Publishers, 1998) (AS I L Certificate of Merit for 1999's outstanding book in International law)

Timothy L. H. McCormack and Gerry J. Simpson, ed., The Law of War Crimes: National and International Approaches (Kluwer 1997). Location: Lower Mezzanine K5301.L39 1997

Michael P. Scharf, Balkan Justice : The Story behind the First International War Crimes Trial since Nuremberg (Carolina Academic Press, 1997)

Collections of primary material:

Brownlie, Ian, ed. Basic documents on human rights (Oxford University Press, 1992).

Human rights documents: compilation of documents pertaining to human rights: U.S. laws on human rights; Basic UN human rights instruments; UN instruments in selected human rights (U.S. G.P.O., 1983).

Sharp, Walter G. ed., United Nations peace operations: a collection of primary documents and readings governing the conduct of multilateral peace operations (American Heritage, Custom Publishing Group, 1995). Location: Upper Mezzanine KZ6376.U55 1995

Judgments of the International Court of Justice and the European Court of Human Rights are also held by the NESL library. Location: Stack 250

Historical War Crimes:

Trial of the major war criminals before the International Military Tribunal, Nuremberg, 14 November 1945–1 October 1946 (Hein, 1995).

International Military Tribunal for the Far East, The Tokyo major war crimes trial: the transcripts of the court proceedings of the International Military Tribunal for the Far East (Mellen Press, 1998)

Genocide:

Kurt Jonassohn, Genocide and gross human rights violations in comparative perspective (Transaction Publishers, 1998)

Steven R. Ratner, Accountability for human rights atrocities in international law: beyond the Nuremberg legacy (Oxford University Press, 1997)

Robert I. Rotberg, Thomas G. Weiss, eds. From massacres to genocide: the media, public policy, and humanitarian crises (Brookings Institution, 1996)

David Wippman, ed. International law and ethnic conflict (Cornell University Press, 1998) Location:

Finding the codes for particular countries:

Reynolds and Flores, Foreign law: current sources of codes and basic legislation in jurisdictions of the world (Rothman, 1989). (Multiple volume set).

Tip: This work is especially helpful because it identifies the translations as well as the original codes.

Accessing Articles:

Internet links: http://www.nesl.edu/research/indices.cfm Internet access is from the library only.

LegalTrac (Infotrac) 1980–Present

Networked CD-ROM, print, and Internet available.

Index to Legal Periodicals (Wilsondisc) 1981–Present

Articles from over 762 law reviews and books. Internet and print access.

Index to Foreign Legal Periodicals 1985–Present

Articles and book reviews from more than 450 foreign legal periodicals—countries other than the United States, British Isles, and British Commonwealth. Internet and print access.

Current Index to Legal Periodicals 1997–Present

Available through the NELLCO and Suffolk Law Library web site. Internet and print access.

Carl Uncover—multi-disciplinary—Internet only.

Articles First—connect from other databases.

Accessing Online Resources for War Crimes Research

LEXIS/NEXIS Resources:

On the Web Version of the Lexis software (paths to follow):

From the top level: area of law by topic; international; then choose treaties, cases, law reviews, or news

From the top level: country & region (excluding US); then choose World News, Bus Anal. & Country Info, or a specific Country & Region

From the top level: news, by country, world news, current

Country Reports: Country & Region (excluding U.S.): Middle East & Africa: Country Reports

Using the paper Directory to Lexis sources, identify Library and file name; go to "search sources" and select "short form"; type in this format:

LAWREV; INTLR

WORLD; ALLWLD

INTLAW; ASIL

Country Reports: The World Factbook (WORLD; WOFACT)—or Country Profiles
(WORLD; PROFIL)

Internet Resources

http://www.nesl.edu/center/index.cfm (table of contents to International links)

http://www.nesl.edu/research/warcrim.cfm (war crimes, genocide links)

http://www.nesl.edu/research/intcrim.cfm (International Criminal Justice links)

http://www.nesl.edu/research/hrights.cfm (Human Rights links)

http://www.nesl.edu/research/current.cfm (current awareness news links: note that Court TV posts documents from war crimes trials that never make it on Lexis).

Megasites with excellent war crimes links:

http://www.lib.uchicago.edu/e/law/home.html—University of Chicago

http://www.hg.org—Hieros Gamos, subject areas for both Human Rights and "War and Peace"

http://www.washlaw.edu/forint/alpha/w/warcrimes.htm —Washburn U. School of Law

Human Rights Collections (Diana):
http://www.yale.edu/lawweb/avalon/diana/index.html.

International Organizations:
http://www.nesl.edu/research/intorgs.cfm—(NESL collection of links to International Organizations.)

The United Nations Security Council has taken action repeatedly to deal with large-scale violations of human rights. These measures are taken under the powers conferred by the UN Charter. For an excellent research guide into the structure, organization and resolutions of the United Nations, see the Duke Research Guide at: http://www.law.duke.edu/lib/libser/publicat/ResearchGuides/unitednations/un.html.

ASIL publications: The American Society of International Law

http://www.asil.org/asilex.htm (search asil publications).

The ASIL publishes much information, including ILM. Other Research Guides for International Law generally can be found at http://www.nesl.edu/research/rsguides.cfm

Foreign Government information:

http://www.library.nwu.edu/govpub/resource/internat/foreign.html (Northwestern U.)

War Crimes Tribunals:

http://www.nesl.edu/research/warcrim.cfm#ict The NESL war crimes page has links to the tribunals and some procedural material.

Foreign Law:

Laws of specific countries, in English, are linked from http://www.nesl.edu/research/foreign.cfm.

Students who need to identify laws even if not in English are directed to the Megasites also linked from that page.

For information on the economic or political situation in a particular country:

Dept. of State http://www.state.gov

Dept. of State Human Rights Reports: http://www.state.gov/www/global/human_ rights/hrp_reports_mainhp.html

CIA Factbook http://www.cia.gov/cia/publications/factbook/index.html

Selected Print Resources

Ambos, K. "Establishing an International Criminal Court and International Criminal Code: Observations from an International Criminal Law Viewpoint." 7 *European Journal of International Law* 519–544 (1996).

Ambos, K. "General Principles of Criminal Law in the Rome Statute." 10 *Criminal Law Forum* 1–32 (1999).

Andreasen, Scott W. "The International Criminal Court: Does the Constitution Preclude Its Ratification by the United States?" 85 *Iowa Law Review* 697 (January 2000, no. 2).

Ball, Howard. *Prosecuting War Crimes and Genocide: The Twentieth-Century Experience.* Lawrence: University Press of Kansas, 1999.

Barkan, Elazar. *The Guilt of Nations: Restitution and Negotiating Historical Injustices.* New York: W. W. Norton, 2000.

Bass, Gary. *Stay the Hand of Vengeance: The Politics of War Crimes Tribunals.* Princeton, NJ: Princeton University Press, 2000.

Bassiouni, M. Cherif. A *Draft International Criminal Code and Draft Statute for an International Criminal Tribunal.* 2nd rev. and updated ed. Dordrecht and Boston: M. Nijhoff, 1987.

———. "Enforcing Human Rights Through International Criminal Law Through an International Criminal Tribunal." In *Human Rights: An Agenda for the Next Century,* ed. Louis Henkin and John Lawrence Hargrove. Washington, DC: American Society of International Law, 1994.

———. "From Versailles to Rwanda in Seventy-Five Years: The Need to Establish a Permanent International Criminal Court." 10 *Harvard Human Rights Journal* 11–62 (1997).

———. *Crimes Against Humanity in International Criminal Law.* 2nd rev. ed. Kluwer Law International, 1999.

———. "Former Yugoslavia: Investigating violations of international criminal tribunal" 18 *Fordham International Law Journal* 1191 (April 1995).

Bedant, Barbara. "Gender-Specific Provisions in the Statute of the International Criminal Court." In *Essays on the Rome Statute of the International Criminal Court,* vol. 1, ed. Flavia Lattanzi and William A. Schabas. Ripa Fagnano Alto: Editrice il Sirente, 2000.

Benison, Audrey I. "War Crimes: A Human Rights Approach to a Humanitarian Law Problem at the International Criminal Court." 88 *Georgetown Law Journal* 141–176 (1999).

Best, Geoffrey. *Humanity in Warfare: The Modern History of the International Law of Armed Conflicts.* London: Methuen, 1983.

———. *War and Law Since 1945.* Oxford, UK: Clarendon Press, 1994.

Bowden, Mark. *Black Hawk Down: A Story of Modern War.* Boston: Atlantic Monthly Press, 1999.

Brackman, Arnold C. *The Other Nuremberg: The Untold Story of the Tokyo War Crimes Trials.* New York: William Morrow, 1987.

Brownstone, David, and Irene Franck. *Timelines of War: A Chronology of Warfare from 100,000 BC to the Present.* Boston: Little, Brown, 1994.

Buckley, William J., ed. *Kosovo: Contending Voices on Balkan Interventions.* Wm. B. Eerdmans, 2000.

Cassel, Douglass. "Empowering United States Courts to Hear Crimes Within the Jurisdiction of the International Criminal Court." 35 *New England Law Review* 421–445 (2001).

Charney, Jonathan I. "International Criminal Law and the Role of Domestic Courts." 95 *American Journal of International Law* 120–124 (January 2001).

Clarke, Walter, and Jeffrey Herbst. *Learning from Somalia: The*

Lessons of Armed Humanitarian Intervention. Boulder, CO: Westview Press, 1997.

Cogan, Jacob Katz. "The Problem of Obtaining Evidence for International Criminal Courts." 22 *Human Rights Quarterly* 404 (2000).

Cohen, Roger. *Hearts Grown Brutal: Sagas of Sarajevo.* New York: Random House, 1998.

Cooper, Belinda, ed. *War Crimes: The Legacy of Nuremberg.* New York: TV Books, 1999.

Deming, Stuart H. "War Crimes and International Criminal Law." 28 *Akron Law Review* 421 (1995).

Edwards, Charles S. "Grotius and the Law of War." In Edwards, ed., *Hugo Grotius, the Miracle of Holland: A Study in Political and Legal Thought* (Chicago: Nelson-Hall, 1981).

Falk, Richard A., Gabriel Kolko, and Robert Jay Lifton, eds. *Crimes of War: A Legal, Political-Documentary, and Psychological Inquiry into the Responsibility of Leaders, Citizens, and Soldiers for Criminal Acts in Wars.* New York: Vintage Books, 1971.

Fein, Helen. "Discriminating Genocide from War Crimes: Vietnam and Afghanistan Reexamined." 22 *Denver Journal of International Law and Policy* 29 (1993).

Freeman, Lawrence, ed. *War.* New York: Oxford University Press, 1994.

Friedman, Leon, ed. *The Law of War: A Documentary History,* 2 vols. New York: Random House, 1972.

Goldstone, Richard. "Assessing the Work of the United Nations War Crimes Tribunal." 33 *Stanford Journal of International Law* 1 (1997).

———. *For Humanity: Reflections of a War Crimes Investigator.* New Haven, CT: Yale University Press, 2000.

———. "Prosecuting War Criminals." David Davies Memorial Institute of International Studies Occasional Paper No. 10, Yale University, 1998.

Goldstone, Richard, and Nicole Fritz. "'In the Interests of Justice' and the Independent Referral: The International Criminal Court Prosecutor's Unprecedented Power." 13 *Leiden Journal of International Law* 655 (2000).

Gourevitch, Philip. *We Wish to Inform You That Tomorrow We Will Be Killed with Our Families: Stories from Rwanda.* New York: Farrar Straus and Giroux, 1998.

Griffin, John Blount. "A Predictive Framework for the Effectiveness of International Criminal Tribunals." 34 *Vanderbilt Journal of Transnational Law* (March 2001).

Gutman, Roy. *A Witness to Genocide.* New York: Macmillan, 1993.
Haas, Richard N. *Intervention: The Use of American Force in the Post–Cold War World.* New York: Carnegie Endowment for International Peace, 1994.
Hanson, Victor Davis. *The Soul of Battle: From Ancient Times to the Present Day, How Three Great Liberators Vanquished Tyranny.* New York: The Free Press, 1999.
Healey, Sharon A. "Prosecuting Rape Under the Statute of the War Crimes Tribunal for the Former Yugoslavia." 21 *Brooklyn Journal of International Law* 327 (1995).
Hirsch, John L., and Robert B. Oakley. *Somalia and Operation Restore Hope: Reflections on Peacemaking and Peacekeeping.* Washington, DC: United States Institute of Peace, 1995.
Hochschild, Adam. *King Leopold's Ghost.* New York: Houghton Mifflin, 1999.
Holmes, Richard. *Acts of War: The Behavior of Men in Battle.* Paperback ed. New York: The Free Press, 1989.
Holmes, Robert L. *On War and Morality.* Princeton, NJ: Princeton University Press, 1989.
Honig, Jan Willem, and Norbert Both. *Srebrenica: Record of a War Crime.* New York: Penguin USA, 1997.
Howard, Michael, George J. Andreopoulos, and Mark R. Shulman, eds. *The Laws of War: Constraints on Warfare in the Western World.* New Haven, CT: Yale University Press, 1994.
Ignatieff, Michael. *Virtual War: Kosovo and Beyond.* Metropolitan Books, 2000.
———. *The Warrior's Honor: Ethnic War and the Modern Conscience.* Metropolitain Books, 1998.
Jacobs, Dan. *The Brutality of Nations.* New York: Alfred A. Knopf, 1987.
Johnson, James Turner. *Morality and Contemporary Warfare.* New Haven, CT: Yale University Press, 1999.
Kagan, Donald. *On the Origins of War and the Preservation of Peace.* New York: Doubleday, 1995.
Kalshoven, Frits. *Constraints on the Waging of War.* Geneva: International Committee of the Red Cross, 1987.
Keegan, John. *A History of Warfare.* New York: Vintage Books, 1994.
———. *The Face of Battle.* New York: Viking Press, 1995.
Kochavi, Arieh J. *Prelude to Nuremberg: Allied War Crimes Policy and the Question of Punishment.* Chapel Hill: University of North Carolina Press, 1998.
Krass, Caroline D. "Bringing the Perpetrators of Rape in the

Balkans to Justice: Time for an International Criminal Court." 22 *Denver Journal of International Law and Policy* 317.

Lawrence, *Philip K. Modernity and War: The Creed of Absolute Violence.* New York: St. Martin's Press, 1997.

Loyd, Anthony. *My War Gone By, I Miss It So.* New York: Atlantic Monthly Press, 1999.

Lyons, Gene M., and Michael Mastanduno, eds. *Beyond Westphalia: State Sovereignty and International Intervention.* Baltimore: Johns Hopkins University Press, 1995.

Maguire, Peter. *Law and War: An American Story.* New York: Columbia University Press, 2000.

Maass, Peter. *Love Thy Neighbor: A Story of War.* New York: Vintage Books reprint edition, 1997.

Meron, Theodor. "Answering for War Crimes." *Foreign Affairs* 76, no. 1 (January/February 1997): 2.

Minow, Martha. *Between Vengeance and Forgiveness: Facing History After Genocide and Mass Violence.* Boston: Beacon Press, 1999.

Moore, Jonathan, ed. *Hard Choices: Moral Dilemmas in Humanitarian Intervention.* Lanham, MD: Rowman and Littlefield, 2000.

Moshan, Brook Sari. "Women, War, and Words: The Gender Component in the Permanent International Criminal Court's Definition of Crimes Against Humanity." 22 *Fordham International Law Journal* 154 (November 1998).

Neier, Aryeh. "Waiting for Justice: The United States and the International Criminal Court." 15 *World Policy Journal* 33 (Fall 1998).

———. *War Crimes: Brutality, Genocide, Terror, and the Struggle for Justice.* New York: Times Books/Random House, 1998.

Neuffer, Elizabeth. *The Key to My Neighbor's House: Seeking Justice in Bosnia and Rwanda.* New York: Picador USA, 2001.

Niarchos, Catherine N. "Women, War, and Rape: Challenges Facing the International Tribunal for the Former Yugoslavia." *Human Rights Quarterly* 17, no. 4 (November 1995): 649.

Osiel, Mark J. *Obeying Orders: Atrocity, Military Discipline, and the Law of War.* New Brunswick, NJ: Transaction Publishers, 1999.

Paust, Jordan J. "Applicability of International Criminal Laws to Events in the Former Yugoslavia" 9 *American University Journal of International law and Policy* 499 (1994).

Peterson, Scott. *Me Against My Brother: At War in Somalia, Sudan, and Rwanda.* London: Routledge, 2000.

Rieff, David. *Slaughterhouse: Bosnia and the Failure of the West.* New York: Touchstone Books, 1996.

Roberts, Adam, and Richard Guelff, eds. *Documents on the Laws of War.* 3rd ed. Oxford and New York: Oxford University Press, 2000.

Robertson, Geoffrey. *Crimes Against Humanity: The Struggle for Global Justice.* The New Press, 1999.

Rogers, A. P. V. *Law on the Battlefield.* Manchester, UK: Manchester University Press, 1996.

Rohde, David. *Endgame: The Betrayal and Fall of Srebrenica, Europe's Worst Massacre Since World War II.* Boulder, CO: Westview Press, 1998.

Scharf, Michael. *Balkan Justice: The Story Behind the First International War Crimes Tribunal Since Nuremberg.* Columbia, SC: Carolina Academic Press, 1997.

Scheffer, David J. "Challenges Confronting International Justice Issues." 4 *New England International and Comparative Law Annual* (1998).

Schmandt, Lisa L. "Peace With Justice: Is It Possible for the Former Yugoslavia?" 30 *Texas International Law Journal* 335 (1995).

Sewall, Sarah B., and Carl Kaysen, eds. *The United States and the International Criminal Court: National Security and International Law.* American Academy of Arts and Sciences/Rowman and Littlefield Publishers, 2000.

Silber, Laura, and Allan Little. *Yugoslavia: Death of a Nation.* New York: Penguin USA, 1997.

Solis, Gary D. *Son Thang: An American War Crime.* New York: Bantam Books, 1998.

Stover, Eric, and Gilles Peress. *The Graves: Srebrenica and Vukovar.* Scalo Verlag, 1998.

Sudetic, Chuck. *Blood and Vengeance: One Family's Story of the War in Bosnia.* New York: Penguin USA, 1999.

Triffener, Otto. *Commentary on the Rome Statute of the International Criminal Court—Observers' Notes, Article by Article.* Baden-Baden: Nomos, 1999.

Turns, David. "War Crimes Without War? The Applicability of International Humanitarian Law to Atrocities in Non-international Armed Conflicts." 7 *African Journal of International and Comparative Law* 4, 804 (1996).

Van Creveld, Martin. *The Transformation of War.* New York: The Free Press, 1991.

von Sternberg, Mark R. "A Comparison of the Yugoslavian and Rwandan War Crimes Tribunals: Universal Jurisdiction and the 'Elementary Dictates of Humanity.'" 22 *Brooklyn Journal of International Law* 111 (1996).

Vulliamy, Ed. *Seasons in Hell: Understanding Bosnia's War.* New York: Simon and Schuster, 1994.

Wade, Daniel L. "A Basic Guide to the Sources of International Criminal Law." In *Contemporary Practice of Public International Law,* ed. Ellen G. Schaffer and Randall J. Snyder. Dobbs Ferry, New York: Oceana Publications, 1997, pp. 189–220.

Wakin, Malham M., ed. *War Morality and the Military Profession.* Boulder, CO: Westview Press, 1979.

Walzer, Michael. *Just and Unjust Wars: A Moral Argument with Historical Illustrations.* 3rd ed. New York: Basic Books, 2000.

Warbrick, Colin. "The United Nations System: A Place for Criminal Courts?" 5 *Transnational Law and Contemporary Problems* 237 (1995).

Nonprint Resources

American Society of International Law
http://www.asil.org. Actively pursues and publishes information pertaining to the International Criminal Court.

Amnesty International Campaign for a Permanent International Criminal Court
http://www.amnesty.it/campaign/icc/en/index.html.

ASIL Insights (American Society of International Law)
http://www.asil.org/insights.htm. ASIL Insights are brief essays on current topics by international law experts. Insights are not designed to argue a position but rather to inform decisionmakers and the public of the relevance of international law to current events.

Coalition for an International Criminal Court (CICC)
http://www.igc.org/icc. This is the primary NGO provider of online information about the permanent International Criminal Court. It includes the text of all UN documents related to the formation of the Court, such as the Rome Statute (gopher://gopher.igc.org:70/00/orgs/icc/undocs/rome/romestatute.txt), an Index to the Rome Statute (gopher://gopher.igc.apc.org:70/00/orgs/icc/ngodocs/romeindex.txt), a Rome Statute Signature and Ratification Chart (http://www.igc.org/icc/rome/html/ratify.html), the draft statutes, session documents of the preparatory committee; (http://www.igc.org/icc/html/monitor.htm) is an

electronic journal featuring articles and perspectives worldwide. In addition, the CICC has prepared current awareness summaries and explanations of the UN deliberation process in this matter. It has also collected reports, opinion papers, and statements from NGOs such as Amnesty International, the Lawyers Committee for Human Rights, and the International Committee of the Red Cross.

Council of Europe: European Treaties
http://conventions.coe.int. Provides the text of the Statute of the Council of Europe, as well as signatures and ratifications. A complete list of the Council of Europe's Treaties (http://conventions.coe.int/treaty/EN/cadreprincipal.htm) is arranged chronologically.

Council of Europe: International Criminal Court
http://www.legal.coe.int/criminal/icc.

Countries of the World
http://www.uncjin.org/country/country.html. Includes general country information, maps of the world, U.S. Department of State Human Rights Reports, and a complete list of links to countries on which the United Nations Crime and Justice Information Network has compiled information.

European Union
http://europa.eu.int. This is an umbrella site for all of the European Union's institutions and organizations. It includes the text of European Union founding treaties, policies, institutional documents, press releases, and gateways to CELEX and SCAD, which index European Union documents, reports, and articles.

Greek's Criminal Justice Links: International
http://www.criminology.fsu.edu/cjlinks/world.html. Created and maintained by Dr. Cecil E. Greek at the School of Criminology and Criminal Justice, Florida State University. This well-known, comprehensive list links to websites for criminal law, law enforcement, crime prevention, and peacemaking and includes regional source lists for the United Kingdom, Europe, Canada, Australia, Africa, Asia, and South America. A list, focusing primarily on American resources, entitled "Criminal Justice Links" (http://www.criminology.fsu.edu/cjlinks) is also maintained by Dr. Greek.

Human Rights Watch Campaign to Establish an International Criminal Court
http://www.hrw.org/campaigns/icc.

International Court of Justice (ICJ)
http://www.icj-cij.org. All ICJ judgments delivered since its inception in 1946 are listed, along with information on the background of the court, its current docket, procedures, jurisdiction, and rules. Recent cases pertaining to international criminal law include the aerial incident at Lockerbie and the application of the Convention on the Prevention and Punishment of the Crime of Genocide (*Croatia v. Yugoslavia*).

The International Court of Justice Website at Cornell Law Library
http://www.lawschool.cornell.edu/library/International_Resources/icj.htm. The website is the ICJ's official mirror site. The Cornell site also provides ICJ foundational documents and court rules as well as links to research guides and other resources. A complete set of ICJ decisions is available electronically in the INT-ICJ database on WESTLAW, which is a fee-based service.

International Criminal Court
http://www.un.org/icc/romestat.htm. The ICC was adopted on July 17, 1998, establishing "an independent permanent International Criminal Court in relationship with the United Nations system, with jurisdiction over the most serious crimes of concern to the international community as a whole." The following sites will provide a full picture of the issues and debates surrounding the creation of this new court.

International Criminal Court: Resources in Print and Electronic Format
http://www.lib.uchicago.edu/~llou/icc.html.

International Criminal Tribunal for the Former Yugoslavia (ICTY)
http://www.un.org/icty/index.html. This is the official UN website for the ICTY and includes the statute (http://www.un.org/icty/basic/statut/statute.htm), rules of procedure (http://www.un.org/icty/basic.htm), documents establishing the tribunal (http://www.un.org/icty/pub.htm), background information, regulations, summaries of judicial activities,

publications (http://www.un.org/icty/pub.htm), and press releases.

International Criminal Tribunals (University of Minnesota)
http://www1.umn.edu/humanrts/links/intrib.html. An extensive collection of links to basic documents, media outlets, and other sources relating to all International Criminal Tribunal for Rwanda (United Nations) (http://www.ictr.org) or their mirror site at (http://www.un.org/ictr). This is the official UN website for the ICTR and includes, under the link to Cases (http://www.ictr.org), the text of indictments, trial chamber decisions, tribunal judgments, and appeal chamber decisions. Case summaries (http://www.un.org/ictr/casesum.htm), the ICTR statute (http://www.un.org/ictr/english/Resolutions/ 955e.htm), Rules of Procedure and Evidence (http:// www.un.org/ictr/rules.html), Security Council resolutions, press releases, listings of indictments, and hearing transcripts are also included. The ICTR library publishes the *ICTR Quarterly Bibliography* (http://www.ictr.org), which contains references to books, official documents, and periodical articles recently acquired by the library.

International Law Commission
http://www.un.org/law/ilc/index.htm. As early as 1947, the UN General Assembly requested the International Law Commission to formulate a Draft Code of Crimes Against the Peace and Security of Mankind (http://www.un.org/law/ilc/texts/dcodefra.htm). Included here is the text of the 1996 draft code with commentary, an abstract, an analytical guide, and the 1954 draft code.

Justice Information Center, National Criminal Justice Reference Service (NCJRS)
http://www.ncjrs.org. This information clearinghouse, an information service of the NCJRS (http://www.ncjrs.org), "is one of the most extensive sources of information on criminal and juvenile justice in the world." It is divided into sections covering corrections, courts, crime prevention, criminal justice statistics, drugs, international information, juvenile justice, law enforcement, research and evaluation, victims, and current highlights.

Lawyers Committee for Human Rights
http://www.lchr.org.

Lexadin World Law Guide
http://www.lexadin.nl/wlg/courts/nofr/courts.htm.

Major War Criminals/Suspects
http://www.cco.caltech.edu/~bosnia/criminal/criminals.html.

Nuremberg War Crimes Trials
http://www.yale.edu/lawweb/avalon/imt/imt.htm.

Organization of American States (OAS)
http://www.oas.org. The Inter-American Treaties database is an extensive collection of OAS treaties and agreements, including ratification and status information. Treaties can be searched by subject or year. The database can be reached via the OAS homepage by clicking on Documents, then Treaties and Conventions.

Other Treaty Resources.
The Multilaterals Project at the Fletcher School of Law and Diplomacy (http://www.fletcher.tufts.edu/multilaterals.html).

Research Guide to International Law on the Internet, International Criminal Law
http://sun1.spfo.unibo.it/spolfo/CRIMLAW.htm. The University of Bologna's faculty of political science created a series of research guides on topics such as the United Nations, the European Union, International Organizations, Peace and Security, Human Rights, International Criminal Law, Environmental Law, Law of the Sea, Air and Space Law and International Trade Law (http://www2.spfo.unibo.it/spolfo/ILMAIN.htm).

The Rome Statute of the International Criminal Court
http://www.un.org/law/icc/index.html.
Rome Statute (http://www.un.org/law/icc/statute/romefra.htm)
Ratification Status of the Rome Statute (http://www.un.org/law/icc/statute/status.htm)
Rome Conference (http://www.un.org/law/icc/docs.htm)
Preparatory Commission (http://www.un.org/law/icc/prepcomm/prepfra.htm)
General Assembly Resolutions (http://www.un.org/law/icc/gares/garesfra.htm)
Preparatory Commission for the International Criminal Court (http://www.un.org/law/icc/prepcomm/prepfra.htm)

The Preparatory Commission for the Establishment of an International Criminal Court was established by Resolution F of the Final Act of the United Nations Diplomatic Conference of Plenipotentiaries on the Establishment of an International Criminal Court, which adopted the Rome Statute of the International Criminal Court on July 17, 1998. This site, maintained by the UN Office of Legal Affairs, contains selected documents issued since the first session of the Preparatory Commission. In particular, the Proceedings of the Preparatory Commission at its First Session and the Report of the Second Session of the Preparatory Commission for the International Criminal Court discuss proposed rules of procedure and evidence, rules governing appeals, procedures governing investigation and prosecution, rules relating to organization and composition of the court, and elements of crimes. Documents and work plans are available for every session, including sessions currently in progress.

UN Action Against Terrorism
http://www.un.org/terrorism.

United Nations Association of the United States of America—International Criminal Court
http://www.unausa.org.

United Nations Crime and Justice Information Network (UNCJIN)
http://www.uncjin.org. This electronic network was established in 1989 in response to a resolution of the UN Economic and Social Council and is the creation of the UN Centre for International Crime Prevention in Vienna. It encompasses all criminal law information generated by the United Nations and its related bodies, including texts of laws, treaties, and conventions, UN documents, statistical sources, and gateways to affiliated organizations.

United Nations Crime and Justice Information Network: Statistics and Research Sources
http://www.uncjin.org/Statistics/statistics.html.

United Nations Treaty Collection
http://untreaty.un.org. The United Nations has been the forerunner in undertaking actions to combat international crime in all of its forms. Major UN treaties and conventions include the

UN Charter and conventions on apartheid, genocide, war crimes and crimes against humanity, torture, narcotic drugs, slavery, the taking of hostages, aircraft hijacking, and terrorism. Researchers can search for the text of a treaty in the United Nations Treaty Series http://untreaty.un.org/ENGLISH/series/simpleunts.asp), or for unpublished treaties in Recently Deposited Multilateral Treaties (http://untreaty.un.org/ENGLISH/notpubl/notpubl.asp), or for the status of a treaty in Status of Multilateral Treaties deposited with the Secretary-General (http://untreaty.un.org/ENGLISH/bible/englishinternetbible/bible.asp). Sample portions of the database are available at no charge; effective March 1, 2000, access to the complete UN treaty database is by subscription only.

United States Senate Committee on Foreign Relations, Committee Hearings, 105th Congress

http://www.access.gpo.gov/congress/senate/senate11sh105.html. On July 23, 1998, the Senate Foreign Relations Committee conducted hearings on the establishment of the International Criminal Court and the U.S. role in the process. Senate Hearing 105-724 (Is a UN International Criminal Court in the U.S. National Interest?) included testimony from David J. Scheffer, ambassador-at-large for War Crimes Issues, John R. Bolton, former assistant secretary of state for international organization affairs, attorney Lee A. Casey, professor Michael P. Scharf, along with statements submitted by the Lawyers Committee for Human Rights and Human Rights Watch.

University of Minnesota Human Rights Library, War Crimes and Crimes Against Humanity, Including Genocide

http://www1.umn.edu/humanrts/instree/auox.htm.

War Criminal Watch

http://www.wcw.org. This page is designed and maintained by the Coalition for International Justice (http://www.cij.org), which operates this website exclusively dedicated to information relating to the Yugoslavia and Rwanda tribunals, including audio and video files on the tribunal for the former Yugoslavia, the status of cases in national courts and implementing legislation, and other legal resources. The ICTY/ICTR pages offer case files, rules of procedure, manual for practitioners, annual reports, and other related documents.

Web Genocide Documentation Centre
http://www.ess.uwe.ac.uk/genocide/war_criminals.htm.

World Justice Information Network
http://www.wjin.net/ or http://www.justinfo.net; for registered users only. The World Justice Information Network is designed to be an independent global research forum for information on crime, justice, and the rule of law. The system, which is supported and administered by the National Institute of Justice (http://www.ojp.usdoj.gov/nij), builds upon its predecessor, the United Nations Online Crime and Justice Clearinghouse (UNOJUST), and works in close cooperation with the United Nations Crime Prevention and Criminal Justice Programme Network . It serves as a central point of access to a global virtual library containing thousands of professional publications and is a worldwide criminal justice news monitoring tool. Features include a specialized criminal justice search engine and multilingual capabilities. Registration is required, but any individual who is professionally involved in the area of international crime and justice may qualify for a free membership.

Glossary

accused A person against whom an indictment has been submitted, according to the tribunal's rules of procedure and evidence.

act of war A declaration by one nation ending normal international relations with another nation. Article 2 of the United Nations Charter ended this action: "All members shall refrain in their international relations from the threat or use of force against the territorial integrity or political independence of any other State."

armistice An agreement that brings hostilities to an end; an armistice does not terminate a state of war between belligerents.

belligerent status A legal standing for a revolutionary group similar to that accorded a government and bringing the international laws and customs of war into play to cover the war activities of the group, especially Article III of the 1949 Geneva Conventions.

Bosnia Part of the former Yugoslavia, Bosnia consists of two republics, both created in 1995 pursuant to the Dayton peace conference. There is the republic of Bosnia-Herzegovina, populated by Bosnian Muslims and Croats; it is essentially a Muslim Republic. The Republika Srpska, the second territory, is occupied by Bosnian Serbs.

Cambodia Bordered by Thailand, Laos, and Vietnam, Cambodia has been in the throes of civil war for more than forty years. In 1975 the Khmer Rouge, under the leadership of Pol Pot, seized control and turned Cambodia into the killing fields. About 2 million Cambodians and foreign nationals were murdered or starved to death by the Khmer Rouge until its rule ended in January 1979. Between 1974 and 1979 at least 20 percent of Cambodia's population was executed. To date there has been no indictments or trials of the Khmer Rouge leadership for the genocide they planned and implemented using their military forces.

carpet-bombing Air attacks on a city that planners treat as a single target without distinguishing military from nonmilitary targets. In the 1977

Additional Protocol I to the 1949 Geneva Conventions, such bombing was labeled as a prohibited "indiscriminate attack" that violated the laws and customs of war because it would cause an excessive loss of life, injury to civilians, and destruction of enemy civilian, religious, and aesthetic property.

child soldiers A United Nations report indicated that in a single year—1996—more than 250,000 child soldiers were serving in national and rebel armies in Sri Lanka, Vietnam, Liberia, Afghanistan, Cambodia, and the Balkans. The 1977 Geneva Additional Protocols imposed on armed parties in a war the obligation "to take all feasible measures in order that children who have not attended the age of 15 years do not take a direct part in hostilities" and to "refrain from recruiting them into their armed forces."

civil war Internal armed conflict that was not covered in international laws of war until the Additional Protocol II of 1977 amending the 1949 Geneva Conventions.

civilian immunity Pursuant to the 1977 Additional Protocols civilians enjoy total immunity: "They shall enjoy general protection against dangers arising from military operations [and] shall not be the object of attack."

collateral damage Occurs when attacks against enemy belligerents or enemy facilities causes death or injury of civilians and destruction of civilian buildings.

collective criminality A concept created for use by the Allied prosecutors at the Nuremberg trials in 1945. If a Nazi organization was identified as a criminal organization, then members of that organization were subject to punishment if their membership was voluntary, if the member had knowledge of the criminal activities of the group, and if the member was also guilty of some criminal action.

collective punishment When an enemy punishes a civilian for crimes he/she has not committed. Article 33 of the Fourth Geneva Convention (1949) states: "No protected person may be punished for an offense he or she has not personally committed."

combatant status In any armed conflict, only combatants are permitted to take a direct part in the hostilities. Combatants are all the members of a nation's armed forces, except medical and religious personnel.

command responsibility The 1949 Geneva Protocol states: "The fact that a breach of the Conventions . . . was committed by a subordinate does not absolve his superiors from penal disciplinary responsibility as the case may be, if they knew, or had information that would have enabled them to conclude in the circumstances at the time that he was committing or was going to commit such a breach and if they did not take all feasible measures within their power to prevent or repress the breach."

concentration camps First employed by Great Britain during the Boer War (1899–1902) to hold concentrations of Boer women and children in order to deny the Boer soldiers food and intelligence. During World War II the Nazis created a network of concentration camps (*Konzentrationslager*) to hold political prisoners and, later, civilians the Nazis thought unworthy of life, that is, Jews, Gypsies, Poles, and Russians. Six million Jews were exterminated by the Nazis at these camps and at the six major killing centers.

crimes against humanity The foundation for these crimes is found in Article 6(c) of the UN Charter and the Nuremberg Principles of 1946. Murder, extermination, enslavement, deportation torture, and rape "committed against civilian populations, before or during the war; or persecutions on political, racial, or religious grounds in execution of or in connection with any crime within the jurisdiction of the tribunal, whether or not in violation of the domestic law of the country where perpetrated" are crimes against humanity.

crimes against the peace Also known as crimes of aggression. The Nuremberg Tribunal in 1946 said that crimes against peace is the primary international crime, "differing from other war crimes in that it contains within itself the accumulated evil of the whole."

Croatia A republic of the former Yugoslavia that declared independence in 1991. Roman Catholic since the time of the Holy Roman Empire, it allied with Bosnian Muslims in resistance to Serbian claims.

customary law One of the two basic foundation blocks for the laws of war (the other is the written international treaty or convention). Customary law is the result of general and consistent practices of nations when engaged in armed conflict and binds all nations engaged in armed conflict.

Dayton Peace Accord The General Framework Agreement for Peace in Bosnia and Herzegovina, signed in Dayton, Ohio, in November 1995 by Croatia, Bosnia-Herzegovina, and the Federal Republic of Yugoslavia. The treaty recognizes the sovereignty of the Republic of Bosnia-Herzegovina and the existence of its two republics, the Federation of Bosnia-Herzegovina and Republika Srpska. It established a UN presence, the UN International Police Task Force to report human rights violations to the International Criminal Tribunal for the former Yugoslavia, and established NATO's peacekeeping force in the area (IFOR).

death squads During military rule in Guatemala, which began in 1980, *judiciales* (death squads) were responsible for the disappearances—and deaths—of tens of thousands of Guatemalan citizens. It is a violation of the 1949 Geneva Accords that explicitly prohibit executions without a fair trial.

ethnic cleansing According to a United Nations report, ethnic cleansing is defined as "rendering an area ethnically homogenous by using force or intimidation to remove from a given area persons from another ethnic or religious group."

genocide The 1948 Convention on the Prevention Punishment of Genocide defines genocide as "acts committed with the intent to destroy, in whole or in part, a national, ethnic, racial, or religious group."

grave breaches Violations of the 1949 Geneva Conventions, which prohibit a wide range of violent conduct against belligerents and civilians, including killing, torture, inhuman treatment, and willfully causing great suffering.

hors de combat A belligerent who is "out of combat" and entitled to be protected and treated humanely as a prisoner of war in accord with the 1949 Geneva Protocols.

hostages Since the 1949 Geneva Protocols, taking hostages is prohibited. Common Article 3 bans the taking of hostages during time of war or during an internal armed conflict.

irregulars A belligerent who belongs to a paramilitary unit, militia, volunteer brigade, or rebel force. Generally they do not wear uniforms. Such combatants are also known as partisans.

international tribunals (ad hoc) Four ad hoc international tribunals have been created since the end of World War II. These are Nuremberg (1945); Tokyo (1946); Yugoslavia (1993), and Rwanda (1994). They were created to indict alleged war criminals, conduct criminal trials, and sentence those persons responsible for serious violations of international laws and customs of war.

jus ad bellum A set of principles that defined the legitimate and just reasons that a state may engage in armed conflict with another nation.

jus in bello The laws and customs of legitimate and prohibited practices of war. They come into effect once an armed conflict commences. Its primary purpose is to regulate how wars are fought by prohibiting a range of activities that shock the conscience of the international community.

Kosovo An autonomous region of the republic of Serbia in the former Yugoslavia. In 1389 the Ottoman Turks ended the reign of medieval Serbia here by beheading Serb martyr Prince Lazar. In 1987, Serbian President Slobodan Milosevic visited Kosovo to support the Serbian minority living in the largely Muslim province. His visit and acrimonious speech are viewed by many as the beginning of the end of the Federal Republic of Yugoslavia and the start of the four wars that raged in the former Yugoslavia between 1991 and 1999.

levee en masse Mass uprising against foreign troops occupying a conquered territory.

military necessity A term used to justify killing of civilians and destruction of enemy property because of an attack on a legitimate military target.

negative criminality A concept that emerged after World War I that would allow the punishment of military leaders for failure to prevent war crimes and crimes against humanity by their forces in the field or at sea.

no quarter Until the mid–nineteenth century, there was no humane treatment for belligerents who laid down their arms, who were wounded and unable to participate in the battle, or who surrendered. Enemy forces gave no quarter to these troops, that is, they would kill them where they lay injured or where they surrendered. The 1949 Geneva Conventions formally prohibited the execution of defenseless soldiers. The 1977 Additional Protocols stated: "A person who is recognized, or who, in the circumstances, should be recognized as hors de combat shall not be made the object of attack."

non-bis-in-idem "Not twice for the same," referring to double-jeopardy protection under international law. The concept prohibits a second trial before a national court of an individual previously convicted in an international tribunal for war crimes, and vice-versa, provided the prior charge was not an "ordinary crime" and that the tribunal was impartial.

nullum crimen sine lege "There can be no crime without law," a standing principle of domestic and international law.

occupation of territory International law proscribes an occupying power's use of force against the civilian population.

POWs Prisoners of war; combatants captured by the enemy must be accorded humane treatment while in a POW camp. According to the 1949 Geneva Conventions, a POW need give only name, rank, and serial number. The Geneva Conventions mandate proper food, medical, and living conditions for all POWs. At the conclusion of hostilities all POWs must be repatriated.

POW camps Places where POWs are kept, consistent with the 1949 Geneva Conventions. The International Committee of the Red Cross, pursuant to the Geneva Conventions, is mandated to periodically inspect these camps to ensure that military prisoners are treated in accordance with the Geneva Conventions. All camps should be situated in areas far away from the battlefields so as not to endanger the lives of the POWs.

proportionality A principle in the international law of war to determine whether a military action that caused the deaths and/or injuries of civilians was a lawful action or a violation of the laws of war. When a belligerent attacks a military objective, proportionality comes into play when there is collateral damage. An attack is a violation of the laws of war if the collateral damage is excessive in relation to the military advantages achieved by the attack.

proprio motu "On one's own motion"; gives a war crimes tribunal the power to issue warrants for the prosecution and the defense or to give itself power to investigate.

rape The act of rape is a crime against humanity when it becomes systematic in an area occupied by an enemy force. A UN commission investigating war crimes in Bosnia labeled systematic rape "an instrument for ethnic cleansing."

refoulement The forced return of a person to a country where he/she faced prosecution. It is an action that is prohibited under the 1949 Geneva Conventions.

refugees It is estimated that there were 45 million refugees across the world in 2000, the terrible consequence of the nearly 300 wars of liberation and civil wars that have taken place since 1945. The 1949 Geneva Conventions and the 1977 Additional Protocols call for humane treatment for refugees, including not forcing them back to their former country if prosecution awaits them.

reprisal, right of When a belligerent takes action in response to enemy action that violated the laws and customs of war. It may be "in kind" or "not in kind" (violating an unrelated rule). The 1949 Geneva Conventions categorically prohibit reprisals against civilians and civilian objects the belligerent is required to protect.

Republika Srpska A separate independent nation in Bosnia-Herzegovina for Bosnian Serbs created at the 1995 Dayton peace conference; also known as the Serb Republic.

Serbia A republic in the former Yugoslavia that was led by Slobodan Milosevic from 1990 to 1997 after he became president of Yugoslavia. It is strongly identified with the Eastern Orthodox Church.

sick and wounded The 1949 Geneva Conventions recognize that sick and wounded belligerents and/or civilians should be treated equally humanely and with dignity at all times.

siege Since the earliest wars, belligerents have sought to defeat the enemy by blocking all access to cities, then bombarding the encircled town until its inhabitants surrendered. Until post–World War II events, a siege was not per se a prohibited military action. However, the 1949 Geneva Conventions as well as the 1977 Additional Protocols prohibit military actions that attempt to starve civilian populations and allow humanitarian relief agencies to bring food into these besieged towns.

soldiers, rights of Soldiers, as combatants, have rights to take actions during an armed conflict that would be crimes in another context. If captured, combatants have POW status and the right to humane treatment under the 1949 Geneva Conventions.

Srebrenica A Muslim town in Bosnia-Herzegovina that was declared a "safe area" by the United Nations but was overrun by Bosnian Serbs in July 1995. Thousands of innocent Bosnian Muslims were tortured, raped, murdered, and buried in mass graves by the Serb military forces.

suspect A person about whom the prosecutor in an international criminal tribunal has reliable information that tends to show that he/she may have committed a crime over which the tribunal has jurisdiction. A suspect has the right to assistance of counsel and the right to remain silent. The prosecutor is obliged to audiotape or videotape interrogations of a suspect.

terrorism Terrorist acts have been prohibited by a variety of international treaties and conventions, including the 1949 Geneva Conventions and the Additional Protocols of 1977. They ban terrorism during international and internal armed conflict, such as armed attacks directed against civilians and police torture and execution of political prisoners and other enemies of the state. Terrorism against civilians is a particularly shocking event, as seen in Israel when young Palestinians, male and female, strap explosives to their bodies, enter Israel, and blow themselves up along with dozens of innocent Israeli civilians.

torture The 1984 Convention for the Prevention of Torture and Inhuman or Degrading Treatment or Punishment defines torture as "any act by which severe pain or suffering, whether physical or mental, is intentionally inflicted on a person for such purposes as obtaining from him or a third person information or a confession." Torture is universally prohibited and when committed is a war crime; it is a crime against humanity when committed against civilians. The same convention states: "No exceptional circumstances whatsoever, whether a state of war or a threat of war, internal political instability or any other public emergency, may be invoked as a justification of torture."

Truth and Reconciliation Commission An alternative to war crimes trials, or the granting of amnesty after an international or civil war, is the establishment of a Truth and Reconciliation Commission. The most visible of such commissions was that created in South Africa after the brutal system of apartheid ended.

total war The total mobilization of a nation's resources—human and economic—in support of a war effort. It does not mean rejection of the laws and customary principles of war.

universal jurisdiction The prosecutors at Nuremberg argued that the crimes committed by the Nazis—war crimes and crimes against humanity—were universally condemned by the civilized world (alluding to the language of the Martens clause in the 1907 Hague Convention). As such, there was so-called universal jurisdiction by courts, including the international military tribunal sitting in Nuremberg to hear cases involving the perpetration of these crimes.

victims, rights and protections The International Committee of the Red Cross and the UN High Commissioner for Refugees are the two agencies that attempt to provide humane treatment for the innocent victims of international and civil wars. Very little was done for victims of war crimes and genocide, except for the efforts of successive post–World War II German governments to provide reparations to the victims of genocide who died between 1939 and 1945. Japan, for example, has steadfastly refused to provide compensation for civilians who suffered or who were killed by the Japanese military between 1931 and 1945.

violation of laws or customs of war Drawn from international law, the 1907 Hague Convention prohibits the use of force "not justified by military necessity" against villages, dwellings, civilians, as well as enemy belligerents and prisoners of war.

war crimes "Grave breaches" of the laws and customary principles of war generated by the international community in an effort to reduce the excesses of armed conflict perpetrated against belligerents and civilians alike. The 1946 Nuremberg Principles stated that war crimes included murder, ill-treatment, or deportation of civilians in occupied territories; murder or ill-treatment of prisoners of war; killing of hostages; wanton destruction of cities and towns; and any devastation not militarily necessary.

willful killing As seen in the Bosnian wars, willful killing was engaged in by Bosnian Serb sharpshooters whose targets were innocent Bosnian Muslim and Bosnian Croat civilians. Such intentional killing of civilians in any armed conflict is a war crime, as defined in the 1949 Geneva Conventions and the 1977 Additional Protocols. The killing of a civilian, if not justified by military necessity, is a "grave breach" of the laws of war, that is, a war crime.

Index

Accused, defined, 239
Act of War, 239
Aerial bombing, 65, 66, 68, 69, 70, 71
Afghanistan, 22, 25, 38, **46–47,** 83
AFRC. *See* Armed Forces Revolutionary Council
Agent Orange, 77
Aggression. *See* Crime of aggression
Airplanes, 66, 70
  crews, 145
Albanians, 35, 36, 37, 38, 83, 95, 194, 196. *See also* Bislimi, Rexhap; Lajqi, Hajrie
Alexander III (pope), 11
Alien Tort Act (U.S. 1789), 19
Allende, Salvador, 33
Allied Control Commission (1945), 71
Allies, 70, 71
All-People's Congress (APC) (Sierra Leone), 39
Al-Qaeda, 47, 83
Ambulances, 108, 131
American Society of International Law (ASIL), 223–224, 230
Amnesty International, 23, 34, **207–208,** 230
Annan, Kofi, 50, 55–56, **85–86**, 181, 201
Anschluss (1938), 91
Anti-Semitism, 97
Apartheid, 184, 185
APC. *See* All-People's Congress
Arbitration and mediation, 64
Argentina, 47
Arm-badge (brassard), 109
Armed Forces Revolutionary Council (AFRC) (Sierra Leone), 39, 40
Arms reduction, 18
Armistice, 239
Artillery, 66
Aryan race, 140. *See also* Nuremberg Laws
ASIL. *See* American Society of International Law
Atlantic Charter (1941), 88
Austria, 23, 66, 91
Axis, 70, 91

Bacteriological methods of warfare, 68
Balkan Wars (1991–1995), **86–87.** *See also* Bosnia-Herzegovina; Croatia; Serb-Muslim war; Serbia; Slovenia
Balkans, 16, 25
Baltic states, 24
Bangladesh, 25
Barbed wire, 66
Bartetzko, Roland, 44–45
Basic Rules of the Geneva Conventions and Their Additional Protocols (ICRC), 187
  summary, 188–189
Bassiouni, Cherif, **87,** 220
Battle of Solferino (Italy 1859), 23, 62, **89**
Beer Hall Putsch (1923), 90
Belgium, 19–20, 102–104, 174
Belligerent status, 239

Bellum hostile, 12
Bellum Romanum, 11–12
Benenson, Peter, 207
Berlin Wall (1989), 24
Bilateral treaties, 15
Bio, Julius Maada, 39
Biological experiments, 6, 7, 160
Bislimi, Rexhap, 29–31
Boer War (1899–1902)
concentration camps, 241
Bolanos, Aldo, 196
Bolivia, 47
Bolton, John R., 201
Bombardment of undefended towns, 65, 69, 70, 75, 116, 123, 155, 239–240
Bombs. *See* Aerial bombing; Bombardment of undefended towns
Booby-traps, 79, 196
Bosnia-Herzegovina, 35, 80, 178, 239, 245. *See also* Dayton Peace Accord; Serb-Muslim war
Brett, Rachel, 203
Bretton-Woods conference (1944), 96
Brussels Declaration (1874), 14
Bulgaria, 24, 66
Bullets, 8, 18, 63–64
dum-dum, 65
Burundi, 25, 103, 205
Bush, George W., 197, 201
"Butcher of the Balkans." *See* Milosevic, Slobodan

Cambodia, 35, 38, **45–46,** 99, 209, 239
ethnic groups, 100
Campaign to End Genocide, **208**
Carpet-bombing, 239–240
Center for Economic and Social Rights, 208
Central Powers, 66–67
Chad, 200
Chaplains, 131–132, 138
Chemical weapons, 18, 79
Children, 8, 9, 19, 40, 75, 141, 205, 210
soldiers, 240
Chile. *See* Pinochet, Augusto
China
and Japan(1937–1939), 70
Chivalry, 14
Christian nations, 11–12
Churchill, Winston, **87–88,** 93
Ciano, Galeazzo, 91
CIJ. *See* Coalition for International Justice
Civil War, U.S. (1861–1865), 15, 16–17, 21, 62
Civil wars, 31, 62, 78, 204, 240
Bosnia, 35, 80
Cambodia, 45–46
East Timor, 41–44
Kosovo, 44–45
Rwanda, 25, 80–81, **102–104**
Sierra Leone, 39–41
Slovenia, 80
Spain, 69–70
weapons, 79
Civilians, 6, 7, 78–79, 145
coercion, 8, 122–123, 124, 160, 162, 184
collateral damage, 204
defined, 154
deportation or transfer, displacement, 7, 19, 160, 162, 184, 205
executions, 19, 161, 194, 241, 246
immunity, 240
property, 6, 7, 9, 18, 21, 75, **117–118,** 156, 160
protection, **149–159,** 161–162, 183–185, 188–189, 242, 244
refugees, 40, 42, 89, 180, 191, 213, 244, 246
wartime casualties (1900), 1
wartime casualties (1945–1999), 31, 38, 42, 62, 70, 101, 104, 194
wartime casualties (2000-), 1
women, 21, 210
wounded and sick, 149
See also Children; Hostage taking
Clinton, Bill, 88, 89, 197–199, 201
Coalition for an Independent Criminal Court (CICC), 50, **208–209,** 230–231
Coalition for International Justice (CIJ), **209,** 236
Cold War, 24, 49

Collateral damage, 204, 240, 243–244
Collective criminality, 240
Collective punishment, 240
Combatant status, 240
Command responsibility, 240
Commander's Handbook on the Law of Naval Operations (U.S.), 22
Communications, 125
  technology, 17
Communist Party
  Cambodia, 45, 99
  Chile, 33
  Yugoslavia, 34–35
Communists, 71
Complementarity concept, 49
Concentration camps
  in Boer War, 241
  Bosnia, 4, 95–96
  in World War II, 71, 241
Conscription, 17
Convention for the Prevention of Torture and Inhumane or Degrading Treatment or Punishment (1984), 245
Convention on the Rights of the Child (1989), 205
Corell, Hans, 57
Council of Europe, 231
Crime of aggression, 183. *See also* Crimes against peace
Crimean War (1854–1856), 15–16
Crimes against humanity, 5, 18, 26, 71, 73, 74, **140,** 161–162, 175
  defined, 241
  See also International Criminal Court
Crimes against peace, 71, 72–73, **140**
  defined, 241
Croatia, 35, 80, 86, 87, 181, 241
Croats, 4, 25, 35
Cultural property, 6, 7, 21, 65, 75, 76, 116, 156
Customary law, 13–15, 18, 24, 72, 83, 241
  as binding on states not party to treaty, 15
  codification, 17–18, 24
  corollaries, 14
  and scholars and philosophers, 20–21
Czechoslovakia, 24, 70

Darabi, Dr. Homa, Foundation, 210
Dayton Peace Accord (1995), 36, 87, 88–89, **178–181,** 241
Death Squad (Rwanda), 200
Death squads, 200, 241
Declaration of war, 14, 15, 239
Del Ponte, Carla, 25, 38, 196
DeMille, Nelson, 1
Denmark, 91
Deportation. *See* Civilians, deportation or transfer, displacement
Derechos Human Rights, **209–210**
Detainee Management Unit (UN), 42
Dew v. Johnson, 5
Dicker, Richard, 181
Dignity, 8, 9, 149
Disappearances, 47, 184, 185, 215
Disarmament, 64
Discrimination principle, 14
Disease, 16. *See also* Biological experiments
Dr. Homa Darabi Foundation, 210
Doctors Without Borders/ Medecins sans Frontiers, 23, **210**
Double jeopardy. *See Non-bis-in-idem*
Dragons (Les Dragons), 200
Dumont, Henri, 61
Dunant, Henri, 23, **89**

East Timor, 25, 38, 41–44, 209
Economic Community of West African States (ECOWAS), 39–40
Economic embargo, 39
ECOWAS. *See* Economic Community of West African States
Eisenhower, Dwight D., 17
Enslavement, 184
Environmental modification, 77, 157
Ethiopia, 69
Ethnic cleansing, 29
  Bosnia, 4, 5, 36
  defined, 241–242

European Community, 174
European Union, 190
Explosive projectiles, 18, 63–64
Explosives, 66. *See also* Landmines; Mines

Feudal lords, 12
Flag of truce, 7, 65, 116, 122
Fletcher School of Law and Diplomacy Multilaterals Project, 234
Force. *See* Proportionality principle
Forensic process, 193
France
  and Austria, 23
  and Crimean War, 15–16
  military personnel, 22
  and Prussia, 12
  and World War II, 18, 70, 91
Franco, Francisco, 69
Franco-Prussian War (1870–1871), 12, 64
Frank, Hans, 98

Gabriel, Peter, 215
Gas chambers, 71
Gases, 65, 66, 68, 71, **126–127**
General Framework Agreement for Peace in Bosnia and Herzegovina. *See* Dayton Peace Accord
General Protocol for the Prohibition of the Use in War of Asphyxiating, Poisonous or Other Gases, and of Bacteriological Methods of Warfare (1925), **126–127**
Geneva Convention
  1864 (for the Amelioration of the Wounded and Sick of Armies in the Field), 17, 23, 63, 64, 107, **108–109**
  1929 (Relative to the Treatment of Prisoners of War), 68–69, **132–138,** 143
  1949 breaches and violations, 75–76, 77–78, 160–162
  1949 (on the Amelioration of the Condition of the Wounded and Sick in the Armed Forces in the Field), 14, 75, 143, 150, 204
  1949 (on the Wounded, Sick and Shipwrecked Members of Armed Forces at Sea), 6–10, 14, 75, 143, 150, 204
  1949 (Relative to the Protection of Civilian Persons in Time of War), 6–10, 14, 75, 143, **148–152,** 204, 242
  1949 (Relative to the Treatment of Prisoners of War), 6–10, 14, 75, **143–148,** 150, 242
  1997, 10
  See also Basic Rules of the Geneva Conventions and Their Additional Protocols
Geneva Protocol for the Prohibition of the Use in War of Asphyxiating, Poisonous or other Gases and of Bacteriological Methods of Warfare (1949), 68
Geneva Protocol I Additional to the Geneva Convention of 12 August 1949 and Relating to the Protection of Victims of International Armed Conflicts (1977), 77, 78, **153–159**
Geneva Protocol II Additional to the Geneva Convention of 12 August 1949 and Relating to the Protection of Victims of Non-International Armed Conflicts (1977), 14, 77–78, 153, 205, 206
Geneva Protocols (1949, 1977), 14, 49, 77–78, 204
Genocide, 5, 26, 45, 71, 93–94, 104, 174, 175, 246
  Conventions (1948), 18, 22, 49, 54, 73–75, 140–142
  defined, 74–75, 141–142, 161, 242
  name origin, 73, 93
  NGOs, 208
  print sources, 221–222, 237
  See also International Criminal Court
Germany, 68
  World War I war crimes, 19–20, 26
  See also Nazi Germany; Prussia
Goebbels, Joseph, 97

Goering, Hermann, 186
Goldstone, Richard J., **89–90**
Grave breaches, 242
Great Britain, 33, 40
  and Crimean War, 15, 16
  and World War II, 18, 70
  See also World War I
Greek, Cecil E., 231
Greeks (ancient), 12, 14
Greek's Criminal Justice Links: International, 231
Grossman, Marc, 201
Grotius, Hugo, 20
Grynszpan, Herschel, 97
Guatemala death squads, 241
Guerre couvette, 12
Gulf War (1991), 22, 80
Guzman, Juan, 34
Gypsies, 71, 74, 140, 195

Habeé, Hissène, 200
Habyalimana, Juvenal, 103
The Hague
  1899 (Convention with Respect to the Laws and Customs of War on Land), **110–111**
  1899 (Convention with Respect to the Laws and Customs of War on Land) Annex, **111–118, 121–123**
  1899 (Declaration for the Pacific Settlement of International Disputes), 10, 14, 48, 64, **110**
  1907 (Convention on the Amplification of 1899 Declaration), 10, 14, 48, 61, 64–66, 94, **119–121**
  1923 (Rules of Aerial Warfare), 68
  1954 (Convention for the Protection of Cultural Property in the Event of Armed Conflict), 76, 156
  peace conferences (1899, 1904, 1907), 18
  as seat of UN International Tribunal, 174
  tribunals, 3, 25
Hammer, Joshua, 194
Hartmann, Michael, 44
Heads of State. *See* Individual responsibility for actions
Helsinki Final Accord (1975), 179
Hess, Rudolf, 90, 186
High Commissioner for Refugees (UN), 56, 192, 246
Hindenburg, Paul von, 90, 91
Hindu Code of Manu (c. 200 B.C.E.), 12, 14
Hirohito (emperor of Japan), 24
Hitler, Adolf, 24, 70, **90–91,** 97–98
Holocaust, 91, **96–98**
Hoover, Herbert, 129
Hors de combat, 242. *See also* Prisoners of war
Hospital ships, 19
Hospitals and medical personnel, 7, 20, 23, 108, 116, 131–132
Hostage taking, 6, 9, 20, 149, 160, 242
Human rights, 180
  documents, 221, 231
  Internet-based organization, 209
  organizations and international humanitarian law, 203–207
  violations, 34, 39, 40, 43
Human Rights Watch, 23, 181, 205, **211,** 232
Humanitarian assistance, 6–7, 9, 22–23
Hungary, 24, 66
Hutus, 25, 80, **102–104,** 174
Hydrocarbons, 79

ICC. *See* International Criminal Court
ICJ. *See* International Commission of Jurists
ICRC. *See* International Committee of the Red Cross
ICTR. *See* International Criminal Tribunal for Rwanda
ICTY. *See* International Criminal Tribunal for the Former Yugoslavia
Ideology, 16, 17
IMTN. *See* International Military Tribunal in Nuremberg
Incendiary weapons, 79
Individual responsibility for actions, 24, 72, 139, 162
Indochina War (1949–1954), 76. *See also* Vietnam War

Indonesia, 41–42, 43–44
Institute of War and Peace Reporting (IWPR), **211–212**
Instructions for the Government of Armies of the United States in the Field (Lieber), 21–22, 63
Internal disturbances, 8
International Ad Hoc War Crimes Tribunals (post-1945), 23–26, 242. *See also* International Criminal Court
International Campaign to Ban Landmines (ICBL), 61, 82, 106, **212**
International Commission of Inquiry (for East Timor), 42, 43
International Commission of Jurists (ICJ), **212**
International Committee of the Red Cross (ICRC), 22–23, 61, 62, 64, 76, 78–79, 107, 129, 149, 196, 204, **212–213,** 246
  flag, 109
  Fundamental Rules of International Humanitarian Law Applicable in Armed Conflicts (1978), 187–189
International Court of Justice, 10, 142, 232
International Criminal Court (ICC) (UN), 6, 25, 26, 32, **51–57,** 141, 232
  concept, 48–53
  hybrid, 38–47
  jurisdiction, 185
  location (The Hague), 181
  and national criminal jurisdictions, 183
  operational (2002), 83
  Preparatory Committee (PrepCom), 50, 235
  punishment as imprisonment only, 52
  See also Rome Statute of the International Criminal Court
International Criminal Tribunal for Rwanda (ICTR) (1994), 25, 26, 75, 76, 80–81, 90, 141, 174–175, 200–201, 209, 233, 236
  press release (2000), 199–200
  Statute, 167, **174–178**
  Statute Annex (1994), 177–178
International Criminal Tribunal for the Former Yugoslavia (ICTY) (1993), 3–4, 25, 31, 36, 56, 75, 76, 80, 90, 141, 162–163, 193–197, 209, 232–233, 236
  Statute (1993), 159, 162–163
International governmental organizations
  directory, 207–216
  See also League of Nations; United Nations
International law, 12–23, 26, 61–62
  chronology of treaties and events, 62–83
  and complementarity, 49
  and complicity, 73
  and domestic law, 19, 20, 73
  humanitarian, 203–207
  humanitarian, basic rules of, 188–189
  nonprint resources, 230–237
  Principles of International Law Recognized in the Charter of the Nuremberg Tribunal and in Judgment of the Tribunal, Adopted by the International Law Commission of the United Nations (1950), **139–140**
  violations, 246
  See also Customary law; International Criminal Court
International Military Tribunal—Far East (IMTFE) (1946), 18, 24, 72
International Military Tribunal in Nuremberg (IMTN) (1945), 10, 18, 20, 23–24, 26, 72, 73–74, 92, 139
  opening remarks, 186–187
International Rescue Committee (IRC), **213**
International Task Force on Terrorism, 90
International war crimes tribunal (1919), 67
Internet, 209, 218
IRC. *See* International Rescue Committee
Irregulars, 242

Italy, 22, 23, 69, 70, 91
IWPR. *See* Institute of War and Peace
Izetbegovic, Alija, 86, 87

Jackson, Robert H., 20, 74, **92,** 186
Japan, 68
  and China, 70
  and World War II, 18, 19, 24, 70, 71, 133, 246
Jehovah's Witnesses, 71
Jews, 71, 73–74, 90, 91, 96–98, 140
Judicial tribunals, 19–20
Jus ad bellum, 242
Jus in bello, 2, 5, 242
Justice, 31–47, 56, 57
Justice Information Center, 233

Kabbah, Ahmad, 39
Kambanda, Jean, 199–200
Kampuchea, 99
Karadzic, Radovan, **92–93**
Kellogg-Briand Pact for the Renunciation of War as an Instrument of National Policy. *See* Treaty of Paris (1928)
Kerrey, Bob, 2–3, 4–5
Khmer Rouge, 45, 46, 99–101
Killing centers, 71
Kirsch, Philippe, 58
Koroma, Johnny Paul, 39
Kosovo (Serbia), 29–31, 35, 36–37, 38, **44–45,** 83, 189–190, 242
  Liberation Army, 44, 191, 192
  Peace Accord (1999), 190–193
  war crimes forensic evidence, 194–197
Kostunica, Vojislav, 36
Kristallnacht/Night of Broken Glass (1938), 97
Kuwait. *See* Operation Desert Storm

Lajqi, Hajrie, 189
Landmines, 18, 61, 80, 81–82, 212
Lasers, 79
Law of Land Warfare (U.S.), 21
Laws of humanity, 18, 175–176
Laws of war, 2, 5–10, 26–27, 107
  codification, 17–18
  establishment, 10–23
  violations, 160–161
Lawyers Committee for Human Rights, **213–214,** 215, 233
League of Nations, 22, 49, 68
Legal rights, 6, 7–8, 9–10
Lempkin, Raphael, 73, 74, **93–94**
Levee en masse, 242
Lexadin World Law Guide, 234
Liberian mercenaries, 39
Lieber, Francis, 21, 22, 62, **94**
Lincoln, Abraham, 21, 62
Lomé (Togo) Treaty (1999), 40
London Charter (1945), 71
Ludendorff, Erich, 90
Lusitania sinking (1915), 19

MacArthur, Douglas, 72
MacBride, S., 208
Machete War (Rwanda) (1994), 80–81
Machine guns, 66
Maritime law, 62, 64–65, 81
Martens, Feodor de, 10, **94,** 110
Martens clause, 10, 94, 110, 119, 120, 245–246
McDonald, Gabrielle Kirk, 56–57
Medical and scientific experiments, 6, 7, 71
Mein Kampf (Hitler), 90
A Memory of Solferino (Dunant), 23, 89
Mercenary forces, 13, 39
Merchant marine, 145
Merchant shipping, 69
Middle Ages, 11–12
Military courts-martial, 19
Military insignia and uniforms, 7
Military law manuals, 2–3, 12–13, 21–22, 62–63
Military necessity, 204, 243
Military personnel
  casualties (1900), 1
  casualties (1914–1918), 66
  casualties (2000), 1
  combatant status, 240
  rights, 244–245
  surrender, 7, 65, 122, 144, 188, 243
  wounded and sick, 17, 18, 23, 68–69, 75–76, 78–79, **108–109,** 115–116, 144, 188, 243, 244
  See also Militia; Prisoners of war; Volunteer corps

Military policy, 4–5
"Military-industrial complex," 17
Militia, 121–122, 145, 242
Milosevic, Slobodan, 4, 5, 25, 29, 31, 32, 34–38, 87, **94–95**
Mines, 65, 79, 80
Mladic, Ratko, **95–96**
Montesquieu, Baron de (Charles de Secondat), 20–21
Morgenthau, Henry, Jr., **96**
Moynier, Gustave, 23, 89
Multilateral treaties/conventions, 17–20, 21, 234
Muslim nations, 11. *See also* Afghanistan; Serb-Muslim war
Muslims, 4, 35, 100. *See also* Taliban
Mussolini, Benito, 69, 70
Mutilation, 7, 9, 149

Napalm, 79
National Criminal Justice Reference Service (NCJRS), 233
National Institute of Justice, 237
National Provincial Ruling Council (Sierra Leone), 39
NATO. *See* North Atlantic Treaty Organization
Nazi Germany, 18, 19, 20, 23–24, 70–71, 73–75, 90–91, 133
NCJRS. *See* National Criminal Justice Reference Service
Ndadaye, Melchoir, 103
Negative criminality, 243
The Netherlands, 22
Neutrality/neutrals, 19, 27, 62, 64, 65, 108, 118
Newsweek, 194–197
NGOs. *See* Nongovernmental organizations
Nicholas II (czar of Russia), 110, 119
Nightingale, Florence, 16, **98**
"No peace without justice," 31–47, 57
Nobel Prize
  1901, 23
  1953, 88
  1974, 208
  1997, 61, 106, 208
  1999, 87
  2001, 85
Non-bis-in-idem, 163, 243
"Nongovernmental Human Rights Organizations and International Humanitarian Law" (Brett), 203–207
Nongovernmental organizations (NGOs), 22–23, 50–51, 61, 76, 78
  directory, 207–216
  human rights, 203–207
Noninternational armed conflicts. *See* Civil wars
North Atlantic Treaty Organization (NATO), 36, 37, 38, 44, 45, 83, 86, 89, 190, 191, 194
  Implementation Force, 85
  stabilization force (SFOR), 178
Norway, 91
Nsengimana, Hormidas, 200–201
Ntaryamira, Cyprien, 103
Nuclear electric power, 157
Nuclear weapons, 18, 83
Nullum crimen sine lege, 243
Nuremberg. *See* International Military Tribunal in Nuremberg
Nuremberg Laws (1935), 91, 97
Nuremberg Principles (1946, 1950), 18, 24, 72–73, **138–140**

OAS. *See* Organization of American States
Occupying power, 27, 65, 71, 108, **117–118,** 123–125, 150–152, 242, 243
  and state property, 125
  and taxes, 124
Ogata, Sadako, 56
Olympic games, 12
Omarska (Serb prison camp), 4
On the Law of War and Peace (Grotius), 20
"On the Trail of the Hard Truth" (Hammer), 194–197
"One Sad Night" (Lajqi), 189–190
Operation Desert Storm (1991), 22, 80
Operation Enduring Freedom (2001–), 22, 46, 47, 83
Organization for Security and Cooperation in Europe, 179

Organization of American States (OAS), **214,** 234
Inter-American Commission on Human Rights, 46
Ottawa Convention on the Prohibition, Use, Stockpiling, Production, and Transfer of Anti-Personnel Mines and on Their Destruction (1997), 61, 81–82
Oxford Manual (1880), 14

Pagans, 11
Palestine, 16
Papen, Franz von, 90
Paramilitary unit, as irregulars, 242
Paris Declaration Respecting Maritime Law (1856), 16, 17, 62
Partisans, as irregulars, 242
Peace Brigades International, **214**
Petain, Henri, 91
PHR. *See* Physicians for Human Rights
Physicians for Human Rights (PHR), **214–215**
Pillaging, 8, 9, 11, 19, 20, 116, 123
Pinochet, Augusto, **31–34,** 200
Poison, 8, 14, 19, 65, 66, 68, 115, **126–127**
Pol Pot, 45, **98–101**
Poland, 24
and World War II, 70–71, 91
Poles, 74
Popular Unity government (Chile), 33
Portugal, 22, 41
Powell, Colin, 201
Pregnancy, forced, 184, 185
Prisoners of war (POWs), 12, 243
camps, 133, 136–138, 243
categories, 145–146
and clothing, 137
escaped, 113
officers, 115, 132
and parole, 113–114
and relief societies, 114, 132
rights, 112–113
and rules of war, 1, 6, 15, 65, 78, **112–115,** 130, 188
Russian, 71
treatment, 2, 4, 12, 18, 21, 23, 68–69, 75, 78–79, 115, 117, 122, 130, **132–138, 143–148,** 160
and work, 132
Propaganda, 17
Propio motu, 244
Proportionality principle, 14, 243–244
Prosper, Pierce-Richard, 201
Prostitution, enforced, 184
Protocols (1977), 14
Prussia, 12, 15, 64

Quarter given/no quarter, 7, 9, 11, 20, 21, 122, 243

Railroads, 17
Rambouillet agreement (1999), 192
Rape, as war crime, 4, 8, 20, 40, 162, 184, 244
Rath, Ernst vom, 97
Rebel force, as irregulars, 242
Red Crescent Movement, 213
Red Cross. *See* International Committee of the Red Cross
Red Cross Convention Regarding the Amelioration of the Condition of Wounded and Sick of Armies in the Field (1929), 68–69, **139–132**
Red Cross Fundamental Rules of International Humanitarian Law Applicable in Armed Conflicts (1978), 78–79
Reebok Foundation, 215
Refoulement, 244
Refugees. *See under* Civilians
Religious property, 6, 7, 20, 21, 65, 116, 156
Reprisal, right of, 244
Research Guide to International Law on the Internet, 234
Restraining principle, 13–14
Revolutionary United Front (RUF) (Sierra Leone), 39, 40, 41
Rexhepi, Bajram, 45
Roman law, 14
Romania, 24

Rome Statute of the International Criminal Court (1998), 6–10, 15, 25, 51–57, 76, 82, **181–185**
  as customary law, 15, 22
  document sources, 234
  ratified (2002), 25
  section 8, 5
  Singapore Compromise, 55
Roosevelt, Franklin D., 88, 92, **101–102**
Roosevelt, Theodore, 61, 101, 119
Rousseau, Jean-Jacques, 21
RUF. *See* Revolutionary United Front
Rugova, Ibrahim, 45
Rules for Military War Tribunals (U.S.), 47
Rules of Engagement (U.S.), 2–3
Ruses of war, 123
Russia, 178, 182, 190. *See also* Russia (Czarist); Soviet Union
Russia (czarist), 15–16
Russians, 71
Rwanda, 25, 80–81, **102–104,** 174–175, 199–201

Saboteurs, 150
St. Petersburg Declaration Renouncing the Use of Explosive Projectiles (1868), 17–18, 63–64
San Remo Manual on International Law Applicable to Armed Conflicts at Sea (1994), 81
Sankoh, Foday, 39, 40
Secondat, Charles de (Baron de Montesquieu), 20–21
Sejersted, Francis, 106
Serbia, 4, 25, 29, 35, 45, 80, 83, 86, 105
  "Greater," 35
  military manual, 22
Serb-Muslim war (1992–1995), 4, 25, 35–36, 83, 86–87, 244. *See also* Dayton Peace Accord; "One Sad Night"
Sexual slavery, 8, 184
Siege warfare, 12, 16, 116, 123, 244
Sierra Leone, 25, 38, **39–41,** 48, 209
Sierra Leone People's Party (SLPP), 39
Sihanouk, Norodom (Cambodian king), 46
Slave labor (Cambodia), 100
Slave trade, 19
Slovenia, 35, 80
SLPP. *See* Sierra Leone People's Party
Soldiers. *See* Military personnel
Solidarity movement (Poland), 24
SOS Torture network, 216
"Sovereign immunity," 72
Soviet Union, 24
  collapse of (1991), 25, 49
  and Spain, 69
  and World War II
  See also Russia; Russia (czarist)
Spain, 17, 19, 33
  civil war (1936–1939), 69–70
  military manual, 22
Spanish Civil War (1936–1939), 69–70
Spanish-American War (1898), 17
Speer, Albert, 186
Spies, 116–117, 150
  as POWs, 117
The Spirit of the Laws (Montesquieu), 21
Srebrenica (Bosnia-Herzegovina), 245
Srpska, Republika (Bosnian Serb republic), 36, 178, 179, 244
Stalin, Josef, 91, **105**
Starvation, 8, 16, 156
State sovereignty, 15
Steiner, Michael, 45
Sterilization, 8, 184
Stimson, Henry L., 129
Stocchi, Paolo Pastore, 194, 195, 196–197
Strasser, Valentine E. M., 39
Straw, Jack, 33, 34
Submarines, 19, 66, 69
Sudetenland, 70, 91
Suffering, 6, 7, 8, 18, 65, 83, 122, 160, 184
Sun-tzu, 14
"Superior Orders," 72
Supply centers, 145
Supreme Court (U.S.), 19, 20, 92
Suspect, 245

Tadic, Dusko, 3–4, 36, 56
Taliban, 38, 46–47
Tanks, 66
Technology, 16–17, 66
Terrorism, 90, 245
Tito, Josip Broz, 35, **105**
Torture, 6, 9, 19, 34, 149, 160, 162, 184–185, 214–215, 245. *See also* International Criminal Court
Total war, 15, 16–18, 66, 70, 245
Transitional Judicial Service (UN), 42
TRCs. *See* Truth and Reconciliation Commissions
Treaty of Amity and Commerce (1785), 15
Treaty of London (1936), 69
Treaty of Neuillu-Sur-Seine (1919), 66
Treaty of Paris (1856). *See* Paris Declaration Respecting Maritime Law
Treaty of Paris (1928), 68, **127–129**
Treaty of Saint-Germaine-En-Laye (1919), 66
Treaty of Sevres (1920), 66
Treaty of Trianon (1920), 66
Treaty of Versailles (1919), 18, 26, 48, **66–68**
Trench warfare, 66
Trinidad and Tobago, 49
Tripartite Pact (1940), 91
Truce of God (11th century), 11
Truth and Reconciliation Commissions (TRCs), 32, 40, 41, **47–48,** 245
Tudjman, Franjo, 87
Turkey, 66
  Ottoman Empire, 15, 16
Tutsis, 25, 80, **102–104,** 174, 200

U-boats, 19
UN Assistance Mission for Rwanda, 174–175
UN Commission of Experts, 87
UN Convention on Privileges and Immunities (1946), 173–174
UN Convention on the Prevention and Punishment of the Crime of Genocide (1948), 18, 22, 49, 54, 62, 73–74, **140–142**
UN Convention on the Prohibition of Military or any Other Hostile Use of Environmental Modification Techniques (1976), 77
UN Convention on the Prohibition or Restriction on the Use of Blinding Laser Weapons (1995), 79
UN Convention on the Prohibition or Restriction on the Use of Certain Weapons Which May Be Deemed to Be Excessively Injurious or to Have Indiscriminate Effects: Non-Detectable Fragments (1980), 79
UN Convention on the Prohibition or Restriction on the Use of Incendiary Weapons (1980), 79
UN Convention on the Prohibition or Restriction on the Use of Mines, Booby-traps, and Other Devices (1980), 79
  Amended Protocol II (1996), 80
UN Convention on the Safety of UN and Associated Personnel (1994), 81
UN Mission in Sierra Leone (UNAMSL), 40
UN Statute of the International Criminal Tribunal for Rwanda (1994), 167, **174–178**
UN Statute of the International Criminal Tribunal for the Former Yugoslavia (1993), **159–174**
  investigation, 169–170
  judges, 164–168, 170
  languages, 174
  organization, 163–164
  penalties, 171–172
  prosecutor, 168, 169, 173
  registry, 169, 173
UN Transitional Administration in East Timor (UNTAET), 42, 43
UNAMSL. *See* UN Mission in Sierra Leone

UN-East Timorese Crimes
Tribunal, 43
United Nations (UN)
Action Against Terrorism, 235
Charter, 55, 142, 176, 179, 191
Commission on Human Rights, **215**
Crime and Justice Information Network, 231, 235
Crime Prevention and Criminal Justice Programme Network, 237
High Commissioner for Human Rights, **215**
initial meeting (1945), 71
and international law, 61–62, 138–140
International Law Commission, 138–140, 233
international war crimes tribunals, 3–4, 10, 38, 43, 23–26, 36, 80–81, 160–174
member states, 50
Online Crime and Justice Clearinghouse (UNOJUST), 232
peacekeeping forces, 42–44, 45, 81, 85, 96, 174
Resolution No. 96(I) (1946), 75
Resolution No. 827 (1993), 160
Resolution No. 1166 (amendment of Resolution No. 827; 1998), 160
Resolution No. 1329 (amendment of Resolution No. 1166; 2000), **160–174**
Secretary General. *See* Annan, Kofi
Security Council, 39, 55, 57, 166, 185, 191, 192
Transitional Judicial Service, 42
Treaty Collection, 235–236
See also International Criminal Court
United States
and Afghanistan, 22, 46–47
ambassador for war crimes, 201
Civil War, 15, 16–17, 21
Department of State Human Rights Reports, 231
and Gulf War, 22
and international law, 19
and landmines, 82
and League of Nations, 68
military policy, 2–3, 4–5
Navy, 2–3, 22
and Prussia, 15
and Rome Statute of the ICC, 53, 54, 55, 58, 181, 182, 197–199, 201
and Rwanda, 174
Senate Committee on Foreign Relations, Hearings (1998), 236
and Soviet Union, 24
and Spain, 17, 19
United Nations Association, 235
and World War I, 17, 19
and World War II, 18, 70, 102
United States v. Armistad (1841), 19
Universal jurisdiction, 49, 245–246
University of Minnesota Human Rights Library, War Crimes and Crimes Against Humanity, 236
UNTAET. *See* UN Transitional Administration in East Timor
Up Country (DeMille), 1
U.S. Rules of Engagement for Operation Desert Storm, 22
U.S. Rules of Engagement for Operation Enduring Freedom, 22
Usufruct, 125

Vietnam, 45, 76, 100–101. *See also* Vietnam War
Vietnam War (1963–1975), 77, 79
war crimes, 2–3
Voluntary Aid Societies, 132
Volunteer corps, 121–122, 145, 242

Wallace, William, 12
War, renunciation of, 68, **127–129**
War correspondents, 145
War crimes, 18, 73
brutality, 1–2, 4, 5, 7, 10–11, 25, 38, 242, 246
database sources, 217, 218, 219
defined, 5–10
Internet sources, 218, 219–220, 222–223

key words search, 220
nonprint sources, 230–237
principles (1930), 139–140
print sources, 217–230
reports, rules, and speeches, 186–201
trial (first recorded), 12
tribunals, 10, 18, 19–20, 23–26
types. *See* Crimes against humanity; Crimes against peace; War crimes
victims, 246
victims and perpetrators determination, 193–197
See also Laws of War
War Criminal Watch, 236
War criminals, 2–4, 31, 71, 89, 92–93
War fighting administrative improvements, 16
Weapons, 8
bans, 18, 79, 189
technology, 16, 17
Westphalia Treaty (1648), 15
Wilful killing, 6, 9, 11, 160, 246
Wilful suffering, 6, 7, 8, 160
Wilhelm (William) II (German kaiser), 26, 67
Williams, Jody, 61, **105–106**
Witness Program, **215**
World Federalist Association. *See* Campaign to End Genocide
World Justice Information Network, 237
World Organization Against Torture, **215–216**
World War I (1914–1919), 18, 66
war crimes, 19–20, 26
World War II (1939–1945), 17, 70–71

Xyklon gas, 71

Yugoslavia, 35, 80, 192. *See also* Bosnia-Herzegovina; Kosovo; Serb-Muslim war; Serbia

About the Author

Howard Ball is professor emeritus of political science and University Scholar at the University of Vermont. In 2002–2003, he is professor of government at Dartmouth College. He is also an adjunct professor at the Vermont Law School, where he teaches a seminar on the U.S. Supreme Court's processes and politics. Ball received his B.A. in history from Hunter College–CUNY and his M.A. and Ph.D. in political science from Rutgers University. His scholarship and teaching is in the field of law and politics. He is a member of the American Political Science Association and the International Political Science Association.

Ball is the author of two dozen books and dozens of articles in political science, law, and public administration journals. His books include *Hugo L. Black: Cold Steel Warrior* (1996), *Cancer Factories* (1992), *Of Power and Right: Justices Hugo Black and William O. Douglas and America's Constitutional Revolution* (1992), *Justice Downwind: America's Atomic Testing Program in the 1950s* (1988), *The U.S. Supreme Court: From the Inside Out* (1996), *Compromised Compliance: Justice Department Implementation of Section 5 of the Voting Rights Act* (1982), *Court and Politics* (1987), *Constitutional Powers* (1980), *Prosecuting War Crimes and Genocide: The Twentieth Century* (1999), and *The Bakke Case: Race, Higher Education, and Affirmative Action* (2000). His *A Defiant Life: Thurgood Marshall and the Persistence of Racism in America* (1999) was a featured book for both the Book of the Month Club and the History Book Club. He has four more titles in the works.